The Emergence of
Black Politics in Senegal

# The Emergence of
# Black Politics in Senegal

THE STRUGGLE FOR
POWER IN THE FOUR COMMUNES,
1900–1920

## G. Wesley Johnson, Jr.

*Published for the*
*Hoover Institution on War, Revolution and Peace by*
STANFORD UNIVERSITY PRESS
*Stanford, California*
1971

Sources of photographs and illustrations: No. 1,
from an early nineteenth-century map engraving by
A. Vuillemin; Nos. 2, 3, 6, 7, 8, 9, 13, 14, 15,
16, 17, Collection Viollet; No. 4, from a 1925
advertising flier published by *L'Ouest Africain
Français* (Dakar) and Imprimerie de Vaugirard (Paris);
No. 5, drawing from Abbé P.-D. Boilat, *Esquisses
sénégalaises* (Paris, 1853); No. 10, courtesy of the
staff at the Archives of the Republic of Senegal;
No. 11, courtesy of Mme. Félix Brigaud, Dakar.

Stanford University Press
Stanford, California
© 1971 by the Board of Trustees of the
Leland Stanford Junior University
Printed in the United States of America
L.C. 73-150326
ISBN 0-8047-0783-9

For My Parents

# Preface

I did not create the voters, as has been charged;
I found them ... and I want them to keep the
full measure of their rights.

*—Blaise Diagne*

THE FOUR COMMUNES of Senegal occupy a small but important place in the modern political history of Black Africa, for it was in these settlements, France's oldest African holdings, that Western politics first took root in the eighteenth century. Saint-Louis and Gorée had African mayors by the time of the French Revolution and elected a deputy to the National Assembly in Paris in 1848. The addition of a General Council (colonial assembly) in 1879 gave the Four Communes effective institutions of local government controlled by the urban inhabitants.

True local democracy was thwarted for decades because the great majority of the electorate, the indigenous black Africans, were dominated by a small clique of French and Creole politicians until 1900. After the turn of the century, the African voter began to assert himself and take a greater interest in communal politics—just as French colonial authorities decided that the policy of assimilation, which had created black voters, had gone too far and was a dangerous example for France's newer African colonies. A campaign was launched to deprive the Senegalese voter of his political rights, which set the stage for a complex struggle between French colonial officials, French colonists, Creoles, and indigenous Senegalese for the mastery of local political affairs.

How these urban Africans, called *originaires*, obtained political rights before 1900 and expanded them by 1920 is the subject of this study. It was this group of political mavericks that Blaise Diagne found upon his return to Senegal in 1914; and under his leadership they won a series of electoral victories that confirmed the Africans' right to vote and hold political office and enabled them to replace the French and Creole elite as arbiters of local politics. The fact that this took place several decades before 1945, the generally accepted date for the beginning of African nationalistic movements, is significant. And the fact that neither French nor African scholars have written about the creation of the first African-elected and African-led government in a French colony is an omission that deserves to be filled.

In approaching this study, I was originally interested in the postwar period of Senegalese history—in Léopold Senghor, *négritude*, and the movement toward political independence. But when I found that Senegalese politics had started long before 1945, and that the first crucial period for gaining independence had come decades earlier, I changed the focus of my investigation. Research in the archives of Senegal and France, and my interviews with Senegalese participants in early urban politics, indicated that the significance of this first African political awakening in 1900–1920 had not been fully perceived by French scholars and authorities, and that little had been written about it. Perhaps the perspective of post-independence Africa makes it easier to look back and fit a number of events and occurrences into a meaningful historical pattern.

Whether or not the political pattern of 1900–1920 was incipient nationalism (which I was originally looking for) is difficult to say. My research suggested that nationalism was not necessarily the key factor in explaining the political past; and that other influences, such as assimilation, urbanism, elitism, and religion, were equally important in Senegal's political beginnings. Historians have now moved beyond the nationalistic parameters set by political scientists in the late 1950's and have analyzed the messianism, protests, and rebellion that make up the background of African political activity all over tropical Africa. The Senegalese case was probably unique, however, because in the Four Communes political activity was allowed rather than being proscribed. Consequently, I have thought of this study as a political history rather than an investigation into nationalism or Senegalese resistance to the French. The French assimilation policy in Senegal offered Africans a stake in the French state as their ultimate political reward. The quest for political assimilation was the theme of the early political struggles in Senegal, and the word "independence" was rarely spoken in public. This does not mean that early Senegalese leaders were collaborators with the colonial government, for most were not. Their style of militancy, methods of opposing the regime, and strategies for gaining power were not those of the 1970's, but they were effective, audacious, and ambitious for the times. Political activity within the colonial system, in fact, was an attractive opportunity for the Senegalese in a day when most colonial subjects were deprived of political and human rights. The African awakening of 1900–1920 should, in my opinion, be understood and analyzed within its historical context.

This is the first of two planned volumes on the rise of politics in Senegal before World War II, when that colony was almost the only one in Africa to have local political institutions. The second volume will examine the consolidation of African politics from 1920 to 1945.

Most materials on Senegal concern the French conquest, French administration, or French concern with colonial development. Little attention was paid in most of the colonial literature to the problems of local politics unless these greatly affected the plans of the Governor-General or Governor. Consequently, much of this study is based on oral history. Some private material, both oral and written, was given to me with the understanding that it would not be cited. However, there is a substantial body of archival and published material that reinforces evidence from both these sources.

I received excellent cooperation from the two primary archives used during this study. In Paris, Monsieur Carlo Laroche, Mlle. Menier, and the staff of the former Ministry of Colonies archives (now filed by the French National Archives) were most helpful, and allowed me to see certain materials not yet classified that contributed greatly to my knowledge of Blaise Diagne. (Diagne died in 1934, and much of the material relating to his career has not yet been processed for research; hence I have not always been able to give specific references.) In Senegal, Monsieur Jean-François Maurel of the Republic of Senegal Archives was invaluable in furnishing materials on African politics. His Senegalese assistants, Oumar Bâ, Fily Bâ, and Gambi N'Diaye were extremely helpful in locating specific unclassified materials and in locating odd bits of information that helped to piece together gaps in the archival documentation.

Research for this study was made possible by grants from the Foreign Area Fellowship Program, the Hoover Institution, and the Committee on International Studies of Stanford University. It is impossible to acknowledge all the persons who helped and lent assistance to the project, but I should like to mention a few. A special note of thanks to my mentors at Columbia University, who first encouraged me: Shepard B. Clough, L. Gray Cowan, and Immanuel Wallerstein. A term spent at the UCLA African Studies Center with Leonard

Thompson and James Coleman was invaluable. And in Paris, Henri Brunschwig, Albert Charton, François Crouzet, Hubert Deschamps, Roger Pasquier, and Robert Delavignette were particularly helpful.

In Senegal, a number of friendly and interested persons contributed information and ideas to help flesh out the skeletal outline furnished by the archives and newspapers. The late president of the National Assembly, Lamine Guèye, and the former vice-president, André Guillabert, were particularly helpful; so were Louis Legros, Félix Brigaud, Robert Delmas, Aby Kane Diallo, Armand Angrand, A. Kader Diagne, Charles Graziani, Maurice Guèye, and a number of other Senegalese and Frenchmen who are listed among the interviews in my Bibliography. Moussa N'Diaye of Dakar deserves a special note of thanks for his personal support and encouragement.

Once research in the field is over, analysis and interpretation follow. For this stage of the volume I owe a special debt to the following persons for their advice, counsel, and criticism: Peter Duignan and Lewis Gann of Stanford, Martin Klein of Toronto, and William Foltz of Yale. Also Graham Irwin, Robert Griffeth, Robert July, H. O. Idowu, Michael Crowder, Jacob Ajayi, Boniface Obichere, Denise Bouche, John Ballard, Mercer Cook, Sheldon Gellar, Donald Easum, Cheikh Tidiane Sy, David Gelsanliter, and the editorial staff of the Stanford University Press. I am responsible for the interpretation, of course, and for any possible inaccuracies.

At Stanford, I have been greatly helped by my students and research assistants, in particular Sue Malone, Meredith Barker, Elizabeth Groff, and John Zarwan. And my wife and fellow Africanist Marian A. Johnson has been a continual source of enthusiasm and ideas since the inception of this study.

G.W.J.

# Contents

# PART I

# The Colonial Political Situation
## by 1900

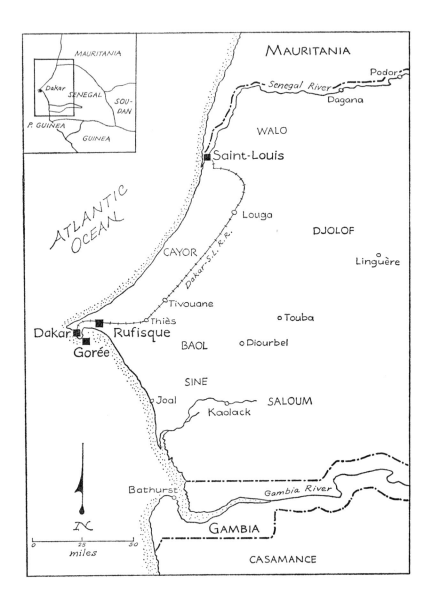

MAURITANIA

SENEGAL

SOU-
DAN

P. GUINEA

GUINEA

Dakar

MAURITANIA

Senegal River

Podor

Dagana

WALO

Saint-Louis

Louga

DJOLOF

Linguère

ATLANTIC
OCEAN

CAYOR

Dakar-S.L.R.R.

Tivouane

Touba

Thiès

Dakar

Rufisque

BAOL

Diourbel

Gorée

SINE

Joal

SALOUM

Kaolack

Gambia River

Bathurst

GAMBIA

0        25        50
miles

CASAMANCE

◇◇◇◇◇◇◇◇◇◇◇◇◇◇◇◇◇◇◇◇◇◇◇◇◇◇◇◇◇◇◇◇◇◇◇◇◇◇◇◇◇◇◇◇◇◇◇◇◇◇

CHAPTER 1

# The Historical Background

THE UNUSUAL status of Senegal among French colonies was first called to the attention of the European public in 1901, when Pierre Mille, a well-known French journalist, published an article describing his visit to the colony's capital city, Saint-Louis. Mille was struck by the fact that black Africans living in the Four Communes, the principal towns of the colony, had long possessed the right to elect local officials. This practice was unknown in France's other tropical African colonies; indeed, it was unknown in the African colonies of any nation. After watching a local campaign, Mille concluded:

It does not seem as though this experiment has been entirely successful from a political point of view because, if the Colony of Senegal has managed to put its house in order and finds itself today in a fairly flourishing condition financially, it is largely due to the circumstance that the native voters are "clients" of an influential white *gens* and vote as they are told to vote. . . . France had made a mistake in granting suffrage to the natives. She did not withdraw her present, but took care not to repeat it elsewhere.[1]

Mille assumed that France's lapse in policy in Senegal was compensated for by the French commercial interests there, who would keep the native electorate in line. He also praised the Creoles, the Senegalese of mixed parentage who were the French merchants' allies in managing local politics. But his disdain for the black African voters who made up the bulk of the electorate was scarcely disguised, and this attitude was shared by most other visitors to Senegal during the next decade. The cultural ethnocentrism of the day inhibited these observers from seriously considering the idea that black Africans might aspire to office and become local political leaders. The earlier French policy of assimilation was now in disrepute; and to Mille and others, the rotten-borough politics of Senegal furnished proof that Africans could not be assimilated. However, these short-term visitors did not look beyond the facade of local politics; and because they ignored the cultural, social, and historical background of the Four Communes they overlooked the power struggle that was developing as the African majority awakened from a long period of French and Creole domination.

### The Unity of Senegalese Geography

Many African states of today, such as Nigeria, Cameroun, and Ivory Coast, have suffered from a geographical diversity inherited from colonial times. But the boundaries of Senegal as drawn by France are roughly in accord with traditional frontiers separating its peoples and cultures from the Moors to the north, the Sudanic peoples to the east, and a variety of ethnic groups to the south. As a result, Senegal to date has not experienced the irredentism and tribal conflicts that have plagued most African nations, and she has a sense of unity few African countries possess.

The heartland of Senegal is a large plain spread between two major river systems, the Senegal on the north and the Gambia on the south.[2] A narrow Atlantic littoral lies on the west; and in the east the heartland merges into the Ferlo desert, a region of sparse vegetation and sand dunes. Southeastern Senegal and the Casamance region, severed from the heartland by the Gambia, have been marginal to the mainstream of Senegalese history. The plains of Senegal are sandy and are typically covered with thornbushes and baobab trees; but during the rainy season luxuriant grasses appear. Both soil and climate are well suited to peanut culture, which has become the economic mainstay of the country.[3]

Senegal is basically a savannah land, and there is little relief except for the low hills around the city of Thiès. Consequently, the inhabitants have always enjoyed easy communications. Whether for war, trade, or day-to-day visits, the dominant Wolof and Serere peoples of the heartland have maintained contact with their neighbors: the Toucouleurs to the north on the Senegal River, the Lebous on the Cape Verde peninsula, the nomadic Fulbe to the east, and the Malinké to the southeast. Only the Diola and other peoples in the Casamance have been isolated.

Most of Senegal (excepting Casamance and Cape Verde) has a hot, dry climate typical of the Sudanic belt. There is only one rainy season, from June to October, and the dry season lasts for the remainder of the year. The absence of tropical humidity during Europe's winter months gives parts of Senegal a climate much like that of the Mediterranean. The *harmattan*, a parching desert wind from the Sahara, heats the interior, whereas winds blowing south from the Canary

Islands cool the Atlantic littoral and Cape Verde during the dry season.

The weather consistently regulates the activity of Senegal's inhabitants. Crops are planted in May and June, and are watered by heavy rains from June to October. Harvesting begins in November, and by May the last of Senegal's peanuts have been sold and shipped on to European markets. From February through May, the dry weather is oppressively hot in the interior, and there is little work for the peasant. With the onset of the rains, the withered landscape of the central plains becomes a verdant parkland not unlike Western Europe in early summer. But the rains also bring an oppressive tropical humidity to the coastal cities. Ironically, the name given this humid summer period is *hivernage*, quite the opposite of the term's French connotation. Every hivernage the colony of Senegal was temporarily abandoned to the Africans, who helped manage businesses, filled vacant posts in the administration, and generally kept things running until the French returned from Europe.[4]

In contrast to the heartland area, Casamance is moist and tropical: rains begin earlier and last longer, and much of the country is a tropical rain forest where raffia and rattan palms, mahogany, and teak grow in abundance. The bamboo thickets, mangrove swamps, and thick forests preclude much travel even during the dry season. And ethnically speaking, the polyglot tribes of Casamance are quite distinct from the rest of Senegal's people. Not until the twentieth century was there much contact between the heartland and Casamance.[5]

Two navigable rivers lie within the boundaries of Senegal. The Gambia, in the south, is navigable in all seasons for 200 miles inland. But it has never been controlled by France for any significant length of time, and the navigable stretch of the river formed a British enclave in French Senegal throughout the colony's existence. Senegal's great highway to the interior for much of its history was the Senegal River, which rises in the mountainous Fouta Djalon of Guinea and descends gently for 1,056 miles, reaching the Atlantic Ocean near the old colonial capital, Saint-Louis. The Senegal, unlike the Gambia, is navigable only during certain seasons. From July to October the river runs rapidly, flooding its long valley with alluvial soils much as the Nile does, and large vessels can then mount as far as Kayes in modern Mali, 550 miles from the sea. But by April the river is so low that even small boats have difficulty reaching Podor, 110 miles upstream from Saint-Louis. The Senegal's picturesque valley, known as the Fouta, is the traditional home of the Toucouleur peoples and was the seat of the great medieval state of Tekrour; it also served as a route for the diffusion of Islam among West African Negroes. The river has always been an important means of communication between the interior Sudanic areas and the Atlantic littoral, since it cuts through the Sahara desert to the north and the Ferlo desert to the south. After the heartland, the fertile river valley is second in importance to Senegal's agriculture.[6]

The Atlantic coastal strip (including Cape Verde), extending from Saint-Louis to the Gambia, is a flat country punctuated with sand dunes and shallow ponds. Palms, ironwood, citrus trees, and European vegetables grow under careful cultivation. Owing to its sub-Canarian climate and gentle winds the area is hospitable to Europeans, which partially explains why the French lingered on the coast for centuries before moving inland. In pre-colonial days, Senegal's indigenous population was concentrated in the northern heartland and on the Senegal River. But during the past century continuous migrations of Africans toward the rich peanut-growing lands of the south have shifted the center of peasant population to a coastal area bounded by the cities of Thiès, Diourbel, and Kaolack.[7] Much of this growth may be ascribed to the attractions of the nearby capital, Dakar, with its government work, port, and small industries.

The geography of Senegal thus provided a central region where both agriculture and grazing could be pursued in a stable subsistence economy. The Wolof, Toucouleur, and Serere peoples of the heartland were traditionally farmers. The nomadic Fulbe, though primarily concentrated in eastern Senegal, traveled around the Ferlo desert and grazed their herds in the river valleys and heartland plains. The heartland was free of the tsetse fly and the stock diseases it carries; hence the Sereres kept large herds of cattle in their villages, and donkeys, horses, and camels could also be raised. The presence of horses meant that many members of the warrior class in Senegal's traditional states were able to fight as cavalrymen, and their highly mobile bands were able to enforce central rule over wide areas. These conditions were analogous to those in other Sudanic areas where great traditional African states arose: Ghana, Mali, Songhai, and Kanem-Bornou.

Senegal's heartland was ideally suited for the development of a cohesive modern nation state. Only the British colonial enclave on the Gambia destroyed this unity: Senegal was deprived of another natural highway to the interior; and many Wolof peoples were separated from their original homeland to the north, although they maintained family, religious, and economic ties with Senegal. Otherwise, Senegal's physical and economic geography has favored the evolution of agrarian kingdoms among the major tribal groups that have dominated the country.

### The Traditional States of Senegal

Four major ethnic groups in Senegal contributed to the urban population of the Four Communes: the Wolof and Lebou peoples were the most important, but the Serere and Toucouleur peoples were present in significant numbers. These four groups were related in language and social customs, and they have maintained close political and religious ties. Each group at one time produced one or more nation-states in Senegal. These are worthy of closer examination, for they indicate the political capacity that rural Africans brought with them when they migrated to the Communes. Detailed information on Senegal's traditional states is only now being brought to light by specialists in oral tradition and ethnohistory, but the written record from Arabic and European travelers suggests that the Senegal area has been a center of organized political activity since at least A.D. 1000.

It is not my purpose to establish a direct link between traditional politics and the politics of the Communes. But the reader should be aware that each major ethnic group involved in communal politics had its own political traditions. Africans in the Communes were no strangers to organized politics, although they needed a certain degree of acculturation to understand the peculiarities of Western political institutions. (Indeed, to take a leading role in the political life of the Communes an African had to be partly assimilated to French culture.) It is doubtful that traditional politics provided an adequate training ground for urban politics: traditional political roles were ascribed, whereas those in the urban areas were achieved by personal merit. However, the concept of the political process as one form of a struggle for power was familiar to every African.

*The Toucouleur states of the Fouta Toro.* The middle valley of the Senegal River, the Fouta Toro, has been the home of the Toucouleur peoples for over a thousand years;[3] and it formed the nucleus of Tekrour, one of the earliest recorded Negro states in all Africa. This nation arose sometime before A.D. 1000, and in medieval times its renown was such that "Tekrour" was synonymous with the term "Sudan" in much of West Africa. The Toucouleur were the primary inhabitants of Tekrour, but the population may have included proto-

Wolof and Serere peoples, as well as a few other ethnic minorities. The Fouta Toro was well suited to agriculture and trade, and was not too far distant from salt mines to the north and gold mines to the southeast. It is not remarkable that the kingdom prospered for several centuries.

Sometime after 1000 the king and court of Tekrour were peacefully converted to Islam by emissaries from Mauritania, and the kingdom at large soon followed. Tekrour's power waned after the twelfth century, and the state fell successively under the influence of the neighboring Mali and Djolof empires. In the sixteenth century, after a brief interlude of independence, Tekrour was conquered by the Denianké, an animistic Fulbe dynasty, and an era of non-Muslim rule began. But the people remained loyal to Islam despite the pagan practices and harsh exactions of their new rulers; and in 1776 a group of Toucouleur *marabouts* led a successful rebellion. The Denianké rulers were deposed, and an elective theocracy called the Almayat was set up.[9] Power was divided among members of the maraboutic party (*torodbé*), who collectively ruled the different communities along the river valley. After this, Toucouleur independence was intimately associated with Islam. And at the same time, the Fouta Toro began to send forth increasing numbers of marabouts to preach the Koran throughout Senegal.

The most notable Toucouleur leader in the nineteenth century was Al Hajj Umar Tall, who made his pilgrimage to Mecca in the 1820's, joined the militant Tijaniyya brotherhood, and returned to act as that sect's Khalife in the western Sudan. Umar wanted to revive the ancient glory of Tekrour by creating an empire similar to the Hausa-Fulani state in northern Nigeria, which he had visited; and gathering a host of enthusiastic followers, he declared a jihad against both pagans and "lapsed" Muslims. He hoped to make the Fouta Toro his base of operations, but the Toucouleur marabouts had no intention of giving up their theocratic rule in that area. Although many young Toucouleurs joined Umar, the major leaders allied themselves with the French, and Umar's westward advance was stopped at Fort Médine on the Senegal in 1857.

Umar and his legions turned east, conquered a vast area on the upper Niger, and founded a large theocratic state. The Fouta Toro remained independent for the moment. But it was isolated between Umar and the French, and Louis Faidherbe and his successors soon conceived the ambitious scheme of conquering the entire West African hinterland. French annexations proceeded slowly, but by 1891 the entire homeland of the Toucouleur peoples was under French rule.

*The empire and states of the Wolof.*[10] The most numerous and important inhabitants of Senegal are the Wolofs, a proud, handsome people who have been the traditional masters of the northern and central heartland plain. Through war, trade, empire, and marriage, Wolof has become the lingua franca of Senegal, spoken by over one-third and understood by possibly two-thirds of all Senegalese. The Wolofs were the first Senegalese to meet Europeans; and they quickly became French auxiliaries, serving as traders, soldiers, sailors, and interpreters. Consequently, they were the earliest African dwellers in the French settlements.

The recorded history of the Wolof peoples does not extend as far back as that of the Toucouleurs. Some observers believe that the Wolofs once lived in Tekrour; others hold that they originated in Mauritania and later moved south. There is also evidence that the Wolofs may have descended from the Toucouleurs or Sereres (and may possibly be a mixture of both these ancient peoples). The modern Wolof historian Cheikh Anta Diop has speculated that the Wolofs originated on the Upper Nile, basing this hypothesis on certain similarities in language and culture.[11]

Oral tradition simply states that the Djolof empire of the Wolof peoples was founded in the thirteenth or fourteenth century by Ndiadiane N'Diaye, who may possibly have been the son of a Toucouleur cleric. N'Diaye's reputation for bravery and supernatural powers led to his selection as the first Bourba of Djolof (i.e. Emperor of the Wolofs). Gaining control of Djolof and of Walo, the Wolof state near the mouth of the Senegal, he apparently united these with the Wolof states of Cayor and Baol to form the Djolof empire. Soon Tekrour and the southern Serere kingdoms of Sine and Saloum became subject to the Wolof state, which also controlled Fulbe lands to the east and Malinké villages to the southeast. At the beginning of the fifteenth century, after the demise of the Mali empire, Djolof embraced all of modern Senegal's heartland, creating a precedent for the French to build on four centuries later. Wolof culture and language slowly spread to the vanquished peoples, especially in the upper classes, and diverse peoples on the periphery of Wolof culture were wholly or partially assimilated. This process has continued to the present, in part because the Djolof empire, though vanished, still lends its prestige to today's Wolofs.

At its height, Djolof was divided into provinces, each with a governor appointed by the Bourba. Provincial governors collected taxes for the empire from all classes and supported themselves by collecting tribute from the great regional chieftains; they also stood ready to furnish the Bourba with troops for his armies, and especially with the services of their mounted cavaliers (tiédos), an aristocratic class of professional warriors. It is not certain whether Islam penetrated the tiédo class or the Djolof nobility. A thin veneer of Islam spread by Moorish or Toucouleur marabouts may have covered certain northern areas of the empire; but Djolof, unlike Tekrour, was basically an animistic state whose traditions were purely African in origin. Recently, a few Wolof genealogists have claimed that Ndiadiane N'Diaye was directly descended from Abu-Bakr Ibn Umar, the Almoravid conqueror of Ghana. However, this seems to be no more than an attempt to claim greater Islamic legitimacy.[12]

The Djolof empire encountered a time of troubles after the mid-sixteenth century: various of its Wolof provinces (Cayor, Walo, and Baol) broke away to become separate kingdoms; and by the end of the sixteenth century it had also lost control of the non-Wolof lands to the south, including the rich kingdoms of Sine and Saloum. The original state of Djolof remained a strong kingdom, but it never regained its former imperial glory. However, it continued to be the center of Wolof culture, and as late as 1855 the Bourba still commanded more respect than any other traditional ruler in Senegal.

The title of sovereign gives to the Bourba, in relation to his former vassals, a moral superiority that still has a great influence. Not even fifty years ago, the princes of the separated provinces came running to the Bourba for advice on important political questions. It is still acknowledged today, without reservation, that if the kings of Sine, Saloum, Baol, Cayor, and Walo were gathered in the presence of the Bourba, only he would have the right to be seated on a higher throne than the rest.[13]

*The Serere states of Sine and Saloum.* The southern provinces of the Djolof Empire were populated primarily by Sereres, who are possibly the most ancient ethnic group in Senegal.[14] This people appears to have migrated from north of the Senegal sometime after A.D. 1000, presumably because of growing Berber pressure. Today, the Sereres are a sedentary people known for their strong attachment to land, crops, and cattle. More than most Senegalese, they can be regarded as peasants in the popular connotation of the term. They are prudent, thrifty, and suspicious of change: for example, they clung to mixed subsistence farming long after most farmers in Senegal had adopted peanut monoculture, and their economy was thus more resistant to fluctuations in the world market.

Soon after their migration to Senegal, the Sereres founded the states of Sine and Saloum in the southern part of the heartland plain. The power of both kingdoms was eventually derived from the tiédo class, which kept the peace, collected taxes, and protected the peasants from foreign enemies. Although the Serere states were often subjugated by imperial powers like Mali or Djolof, they maintained a separate tradition. And the kings (Bours) of Sine-Saloum, like the Bourba of Djolof, were greatly respected by all Senegalese (indeed, the moral authority of these rulers survived the French conquest).

From their inception on, the animistic Serere states resisted Islam and its institutions. However, Sereres near the Atlantic coast fell under the influence of French Catholic missionaries during the nineteenth century and provided many of Senegal's native converts to Christianity. The villages of Joal and Portudal, long familiar with Portuguese traders and missionaries, acquired French missions. And N'Gazobil became famous as a Catholic school and religious printing house. Although the Christian Sereres numbered less than 10 per cent of the total Serere population, they soon became the dominant majority in Senegalese Catholicism and received favored educational opportunities. They were usually the only Sereres interested in moving to the growing urban centers, for most of this ethnic group remained peasants and clung to animist beliefs. By 1891, Sine and Saloum had become part of the French Protectorate.

*The Lebou republic on Cape Verde.* The fortunes of history allowed the Serere peasants to continue their traditional rural life. But the Lebou peasants of Cape Verde were forced to become the most urban of Senegalese peoples after Cape Verde attracted the most intensive French settlement in Black Africa, for they had no hinterland in which to seek refuge.

The traditions of the Lebous place their origin somewhere north of the Senegal River, but how long the Lebous have been a distinct people is a matter for speculation. Their language is a dialect of Wolof, their customs are a mixture of Wolof and Serere practices, and many of their family names are drawn from these two sources. It is fairly certain that they migrated southward to Lake Guier in the Djolof area sometime in the sixteenth century, eventually crossed into Cayor, and took possession of the sparsely settled Cape Verde peninsula after 1700. Expelling a few wandering Malinké tribes, the Lebous established their own village communities on all sides of the Cape and became subsistence farmers and fishermen.[15]

At this time, the Lebous were still subjects of the ruler (Damel) of

Cayor, who was anxious to retain his authority over them. But in 1790 a small maraboutic party (most Lebous were still animists) began a struggle for independence that lasted almost two decades. The most prominent leader of the rebellion was Dial Diop, who led the Lebou troops against the tiédo warriors of Cayor. And when the Damel acknowledged defeat in 1812, the marabouts proclaimed Diop the leader (Serigne) of the Lebou community and gave him full executive powers.

The new Lebou state was a departure from Senegalese tradition, and French writers often refer to it as "the Lebou Republic." Ultimate political authority resided in an assembly of chiefs composed of two colleges: the Diambour-i-N'Dakarou (Grand Assembly of Dakar) and the Diambour-i-Pintch (Assembly of Neighborhood Notables). The chiefs chose a Serigne N'Dakarou (paramount chief and judge) from one of the aristocratic Lebou families. This officer was the court of last appeal for all disputes within the community; he was also considered the "educator" of the people and was supposed to have a maraboutic background. The chiefs also chose the Diaraf (a title previously given to the Damel's governor), who decided when crops should be planted, settled land disputes and inheritance questions, and kept the peace. The third major official appointed was the N'Deye-dy-Rew (minister of the interior and foreign affairs), who was soon put in charge of maintaining contact with the French administration. The colleges were bound to consult this officer before acting on any matter. He became the *porte-parole* of the people, and was even empowered to summon the Serigne to an accounting if necessary; and he signed all treaties with foreign nations.[16]

The heart of the Lebou community was the class of freemen, or *diambours*—patriarchs, clan leaders, and free yeomen. Since there was no monarchy or nobility, the diambours were the primary source of political and military power; and virtually all the local and national chiefs of the Lebou state as well as those who attended the colleges of the Assembly, were chosen from their ranks. In the Senegalese context, this was truly a "republican" system; and it contrasted notably with the Wolof and Serere kingdoms, which were controlled by quasi-absolutist monarchs backed by an aristocratic warrior class of tiédos.[17]

This tradition of collective government gave the Lebous a strong sense of their own uniqueness and separateness, which served them well after the French annexed Cape Verde in 1857. A people with less group consciousness would have been absorbed or destroyed by the French; but the Lebous chose to stay in their homeland and employ passive resistance. As more Frenchmen, other Africans, and finally Lebanese arrived to crowd Dakar, the Lebous retreated, complaining that their lands were being taken away unjustly. They refused to adjust to the realities of French conquest and urbanization— unlike the Wolofs and Toucouleurs, who poured into Dakar and filled jobs the Lebous spurned.

### The Structure of Traditional Senegalese Society

The traditional social structures of the major Senegalese peoples can be examined together, since they are rooted in a common past and have many similarities.[18] There were basically four social strata, or status groups, each divided into several subgroups. A person's status was fixed at birth, and little mobility outside a given class was possible. Marriage to a member of another tribe or ethnic group was considered normal and even desirable as long as one married within one's class; marriage with a lower-class spouse was generally a social taboo. The four primary strata in this system were nobles, freemen, artisans, and slaves.

*The nobility.* The Senegalese aristocracy was generally composed of families who had connections with the ruling dynasty by birth, marriage, or tradition. The Serere countries were dominated by the Guélowar nobles, who were descended from Mandinka warriors. In the Wolof kingdoms, a noble clan called the Garmi furnished claimants to the royal families and officials for the crown. The great regional chiefs were also drawn from the nobility. Nobility was transmitted in the female line among the Sereres, in the male line among the Toucouleurs, and in both lines among the Wolofs.

Each state had various subclasses of aristocracy. The Sereres had a special class of secondary nobles who derived their Guélowar ancestry from their fathers and thus could never attain royal rank. The Garmi alone were eligible for the various Wolof thrones: in Walo, only a claimant from the Garmi M'Bodj clan could become king; in Cayor, descent from one of seven Garmi families was necessary; and in Djolof, the Garmi N'Diaye families furnished members of the royal household as well as Bourbas. Below the Garmis were lesser ranks of nobility, such as Kagnes, Kangames, and Taras, who were usually given positions of authority as chiefs, bureaucrats, or tax collectors. In the Fouta Toro the large Toucouleur aristocracy even included some fishermen who had gained certain ritual privileges over the centuries.

An important subclass of the nobility in most traditional states was the warrior class of tiédos. These cavaliers appear to have originated as slave retainers owned by the crown; but over the centuries they had gradually risen in status, although they usually continued to take orders from their king. In peacetime the tiédos served as tax collectors and were exempted from taxes themselves; in addition, they customarily subsisted by random pillaging and confiscations from the peasant freeholders who made up the bulk of the population, though a strong ruler could limit their plundering. By the time of the French conquest, the tiédos were considered true aristocrats by many Senegalese. And the traditional sovereigns who attempted to keep the old feudal system intact under French pressure (most notably Lat-Dior of Cayor) built their resistance around quick raids by armies of tiédo cavalry. Many tiédos, too, were converted to Islam, often attaching themselves to marabout leaders rather than traditional kings; and under the French they formed an Islamic rural aristocracy with great influence.

*Freemen.* The highest subgroup in this class were the notables and large farmers, who were called *diambour-boureye* by the Sereres, *guer* by the Wolofs, and *diambour* by the Lebous. In Wolof and Serere country freemen had little political influence, although the Diarafs (local representatives of the Bour) were chosen from this class in Serere lands. In contrast, the diambours were the main body of electors and notables in the Lebou Republic.

Most freemen were *badolos*, or peasants, who comprised the bulk of Senegal's indigenous population. It has been debated in recent years whether rural Africans can really be classed with the peasants of Latin America, Europe, or China.[19] The typical peasant in these areas is tied closely to the land, produces crops within a market system, and occupies a definite place in a long-established social system. Senegalese rural cultivators do meet these criteria, although it is probable that some sedentary Negro peoples in other parts of Africa would not. In traditional society, the badolos suffered the lot of peasants everywhere: they were subject to heavy and usually arbitrary taxes; they had to furnish crops or cattle whenever the king or his tiédos needed supplies for war; and they had few privileges. But they were nevertheless freemen, and were under no social restrictions or taboos.[20]

*Artisans.* Below the freeman class was a small, specialized stratum of the social system. The artisans (called *gnégnos* in Wolof) lived quite apart from the nobility and the freemen, were forbidden to marry outside their group, which made them an endogamous caste. However, they profited from the upper classes' distaste for manual work and trades, monopolizing most nonagricultural and nonpastoral economic roles in traditional society. Like the other social strata, the artisans were divided into several groups, each associated with a given trade, and some trades were dominated by artisans from one particular ethnic group. The most important subgroup in this caste was made up of the *griots*, or praise singers, whose ritual chants, music, and exhortations were an essential part of every public ceremony and festival. To the modern historian, the griots' most important function was their traditional task of memorizing and reciting the oral history and noble genealogies of Senegal.

The artisans adapted to the French conquest with great ease, since urbanization and the growing market economy demanded more and more skilled workers. Moreover, they had the training, motivation, and resources to compete in all areas of modern urban society, whereas the traditional upper classes, lacking these things, sought only political offices or administrative jobs (when they bothered to compete at all). Many artisans were able to pass the caste bar and become freemen in the polyglot urban centers. Others built up small fortunes and succeeded as entrepreneurs and merchants; in fact many present-day Senegalese businessmen can trace their ancestry to artisan forebears.*

*Slaves.* The lowest rung on the social ladder was occupied by the slaves (*diams*). In medieval times, captured enemies who were able-bodied fighting men became slaves of the crown, and eventually tiédos. Many Senegalese societies continued to regard the tiédos as royal bondsmen (at least in theory) until the French conquest. Other high-status slaves included those attached to the royal household or noble families as advisers, bodyguards, and domestics; in this setting, some slaves advanced in status and eventually became freemen. Below these privileged slaves were the many foreign captives who were employed as simple domestics in peasant households. Slaves born in the family (*diamdoudou*) enjoyed greater status and privileges than slaves bought or captured elsewhere (*diamsayor*). African domestic slaves were usually considered members of the extended family; and, although they were at the bottom of the social hierarchy, they at least

---

* See Silla, "Persistence des castes dans la société wolof contemporaine," for an informed recent study on questions of caste in Senegal.

had a recognized place in society. When the French freed slaves in their colonies (1848), many simply stayed with their masters; and as late as 1900, most former slaves in Senegal probably retained some kind of obligatory tie to their old masters.*

The social system so far described is a composite picture of traditional life; one must remember that each ethnic group had its own peculiarities and exceptions. (The Lebous, for example, had no royalty or nobility.) In general, the lower classes had a variety of obligations to those above them. But by the same token chiefs and nobles had definite responsibilities to the people—protection from foreign enemies, gifts and public feasts on festive occasions, and so on. Social standing did not necessarily determine one's economic status or one's influence in political affairs. Many artisans were richer and lived more comfortably than badolo peasants, impoverished nobles, or lazy tiédo warriors; and the griot praise singers, though far down on the social scale, often became advisers to chiefs or kings.

The African extended family was the basic element in traditional social organization.[21] The exact rights and duties in family living depended on whether the kinship structure of the tribe or people involved was matrilineal or patrilineal. The Sereres traced descent in the female line, and a young man looked for leadership to his mother's oldest brother. The Toucouleurs were patrilineally oriented, and the father's dominant role in the family was buttressed by Islamic law. The Wolofs traced descent in both ways, but tended to favor patrilineal institutions as Islam gained ascendancy. In most ethnic groups polygyny was sanctioned as normal and desirable for those who could afford to support more than one wife. For economic reasons, many Senegalese men were monogamous, especially since nonsupport was a real ground for divorce; and in practice only chiefs, headmen, and the wealthy took more than one wife.

Senegalese women nonetheless had a great deal of freedom: they could manage their own business without their husband's interference, keep their own herds, grow their own crops, and enter into contracts with third parties. Women, in fact, dominated the small trade of local markets. The first wife in a polygynous household was in charge of directing the other wives; but the rights of all wives were protected by traditional law, and any of them could resort to a local tribunal for divorce or alimony payments. Michel Adanson,

---

* Many slaves were eventually freed by their masters in traditional society; it was also the custom to give slaves their own lands, to which they could devote as much as one-third of their labor. Carrère and Holle, p. 54.

a French visitor to Senegal in the 1750's, observed that Wolof women "have a great share of vivacity and a vast deal of freedom and ease, which renders them extremely agreeable."[22]

## Islam and Traditional Society

African traditional society had evolved a comprehensive political and social structure long before the advent of Islam. Islam has influenced and changed some indigenous institutions in Senegal; but on the whole it is African culture that has modified and adapted Islamic practices.[23] Orthodox Islamicists often complained that Africans did not really understand Islamic theology and law, that the Koran was rarely memorized correctly, and that African knowledge of Arabic was rudimentary. These critics failed to realize that Islam, as a late arrival in West African society, was perforce grafted onto the tenacious local culture.

In Senegal, the Toucouleurs took the lead in diffusing Islam to other Negro peoples; though Moorish marabouts also did a great deal of proselytizing. Much of the prestige of Tekrour stemmed from the fact it was the first Negro kingdom in West Africa to convert to Islam, and the Toucouleur marabouts cultivated this prestige to their advantage. There is evidence that certain northern Wolof peoples were converted in the fifteenth century, but it was not until the nineteenth century that the Islamization of Senegal began on a significant scale.[24]

Several factors encouraged the Senegalese to turn to Islam: the renaissance of the Islamic party in Tekrour after 1776; the increasing activity of marabouts from Mauritania; and most important, the destruction of traditional forms of society by the French conquest. The French experience in Algeria had bred a certain tolerance for Islam that was not accorded to animistic religions; and many French commanders openly encouraged the work of marabouts, who were free to move about and proselytize without restraint. The most significant conversions took place among the Wolofs, whose nobles and tiédos flocked to Islam as a support against French intrusion, carrying with them the bulk of the population. The Lebous were slowly Islamized after 1812, and many of the pastoral Fulbe were converted; but few Sereres abandoned their traditional animistic beliefs.

A distinguishing characteristic of Senegalese Islam has been the part played by the Islamic brotherhoods (*tariqas*). The Qadiriyya and the Tijaniyya were the major tariqas of the nineteenth century, the first strongest in the countryside and the second dominant in the villages and towns. Both brotherhoods were led by Toucouleurs or Moors. The Qadiriyya was the older sect, and was firmly established in Senegal by the eighteenth century. It emphasized tolerance, piety, and respect for all persons, and denounced such frivolities as dancing, buffoonery, and loudly said prayers.[25]

The Tijaniyya was founded in Algeria in the 1780's and soon spread southward.[26] In the 1850's Al Hajj Umar Tall began to preach Tijani concepts by the sword. His legions spread the Tijaniyya throughout the western Sudanic areas; and his sons and disciples accomplished the task in Senegal, where the ascetic and intellectual Qadiriyya doctrines had less popular appeal. The Tijanis offered a simple, understandable version of Islam, emphasizing prayers and religious duties and preaching a positive moral code. Above all, this brotherhood possessed a spiritual dynamism that attracted many Africans to Islam.[27]

Toward the end of the nineteenth century Senegal developed a new tariqa, the Mouridiyya. This sect broke off from the Qadiriyya under the charismatic leadership of Amadou Bamba, a marabout of Toucouleur-Wolof origins who had followed Lat-Dior, Damel of Cayor, during the last struggles of the Senegalese aristocracy against the French.[28] After Lat-Dior's death, Bamba retired to Diourbel in Baol, gathered a group of disciples, and soon became a quasi-deity in the eyes of his *talibés*, or followers.* In spite of persecution by the French, who feared that Bamba might be building a theocratic state within their protectorate, the new tariqa gained many converts among the rural Wolofs and the tiédos. The Mouridiyya teachings were simple, emotional, and highly personalized—closer to African mysticism than Oriental subtlety. Indeed, this was the most African of all the tariqas. The Mourides were as aggressive as the Tijanis, and soon became the wealthiest and most powerful brotherhood in Senegal.[29]

What influences did Islamic teachings and practice have on traditional life in Senegal? Much depended on the people and the region involved, but in general, African culture was surprisingly persistent. Ritual was changed, and a few social mechanisms (e.g. inheritance customs) were profoundly altered. Islamic doctrine, however, was never taken too seriously for its own sake; the chief element in conversion and loyalty to a tariqa was the convert's personal devotion to his marabout, and to be on the safe side some Africans associated

---

* Bamba was considered heretical by some orthodox observers who thought the position of Muhammed as prophet or "messenger of God" was being undermined.

themselves with several marabouts at once.[30] Senegal's social and juridical systems were little affected by Islam. Indeed, the greatest changes occurred in minor areas like dress and food. The long, flowing robes of North Africa became popular, and Moroccan sandals and a fez were also favored by some men. Pork disappeared from Muslim dishes, and French-introduced wines were forbidden (at least in theory). Given names tended to be Islamized, and infants were called Ibrahima, Ahmadou, Moustapha, and so on. But traditional family names such as N'Diaye, Diagne, and Diop stayed the same. Funerals were usually conducted according to Islamic laws.[31]

### French Contact and the Growth of the Communes

The Four Communes were built by the French and given French government, but they were inhabited principally by Africans. The history of the Communes spans 250 years; and throughout this period, the Communes nurtured the Africans' interest in local government, which eventually became an interest in the political process as a whole.

Senegal was first opened to European trade by the Portuguese in the mid-fifteenth century. France took an interest in the area during the next century, and by the 1650's her plans were fairly clear: mastery of trade on the Senegal river, control of the river mouth, and exclusion of other European merchants. Like the Portuguese before them, the French eventually hoped to penetrate the interior of West Africa and tap the reputed riches of the Sudan. In 1658, Finance Minister Colbert reorganized a Norman trading company that had been operating in Senegal for several decades; backers and directors from Paris took over the management, and preparations for the thrust inland were begun. This firm, the Compagnie du Cap Vert et du Sénégal, was the first of six successive companies that monopolized French trade in Senegal for over a century.

The new company set up its first factory slightly upstream from the treacherous, shifting mouth of the Senegal. After negotiating with the local Wolof chief, the company's craftsmen built a small but substantial fort on a narrow island in the river. This initial post, called Saint-Louis du Sénégal, was too small to house any of the company employees, who were obliged to live like the Africans in reed huts outside its walls.[32] One Sieur de la Courbe, appointed director of the post in 1685, observed on arriving that the fort had had four towers added to it but was still very small. "If the blacks had been malicious they could easily have slaughtered the whites who lived outside the fort, for no watch was ever kept."[33] By this time a chapel, storehouses, and other permanent buildings had been constructed. De la Courbe was also alarmed by the fact that his employees openly kept Negro mistresses in their reed huts. The French, like the Portuguese before them, had quickly succumbed to the charms of the Wolof women, who were regarded as among the most glamorous in Africa. The mulatto class that resulted from these unions was of great importance in Senegal's later political history.

Saint-Louis continued as the center of French operations in Senegal, although the initial French company was soon replaced by others. Trade pushed slowly inland; new forts were built; and gum arabic, hides, and gold from the interior began to reach the coast. The French worked under several handicaps during this period. Contact with France was often broken by European wars, and few Frenchmen cared to spend much time in Senegal in any case. There were never more than a few European troops available, and the powerful local rulers had things pretty much their own way. (For example, in 1701 André Brüe, the new French Governor of the colony, was captured and held for ransom by the Damel of Cayor; his lieutenants at Saint-Louis had no recourse but payment.) Still, trade did expand, and more and more Africans grew accustomed to the presence of Frenchmen.

Gorée, a small, rocky island lying just off Cape Verde, was strategically located near the most westerly point of the African continent. For this reason, it was occupied by Portugal at an early date; but because the nearby Cape Verde Islands were Portugal's prime entrepôts for trade and provisioning. Gorée never became more than a way station. Portugal merged with Spain in the sixteenth century, and the Dutch, capitalizing on the defeat of the Spanish Armada, seized Gorée in 1588 as an opening move in their ambitious scheme to replace the Portuguese as masters of the East Indian trade. Fortifications were built, and when the Dutch West India Company was founded in 1621 Gorée also became a thriving entrepôt for the slave trade.

The Dutch, in turn, were weakened later in the century by their interminable wars with Louis XIV, and Admiral Jean d'Estrées seized Gorée for France in 1677. The Treaty of Nijmegen the next year officially confirmed France's possession of the island and also awarded her Joal, Rio Fresco (later to become Rufisque), and Portudal, three old Portuguese stations lying south of Cape Verde. In 1679, Germain Ducasse, an envoy of the Company, concluded treaties with the Damel of Cayor and the Bour of Sine for trading rights on the *petite côte* (the coast between Cape Verde and the Gambia).* The Portuguese and Dutch were now effectively eliminated from the race, and only the English enclave on the Gambia challenged French supremacy on this portion of the upper Guinea coast.

André Brüe, who was appointed Governor of Senegal in 1697, brought activities at Gorée into concert with operations at Saint-Louis. Strong garrisons were attached to the forts of both towns; provision was also made for doctors and priests in both posts. Craftsmen and workers (both French and African) poured in. One has only to examine the personnel lists set up by Brüe to see why the cost of operating the Senegalese establishments was so high that profits were not always assured.[34] Brüe also managed to establish good relations with the British in Gambia, and a brisk trade soon began, the French exchanging their surplus of gum arabic for more slaves. Gorée became the center of this traffic, as Saint-Louis was the entrepot for trade on the Senegal River.

After Brüe left, French Senegal stagnated for several decades. Adanson, however, found Saint-Louis in 1749 a pleasing city, "the most handsome in Africa."[35] Its population was over three thousand, and many permanent buildings had been added, although most dwellings were still reed huts. When a permanent structure was built, the model was typically French but well suited to the tropics: a two-story building with a shop or business on the ground floor, family apartments placed above to catch the breeze, and a courtyard where slaves and servants were quartered. Such houses were usually owned by French, Creoles, or wealthy African merchants. During this period a group of women called *signares* became important in Senegal's social and economic history. These were African or mulatto women who lived with Frenchmen *à la mode du pays*; some were married, others were not. A few signares were simply mistresses, but many of them became educated, entered commerce, and exerted a real influence in the colony.†

* This treaty's existence is disputed by Abdoulaye Ly in *La compagnie du Sénégal*, pp. 144–46.

† Apparently the institution of signares dated from Portuguese days and was quite common on the upper Guinea coast. Golberry, who traveled this coast in the 1780's, observed that anywhere between the Senegal River and Sierra Leone one found mulattoes and Negroes with Portuguese, French, or English names. Many signares contracted a type of limited marriage that was expected to last until the European returned home; it was agreed that any children would be called after the father. See Golberry, pp. 156–58.

Saint-Louis fell under British domination in 1758 during the Seven Years' War, and the city was retained by Britain after peace was made. Like the French, the British were interested in controlling trade on the Senegal and Gambia rivers; and they held onto Saint-Louis for 21 years, leaving Gorée to the French. In 1779, during the American Revolution, France decided to recapture Saint-Louis, since the British fleet was apparently absent from African waters; and the Marquis de Vaudreuil led an expedition that won back the city at small cost. Later in the year, however, Gorée fell to the British, who were only compelled to return it by the Treaty of Versailles in 1783. A new era now dawned in Gorée and Saint-Louis for officials of the French Crown had taken command during the wars. The Senegal establishments were henceforth a royal colony, not simply an outpost of empire managed by a chartered company.[36]

As the King's officials took over French Senegal, they found that the African inhabitants of Gorée and Saint-Louis were used to a privileged status and expected to be treated with deference. Paul Benis, an African who could neither read nor write, managed an enterprise in 1787 that reputedly equalled the King's company in volume of trade; and many mulattoes were prosperous and respected merchants.[37] Moreover, during the years of company rule and English occupation Africans had been active in civic life. The French had found it useful to appoint a kind of local mayor to handle minor criminal and administrative problems. And in 1765 a free mulatto named Thévenot was apparently acting as both priest and mayor in Saint-Louis during the British occupation.[38] By the 1780's, custom dictated that when the Governor tried capital offenses the mayor of Saint-Louis was to be included on a panel of advisers. "In civil cases, the Governor would sit with three assessors of the same color as the parties; in interracial cases, with assessors of both colors."[39] A convicted African was usually transported to the French Antilles; Frenchmen who had injured local Africans could be sent back to France.

Hargreaves believes that urban Africans were already well on the way to cultural assimilation in the eighteenth century, not only because the urban dwellers were accepting European values but also because they felt that this acceptance should bring them certain rights.[40] The 1758 surrender agreement with the British provided that free Negroes and mulattoes would retain their liberty and property, and that they would not be persecuted because of their Catholic religion. In the next year, the Africans complained that this agreement was being violated; a petition was drawn up, signed by local notables and the Senegalese mayor, and sent to the British commander. In 1776 complaints and petitions were still being presented to the British, and by then they were written in English rather than French. After the French returned to Saint-Louis, a new spirit of independence was evident.

By the end of the Old Regime, assimilation in Gorée and Saint-Louis was an accomplished fact. Not only were Africans and mulattoes interested in civic rights, but their skills and enterprise were vital to French Senegal's economy; for it was mainly the urban Senegalese who went upriver to bargain for gum or hides. Increasingly, the French trusted these local agents to handle trade on a commission basis. In 1785, for example, only one Frenchman visited the interior. Some Africans had converted to Catholicism, though most were still Muslims or animists; but the entire mulatto community passed to the Church.

What was the status of the different non-European groups in French Senegal? First of all, there were the *mulâtres* (offspring of a European and an African) and *métis* (persons of mixed descent, i.e., French father and mulatto mother). Both these groups tended to accept European culture and Christianity; in this study I will refer to them collectively as Creoles, a term commonly used by the French. Second, there were the Christian Africans, or *gourmets*, a small but important group.* These were primarily full-blooded Africans, but occasionally a gourmet might be of remote mixed origin. Third, there were the Muslim Negroes, who were primarily Wolofs or Toucouleurs; this was the group most involved in the river traffic. Any member of these three classes could be called a *habitant* or *enfant du pays*; and any could aspire to the title of *notable*, a term used down to the twentieth century to designate the outstanding merchants and most respected members of the community. It should be noted that the Creoles constantly struggled to rise above this categorization and sought equal status with Frenchmen in all respects.†

Below these groups was the bulk of the African urban population (mostly slaves and domestics in the towns), who were usually animists. If an African fresh from the countryside were to stay in Saint-Louis

---

* The spelling *gourmette* is more common in the later nineteenth and early twentieth centuries.

† See the discussion by Hargreaves, "Assimilation," pp. 177–80. He divides free urban Senegalese into mulattoes, gourmets, and Muslim Negroes, all of whom he calls habitants. But he notes that at some times habitant may have meant a local European resident. I have chosen to group all persons of mixed origin together as Creoles—i.e., mulattoes, métis, and some highly assimilated gourmets.

or Gorée for many years, convert to Christianity or Islam, and become a tradesman or commercial agent, he could expect to become a habitant and scale the social ladder. But migration to the towns was not a simple matter of changing houses. A long process of acculturation to urban mores and values awaited the newcomer, who usually spent years living in African huts on the periphery of the town. Residence and a job in the town proper came only with assimilation and increased status.

The city of Saint-Louis grew steadily. A census taken in 1786 showed approximately 7,000 people living on the island: 660 Europeans, 2,400 free Negroes or Creoles, 3,000 slaves or bondsmen, and the balance unaccounted for.[41] (Even today, censuses are difficult in Senegal, since there is a large floating population that varies from season to season.) The outstanding mayor of Saint-Louis during this period was Charles Cornier, a Creole whose influence was extremely important in Senegal during the French Revolution.

When news arrived in 1789 that the Estates-General would meet at Versailles for the first time since 1614, a group of Saint-Louis notables assembled to draw up a local *cahier de doléance* for forwarding to France. Under the leadership of Mayor Cornier and a French merchant, Dominique Lamiral, this committee drafted a petition demanding free trade and the abrogation of the restrictive *pacte colonial*. The new Governor, François Blanchot, traveled to France the next year in an effort to expedite matters. The first years of the Revolution were filled with new projects, and with dreams that were never fulfilled. Saint-Louis won its right to free trade, and slavery was abolished. Several decrees offered the rights of French citizenship to the people of France's overseas possessions; however, it is doubtful that many Creoles or assimilated Africans in Senegal understood the meaning of these rights and tried to become *citoyens*. Local rights continued to evolve while Senegal was virtually cut off from Paris by the later events of the Revolution, but these rights were largely unrecognized outside the colony. Cornier evidently tried to visit France during this period, but was stopped by certain French officials who claimed that the Old Regime's ban against men of color traveling in France was still in effect.[42]

The British recaptured Gorée in 1800, and minor skirmishes characterized the next few years of the Napoleonic wars in West Africa. Governor Blanchot died in 1807, exhausted by work and the climate; the power of the local government and mayors had increased during his benevolent rule and he was apparently beloved by his Senegalese charges. In 1809, an undefended Saint-Louis also fell to the British, who allowed the Creole mayor, Charles Porquet, to continue in charge of the local administration. The Senegalese Catholics remained loyal to their faith during the occupation despite the efforts of British governors to convert them to Protestantism.[43] In fact, a general liking for French values and institutions was obvious among the urban Senegalese by this time, and the British found them strikingly loyal to their former rulers.

The Treaty of Paris ended the Napoleonic wars in 1814, and France's African possessions were returned; from this time on, her mastery of the Senegalese coast was uncontested.

### French Expansion in the Nineteenth Century

During the years 1817–54, seventeen Governors served in Senegal, some holding the post for only a few months.[44] Many were military commanders awaiting assignment elsewhere. Under this uncertain administration Senegal stagnated as a French dependency; but as in the past, the local Creole and African community continued to grow in economic importance and nurtured a healthy interest in local political affairs. The first French schools were established in Saint-Louis in 1816, and local inhabitants now had the chance to acquire a rudimentary French education. The year 1840 was also an important one for the Communes, for the Ordinance of September 7 in that year reorganized the colony and laid down its fundamental administrative framework for the rest of the century. The Governor was given greater powers, making him less subject to Paris. An administrative council was created to advise him; and a colonial General Council was established, consisting of elected members from the local French and habitant population.[45]

In 1845 Edouard Bouët-Willaumez became chief of naval operations for the French South Atlantic District and established his headquarters at Gorée. The island fortress now controlled all French posts and trading enclaves south of Senegal—Guinea, Ivory Coast, Gold Coast, Dahomey, and Gabon. Gorée had been given its own municipal council, the Conseil d'Arrondissement, at the time of the 1840 reorganization, when Saint-Louis received the General Council.* The

* Gorée was separated administratively from Saint-Louis in 1845 but still remained under the capital's jurisdiction. In 1854 Gorée was given autonomy, and the French naval commander took charge. Faidherbe, on becoming Governor of Senegal, was annoyed that Gorée had been detached and used his influence to have the city restored to Saint-Louis's jurisdiction.

island now enjoyed its golden years as a naval base and trading emporium: official French expeditions southward and unofficial French-Creole trading missions kept the harbor bustling.

Saint-Louis continued as the capital of the Senegal River area and served as headquarters for the French Army in tropical Africa. In 1847 it received a visit from Victor Schoelcher, the editor of the famous Parisian abolitionist journal *Le National*. Schoelcher was shocked to find that so many inhabitants of Saint-Louis—masons, carpenters, porters, and daily workers—were either domestic slaves or indentured workers.[46] His impressions of Senegal reinforced his determination to press for total abolition, which occurred after the revolution of the following year.

The Revolution of 1848 was a landmark for the French empire. The Second Republic sought to outdo its first namesake by giving all colonies deputies to the new Assembly in Paris. Senegal was included, and for the first time a general election was called in the colony; all inhabitants of Gorée or Saint-Louis could qualify to vote by proving a residence of five years or longer. The Republic's concrete actions in enforcing the new ban on slavery and giving representation to the colony far outweighed the republican sentiment of 1789 as an influence in Senegal. Although French Senegal had evolved its own municipal institutions and had been given a General Council and an advisory representative to the Ministry of Marine in 1840, the election of 1848 was the first time the general populace actively engaged in a political contest.*

To be sure, some Frenchmen were skeptical of this experiment in popular democracy on the African continent. Governor A. Baudin observed:

I don't share the view of those in France who think universal suffrage an admirable thing; here [in Senegal] I would go further and call it absurd and nonsensical. If it were possible to explain how the election for the colony's representative took place here, it would frighten even the most dedicated partisan of universal suffrage. The poor blacks were beset by the agents of all the candidates. Ballots printed in advance were handed out to some, torn up by others, redistributed, and recirculated perhaps fifty times in the days preceding the election. On election day, the battle was even more murderous; it got to the point where I would defy any black to know positively

---

* A few Senegalese voted for the municipal councils in the confused decade of the 1790's, some voted in the plebiscite held by Napoleon in 1804, and a handful of notables elected representatives from a list fixed by the Governor in the 1840 General Council organization. But never before had the general populace voted, for most of them had been slaves before 1848.

which candidate he voted for; and if such a business should take place often, all the paper manufacturers in Europe would not be able to meet Senegal's needs.[47]

The Governor's views possibly reflected his disappointment at losing the campaign for deputy to the Creole mayor of Saint-Louis, Durand Valantin. But his statement was only the first of many made by Frenchmen who had small regard for Africans (however assimilated) as participants in European-style politics.

The republicanism of the Second Republic soon gave way to the Second Empire's aggressive dreams of glory and expansion. In 1850, Benoist d'Azy, vice-president of the National Assembly, presided over an interministerial commission that examined all French possessions and spheres of influence in Africa. These discussions evolved a new program for French activity in Senegal: the extension of French authority, by force if necessary, in order to eliminate the customs and tributes so far paid to the African rulers of the interior; the creation of economic institutions for the penetration of the interior; and the establishment of free trade throughout the colony. Specific instructions were given to stop the Moors from encroaching on the left bank of the Senegal, to establish French suzerainty all along the river, and to protect the rural population from raiding nomads. The merchants of Saint-Louis welcomed the new policies and enthusiastically supported Governor Auguste Protet's initial plan, to build a fort at Podor on the middle Senegal. The army engineer who directed the fort's construction, Louis Faidherbe, became the next Governor of Senegal and the most famous Frenchman in the colony's history.

Faidherbe was only 36 when he became Governor. Born in Lille and educated at the elite Ecole Polytechnique in Paris, he was austere and resourceful, with a keen sense of duty. He was also an accomplished scholar and linguist, and produced some of the earliest ethnographic studies of Senegal. During Faidherbe's tenure, French influence was extended up the Senegal, to the Cape Verde peninsula and much of the coast, and into the interior heartland plain. And he inaugurated the idea of enlarging French Senegal from a series of coastal enclaves (the Communes) to a large colony encompassing the traditional native states.

When Faidherbe took over the Communes, Senegal was in transition economically. Many merchants in Saint-Louis had believed that after the abolition of slavery Senegal's only commercial future lay in trading for gum arabic. But already there was a new product on the horizon: the peanut, introduced by the Portuguese several centuries earlier, was first produced commercially in Senegal during the 1840's; and by Faidherbe's time it was apparent that it could be profitably raised for commerce by traditional methods. French and Creoles could organize trade and shipping, depending on peanuts raised by African peasants rather than by European-managed plantations. In fact, in 1859 the Ministry of Marine issued a document, since obscured by colonial history, that was actually the charter of African agricultural protection for Senegal (and by extension, for much of what was to become French West Africa). The Ministry held that Senegal could never become another Algeria because of its climate, rejected the notion of European colonization and settlement, and proclaimed that the land should be left to the Africans. The French were to encourage the Africans to produce suitable cash crops, and were themselves to monopolize trading and marketing, "the only activity that Europeans can carry on in such a climate."[48]

The pacte-colonial, a time-honored system of preferential trading between France and her colonies, expired officially with the advent of free trade in France under the Cobden Treaty of 1860; but in practice it had been dead since 1848. In 1854 Faidherbe founded the Banque de Sénégal at Saint-Louis to provide local credit and reduce the dependence of local merchants on French financiers. His regime supported the vigorous trading activity of the Creoles, as well as the establishment of some large Bordeaux and Marseille firms in Senegal. But the cornerstone of Faidherbe's success in Senegal was his policy of linking the commercial interests of the Saint-Louis merchants with those of the Senegal River peoples.[49] This inaugurated a cordial relationship that lasted for almost a century; and many Africans became trusted auxiliaries, developing a real loyalty to the French. It was primarily from the river area and the southern lands of Walo and Djolof that Africans migrated to Saint-Louis to enter the expanding urban economy.

The harmonious multiracial tradition in Saint-Louis continued as in the past. Faidherbe decided that the Muslim Africans should have access to the French schools, heretofore open only to Christianized Creoles. He organized 13 schools for Africans and staffed them with teachers from France; he then persuaded Catholic officials to open their courses to Muslims (who had been reluctant to attend Catholic schools, fearing pressures for conversion). Evening classes were started for those who worked in the day. However, Faidherbe preferred not to create a secondary school in the colony and continued the practice of sending bright students to France for advanced training. He also gave high priority to the School for the Sons of

Chiefs (founded 1855), which brought young Africans of the nobility from the interior to Saint-Louis. It not only educated potential chiefs and leaders in Western ideas but also trained them to serve as French auxiliaries in the future.

The city of Saint-Louis, in particular, owed much to Faidherbe. Buildings of wood were now replaced by solid brick and stucco edifices. A new bridge connected the island with Guet N'Dar, a growing suburb of Wolof fishermen located on the long sandbar that separates the river from the ocean. Faidherbe built roads, cleared the city of fire hazards, and improved the hospitals. Saint-Louis began to take on the air of a southern European city, though still surrounded by masses of thatched huts. And in 1857, the Governor authorized a handsome new building to house a Muslim tribunal that would handle questions of marriage, death, and inheritance in accordance with Islamic practice.

Faidherbe was a gifted and perceptive amateur scholar—the type of administrative observer who later did so much to record African tradition in both the British and French possessions.[50] He was genuinely interested in trying to understand the Africans and their civilization. His motive was largely intellectual curiosity; but at the same time he was trying to formulate a real "native policy" for France. In fact, Faidherbe was very much a man of his time; he firmly believed in France's civilizing mission in Africa, and his policies reflected this assimilationst ideal. Speaking to an African audience in 1860, he praised the lot of the *assimilé.*

Look what is happening down the coast. . . . Backward tribes, rescued from slavery by the English and profiting from the education provided by abolitionist societies . . . have now become merchants, wholesalers, and shopkeepers; others occupy high positions in colonial society, and men born into savagery in the Congo twenty years ago have now become colonial administrators or magistrates for the English.

Here in Senegal . . . young men from Christian families of Saint-Louis, after studying in the religious schools, go to France to finish their studies and return qualified to fill the most important positions in the colony. Now this road is open to all of you. To every child who shows himself capable in his studies, we are obliged to give the chance of a liberal career—without asking whether he is from Fouta, Bondou, Bambouk, or Saint-Louis. I exhort you to profit from these opportunities, so that we won't see the Wolofs, Fulbe, Mandingoes, and Sarakalets—all superior Sudanic races—outdistanced by the "bushmen" of the lower coast.[51]

French designs on the interior of Senegal, manifest since the 1820's, were now implemented by military conquest. Between Faidherbe's advent in 1854 and the end of the century, France vanquished all the

African states of the interior, either placing them under direct rule or establishing protectorates. The physical boundaries of modern Senegal were largely sketched in by the time Faidherbe retired in 1865; his successors laboriously completed the job in the face of vigorous African resistance.

One of Faidherbe's most important acts was his decision to occupy the Cape Verde Peninsula. His contemporaries in the French administration were still preoccupied with the thought of conquering the lands of the Senegal River. But it was obvious by this time that the newer steam vessels could never pass the bar of the Senegal and reach Saint-Louis; moreover, the trade in gum, hides, and other commodities available on the Senegal was becoming less important. Cape Verde, by contrast, had a fine harbor opposite Gorée Island on the site of modern Dakar; and the economic importance of peanut culture in the lands near the Cape was increasing each year. A small military post was set up at Dakar in 1857, and the rest of the peninsula was gradually acquired from its Lebou inhabitants. Because Cape Verde eventually became the economic and political center of West Africa, the Lebous were to feel the weight of French rule more than most Senegalese peoples.

The Lebous' reaction at the outset was mostly one of indifference and acquiescence, since they were allowed to retain their old right to tax trade passing through the Cape. Initially, the French possessed only the small territory at Dakar; but within several years Frenchmen spread throughout the Cape and down the immediate coast. This inevitable expansion aroused the antagonism of the Lebous, who had supposed that their traditional, sedentary way of life would remain undisturbed. Moreover, the French government did not fully understand that the Lebous regarded themselves as their own sovereigns. Captain J. B. Jauréguibéry, who briefly replaced Faidherbe in 1862, decreed that the Lebous could not dispose of their lands without the consent of the neighboring Damel of Cayor, who was under nominal French protection. But the Lebous had fought for two decades before breaking free of the Damel in 1812. The outraged Lebou populace was finally appeased the next year by Faidherbe, who placed Cape Verde under the Napoleonic Code and decreed monetary compensation for Lebous obliged to move because of French occupation.[52] No mention was made of the Damel.

The new policy brought handsome payments to some Lebou families when the Messageries Maritimes, a large steamship company, and other French concerns decided to buy land for future installations. But a vicious pattern was set in operation: expropriated Lebous soon exhausted the cash they had received; and without their lands they had no means of earning more money, or even supporting themselves. Within a few years the same Lebous would ask for additional funds, arguing that their lands had been taken away without adequate payment. To the European mind this was chicanery bordering on extortion. But from the African point of view, the growth of French towns took away the people's traditional livelihood in return for a token bribe. In effect, the Lebous gained nothing permanent from the exchange. A European in the same position might have used his compensation as investment capital; but traditional life on Cape Verde was based on farming and grazing, and land to support these activities was in short supply.

The Lebous were the only traditionally organized people in Senegal to be taken over so suddenly and completely by the French. Saint-Louis and Gorée had grown slowly, with small annual additions of migrants who were absorbed into urban life by an African majority long used to French laws and customs. But the Lebous were a traditional African society meeting westernization as a group, and they tended to resist every change that threatened their old way of life. With the French moving in on them from the sea and the Damel of Cayor barring them from the interior, their only alternative was passive resistance; and they resisted with dignity and suffering.

## The Urban Consolidation, 1857–1914

From Faidherbe on, as the interior conquest proceeded, the French consolidated their holdings in coastal Senegal, especially in the immediate area of the Communes. Senegal was considered a full-scale colony rather than a coastal enclave, and in 1882 a new administrative organization was adopted. All of the coastal regions from Saint-Louis to the Gambia were amalgamated to form the Territories of Direct Administration, whereas the bulk of the interior so far conquered was organized as a protectorate. This basic organization was modified in 1890 by an *arrêté* that limited direct administration to the Four Communes and their suburbs, together with the areas served by the new Saint-Louis–Dakar railway. The rest of Senegal came under the Protectorate. In the areas of direct administration most Africans eventually gained political rights, but in the Protectorate they remained *sujets français* and were subject to arbitrary justice at the hands of French administrators and military officers.

This administrative division reflected the social and economic changes taking place in Senegal. Modern commerce, small-scale industrialization, Western education, and urbanization were steadily expanding in the coastal areas. In the Protectorate, a few changes were evident. Peanut growing and a cash-crop economy spread slowly through the land after the French conquest, and a few Western ideas were gradually diffused. But in general the rural Senegalese peasant lived much as his forebears had. In the towns, meanwhile, a new urban class was growing, and many of its more alert members were aware of the privileges and priorities allowed them by the French administration. In fact, residents in the Communes were governed by laws that differed little from those in the metropole; and they could participate in local government under Western-style political institutions, which was not possible in the Protectorate.

The old Portuguese enclave of Rio Fresco, on the southern shore of the Cape Verde peninsula, was formally annexed by the French in 1859. It had already been known by the French name of Rufisque since the eighteenth century, and the Portuguese names of some Creole families were the only remaining sign of Portuguese influence. The enclave had been a Lebou preserve for some time, and when the French moved in, the situation was much like that in Dakar: the Lebous were well settled, and French encroachment was a threat to traditional life.

Rufisque soon became the commercial center of southern Senegal. Although not endowed with a good harbor, it was close to the inland areas that were now producing peanuts for market. Unlike Dakar, it was an established city; and it had space for warehouses, offices, and depots that could not be built on the small island of Gorée. After 1870 many Gorée merchants moved their offices to Rufisque. Moreover, the coming of the Third Republic marked a renewed interest in Senegal among the big commercial houses in France, and most of them also chose Rufisque as their base of operations.[53] All this happened despite the announced intention of the central government to make Dakar the main port of Senegal, and it was not until the 1920's, that the economic balance of power shifted from Rufisque to Dakar. Dakar's port facilities were clearly superior by the turn of the century, but French business had too much invested to move overnight.

Most of Rufisque's new prosperity sprang from the great boom in cash-crop peanut farming that had begun in the mid-nineteenth century. Peanuts had been raised in Senegal for centuries, but only to supplement the staple crop of millet.[54] In the 1840's, however, a demand for peanut oil arose in Europe: it was needed in the manufacture of soap, since the expanding Industrial Revolution had cut urban dwellers off from the old supplies of wood ash and animal fats; and the French housewife also adopted it as her primary cooking oil. France could obtain peanuts from Senegal, and from India after the Suez Canal opened in 1869; and after the advent of railroads Senegal gradually became the more important. She soon became the classic example of a colony geared to monoculture and dominant trade with the mother country. The rural Senegalese, especially the Wolofs, lured by the cash rewards of the market, gave up other crops and bought imported rice and millet for food. Only the Toucouleurs of the river and the shrewd Serere peasants retained a balanced farming economy. Elsewhere, all across the sandy heartland plain, the light forest cover was burned off, peanuts were planted, and all the necessities of life were purchased with profits from the crops.[55]

The commercial procedures used for the gum trade were shifted over to the peanut trade. A trading season was proclaimed by the Governor, and certain villages were chosen as collection points where Africans could bring the produce. The administration soon declared that peanuts could be exported free of all customs duties,* and Rufisque became the grand depot where peanuts were sorted and shipped to the oil-extraction plants in Europe. This commerce was not a one-way affair. Ships returned to Senegal laden with textiles, bicycles, pots and pans, canned foods, spirits, and hundreds of other products that could easily be sold to the newly affluent Africans. Western Senegal soon developed a thriving credit economy, which spread as French influence and peanut farming reached the more remote inland regions.

French businessmen flocked to Rufisque, turning it into a city of permanent buildings comparable to Saint-Louis. Dakar was left to the colonial government, which slowly improved the harbor. But the city grew more slowly than Rufisque, since few government officials cared to leave the cultivated *cercles*, military balls, and cafe society of Saint-Louis. Until the turn of the century, travelers commented on Dakar's miserable accommodations, shabby wooden buildings, and filthy streets. The port continued to grow; but most of Senegal's trade still passed through Rufisque, whereas Dakar became a way station for vessels plying the South Atlantic.[56]

---

* For example, an 1848 decree removed the duty on peanuts exported from Cayor; and an arrêté of June 1852 prescribed that on the Senegal River navigation taxes would no longer be collected on peanuts.

The construction of the railroad in 1885 improved the situation, and Dakar began to handle more of the trade in minor commodities; but Rufisque continued to monopolize the peanut trade for several decades. Eventually, though, the advantages of Dakar's port were acknowledged; and in 1902 the city became the capital of all French West Africa. A palace for the Governor-General was built overlooking the Atlantic, and a new railway station and *hôtel de ville* were constructed. By the eve of World War I, Dakar had become a city of squares, parks, theaters, cafes, and streets lined with boutiques. And by the 1920's it was often called the "little Paris" of Africa. Business firms eventually found it advantageous to open Dakar offices, especially firms doing business in Africa for the first time. The city was also crowded by *petits colons* seeking a fortune, many of them former agents of the large Bordeaux and Marseille companies. Syrians and Lebanese began to arrive toward the end of the century, and they became important in the Senegalese economy during World War I, when thousands of Frenchmen left for the trenches of northern France. These Levantines were to create a serious minority problem, for Africans resented their presence.[57]

An influx of Africans started too. The Lebous, for so long in the majority, found themselves surrounded by unfamiliar Africans; they attempted to keep to themselves, moved many of their villages away from Dakar, and tried to retain their unique ethnic identity. Wolofs gained the upper hand; they were the great merchants of traditional Senegal, and it was natural they should flock to the new emporium on Cape Verde. Behind the Wolofs came the Toucouleurs, not nearly as numerous but proud of their own Islamic culture and their centuries of contact with the trading cities of the Western Sudan. Like the Lebous, they clung to their own group, organizing into neighborhoods and seeking much the same employment as the Wolofs. These were the major groups, but many other peoples were represented. The migrations were only beginning in 1900, and the Lebous were still a majority with the Wolofs close behind. But within two decades Dakar's African quarter became heterogeneous and cosmopolitan.[58]

Dakar was not the only city to develop an African urban class. The dominant element in most towns was Wolof, owing to the prominence of Wolof culture and language in traditional Senegal; but it was a rare immigrant, Wolof or otherwise, who did not change in response to the urban milieu. The growing urban class was legally separated from its rural cousins, and its members were exposed to social forces that transformed their attitudes, goals, and style of living. Yet the urbanized African was not quite the same as his Creole neighbors, who considered themselves Frenchmen and wholly adopted French customs, dress, and *mentalité*. On the contrary, he retained his African identity, carefully preserving the social usages of traditional society and wearing traditional dress with pride. And his perceptions and understanding were still African—foreign to the French and comprehended but not emulated by the Creoles.

By late in the nineteenth century, the pattern of urbanization in Senegal was established. Saint-Louis, Gorée, Dakar, and Rufisque were full communes—that is, municipalities whose citizens lived under the same laws and enjoyed the same privileges as communal residents in France itself. In these cities, known as the Four Communes, lived most of Senegal's French and Creole inhabitants; and in them most of the colony's local politics took place. Saint-Louis remained the largest of the Communes until the twentieth century, finally losing first place to Dakar (see Table 1). Gorée declined after Cape Verde was settled, and was eventually amalgamated with the Commune of Dakar in 1929. Rufisque grew quickly, losing ground only after Dakar was chosen as the capital of French West Africa.

The Four Communes, however, were not the only urban areas in Senegal. Toward the end of the century other towns and cities sprang up, marking the inland extension of French administration, peanut culture, and the market economy. Thiès, 35 miles inland from Dakar, is a good example. It was founded in 1862 by Faidherbe to facilitate communications between Saint-Louis and Dakar and to serve as an advanced military post near the hostile state of Cayor. Its importance grew rapidly after 1885 because it lay on the new railway and also communicated with Wolof lands to the east and Serere lands to the south. Streets for the town were immediately laid out and lots were put up for sale; in 1886 the first Catholic mission-

TABLE 1

*Growth of the Four Communes to 1921*

| Commune | 1865[a] | 1878 | 1910 | 1921 |
|---------|---------|------|------|------|
| Saint-Louis | 15,000 | 15,980 | 22,093 | 17,493 |
| Gorée | 3,000 | 3,243 | 1,306 | 917 |
| Rufisque | 300 | 1,173 | 12,457 | 11,106 |
| Dakar | 300 | 1,566 | 24,914 | 30,037 |

SOURCE: Census reports, ARS, 27-G-237-108; *Annuaire du Gouvernement-Général de l'A.O.F.*, 1922.
[a] Estimated figures.

aries arrived. Stone and stucco buildings soon replaced wooden ones, and Rufisque merchants opened branch offices for buying peanuts. In 1893, Thiès was put under the civilian government and joined the other direct administration areas. And in 1903, the beginning of the railway toward Kayes in the French Soudan made Thiès the major rail junction in Senegal.[59]

Nonetheless, the Communes continued to dominate Senegalese politics, each of them acquiring its own distinctive character. Saint-Louis was the first Commune, and it continued to be the most individual. Indeed, one cannot completely understand the history of modern Senegal without understanding the arrogance and sense of apartness engendered by the old city on the banks of the Senegal. A great emigration of Saint-Louisians started at the turn of the century—most of them Africans with some business training or a rudimentary education who moved to the interior or to the new towns along the railway. The Saint-Louisian was the man who organized the peanut trade and served as a link with the peasant cultivator. He was the young schoolmaster who taught in the interior; he was the local agent for French or Creole firms; and he was the prime recruit for the colonial federation's offices in Dakar. Until the independence of Senegal in 1960, Saint-Louisians monopolized the most important positions open to Africans in the Senegalese economic and administrative structure. And Saint-Louis itself was the center of Islamic, Catholic, and lay education in Senegal—the city that attracted most of the young men who came in from the bush to train themselves for liberal careers.

The urban elite of Saint-Louis was a self-perpetuating elite that sought special advantages for its members, especially in government service. For example, when a particular administrative service needed a new worker, the many Saint-Louisians already employed would use their influence to get a family or clan member appointed. Many of the employees in one bureau were often related by blood or friendship. The same was true of workers in civilian enterprises.[60] But Saint-Louis itself was dominated by the French-Creole oligarchy that controlled Senegalese politics. Africans were needed as auxiliaries, but were not recruited for management, which the oligarchy reserved for itself.

Indeed, the Creoles had moved closer to the French and away from the Africans as the century progressed. Africans were in the great majority; but in the world of nineteenth-century Senegal this mattered little, since everyone from French colonial officials in Paris to

Creole *traitants* in the bush felt that Africans should be kept in their place. The Senegalese traditions of multiracial cities and nonsegregation continued, but it became increasingly difficult for Africans to advance. Moreover, as the traditional history of interior Senegal gradually merged with the colonial history of the coastal enclaves, the Creoles were the logical ones to lead Africans into the world of Communal politics. But this process could only open the floodgates to African participation in politics, which would undoubtedly bring a Creole downfall. Instead, the Creoles chose to cling to the status quo and their privileged position in the towns.

CHAPTER 2

# The Evolution of Local Government in the Communes

THE GROWTH of local political institutions in Senegal was influenced by French colonial policy, French administrative needs, and the historic character of the coastal cities. The fact that an African colony developed its own political institutions so soon after its foundation reflects France's desire to have a uniform look about her colonial empire. From an administrative standpoint, local elective officials could handle many routine municipal problems, freeing the French military officials (and later the civil bureaucracy) for other duties. Moreover, the colonized areas of Senegal contained traders, merchants, and notables who wished to have a say in the political and economic affairs of the colony. For these reasons, Senegal had developed local political institutions in the Four Communes long before the conquest of the Senegalese interior or the establishment of French West Africa. Senegal's political history at the local level is consequently bound up with her past and her own interior development. This chapter will consider the origins and development of the three primary institutions of local government: the municipal councils and mayors, the deputyship, and the General Council of Senegal.[1]

### Mayors and Municipal Councils

The Four Communes of Senegal were governed in the same fashion as cities in metropolitan France, and were subject to the same organizing and regulating laws. Because of the French tendency to centralize administrative powers they did not have the same initiative in some matters that English or American cities possessed; but the French system allowed a good deal of participation in local government for interested citizens. The municipal government in each commune consisted of a municipal council elected by the eligible citizens of the city. A mayor and his assistants were chosen from the members of the council, and they, in turn, appointed most of the clerical staff who manned the offices and sections of the *mairie*.

It was the responsibility of the mayor to proclaim decrees from the colonial administration that affected the welfare and business of the citizens in his commune. He was also empowered to make independent executive decisions on many important matters that were left to the commune—e.g., police, public health, streets, utilities, and municipal taxes. He performed marriages, greeted visiting dignitaries, and enjoyed all the perquisites normally associated with the office of mayor in France. His municipal council was empowered to make policy on local affairs, to set the local tax rate, and to entertain questions pertaining to local welfare and expansion. In general, the council met only to discuss policy, and the mayor and his assistants handled the day-to-day operations of the communal government.

In August 1872 the Third Republic gave Senegal a seat in the French Chamber of Deputies and it soon afterward gave Saint-Louis and Gorée the right to organize municipal institutions according to French metropolitan law. The privilege was left open to other cities in Senegal. Rufisque became the third *commune de plein exercice* in 1880, and Dakar, removed from Gorée's jurisdiction, followed in 1887. These facts of municipal organization are available in standard reference works on Senegal's administrative organization and history.[2] Most references, however, omit the crucial point that municipal politics had existed in Senegal for more than a century before the Decree of 1872, which simply gave form to an already strong tradition of local political involvement. The Decree of 1872 ushered in the modern era of politics, defined the municipalities more clearly, and gave the communal governments legal recognition and a uniform plan for administrative organization.

Gorée was probably the first Senegalese town to have its own mayor. Although no definitive statement can be made owing to the scarcity of early records, Jore, who has done the most careful work for the early period, states that sometime before 1763 the Senegal Company appointed a local Gorean to act as a kind of town mayor. (He does not rule out the possibility that the English may have started the institution during their occupation of Gorée in 1758–63.) At any rate, when the French reoccupied Gorée in 1763 they found one Kiaka, a Catholic African, acting as mayor. He had recently replaced another Catholic African, Kieme. The records further indicate that in 1778 a mulatto named Joseph Bonnet was serving as mayor. And in 1807 a visiting Englishman noted that Gorée was governed in local affairs by its own mayor and municipal council, who held their mandate from the local military commander.[3]

It is probable that Saint-Louis also had a mayor after 1760, but the earliest reference known is for 1778, when the wealthy Catholic Creole merchant Jean Thévenot held the office. He was succeeded the next year by Charles Pierre Cornier, the Creole mayor who presided over Saint-Louis's committee for sending a cahier de doléances to Paris in 1789. This protest was aimed especially at abolishing the monopolistic trading privileges of the Senegal Company. Another petition, drawn up by Saint-Louis townspeople in 1791, presented a plan for elective local government in Saint-Louis and Gorée; although the document was referred to a committee for examination, it was never acted upon by the National Assembly.[4] François Blanchot, the Governor of the colony, considered the mayor and his aides a useful institution, since they could provide military aid and backing from the local populace during emergencies. The Minister of Marine in Paris seems to have agreed to this idea, and the mayor was allowed local police powers. By the time the English took over Saint-Louis in 1809, the Creole mayor, Charles Porquet, not only controlled the local police but had also extended his influence throughout the local government.* In fact, the English kept him in office.

We can gain a general picture of the municipal institutions evolved in Saint-Louis and Gorée during the revolutionary years by examining the 1791 project for local government to see what the townspeople wanted ratified in law by the National Assembly. Saint-Louis and Gorée were to be established as municipalities with recognized municipal officials. The officials for each Commune would include a mayor and two aides (adjoints), to be elected by local citizens who were either French or naturalized French and had lived in the Commune at least one year (servants and domestic slaves were excluded). In practice this meant that voting would be restricted to Frenchmen, Creoles, and a few assimilated Africans. The municipalities would have clearly defined powers: to police and guarantee public safety; to keep a register of all foreigners in the communes; to provide order and honest weights and measures in the public markets, and to see that goods offered for sale met certain standards. A mayor was to receive 1,200 francs annual salary, an aide 600 francs,

---

* Jore, p. 297. The mayor was also empowered to represent the local inhabitants, to call them in local assembly, to invite them to official functions, to administer the civil register and the census, to distribute food to the needy, to furnish and inspect weights and measures for the market, to imprison offenders designated by the Governor, and to keep foreigners in the colony under surveillance. See Alquier, p. 298.

and a municipal clerk 1,000 francs; mayors and their aides were to wear tricolor sashes as an indication of their republican authority. Finally, the townspeople requested that the French Governor not interfere in the affairs of the local populace, but that he lend them military aid to repulse attacks from Moors or hostile Senegalese.[5]

There is fragmentary evidence that the Governor and the inhabitants of Saint-Louis, impatient with the delays in Paris, went ahead and organized their own local council in the early 1790's. In fact, several councils seem to have functioned during this decade. It is debatable whether these councils were purely municipal or whether they took on some of the duties of a colonial council. Because the evidence points largely to the former case, the councils will be considered in this section; but they obviously affected the evolution of colonial councils.[6] The evidence for these councils was brought to light in 1922 by P. Alquier, a French colonial official who found registers in the archives at Dakar that contained copies of orders from the governor of Senegal to the mayor of Saint-Louis.[7] Previously, historians and legal scholars had held that no councils were organized in Senegal during the period 1789 to 1814.[8]

Alquier's registers indicate that three different local councils functioned in Saint-Louis, all under the direction of the Governor. First was the Administrative Council (Conseil Civil de la Colonie), which was presumably a general advisory council to the Governor. It dated from the Old Regime and continued to function, under various names, until the twentieth century. It probably had local residents as members, especially in wartime, when few Frenchmen were in Senegal. Second was the Colonial Council (Conseil de la Colonie), which was composed of local residents elected by their fellow citizens. Alquier notes that Governor Blanchot issued the following notice on July 28, 1796:

In the name of the French Republic, one and indivisible: Since the limited terms of the members of the Council have expired, and since the principal inhabitants [*habitants*] are now present in numbers great enough to hold a new election, they are asked to meet with the citizen-mayor tomorrow morning at 10 o'clock in the meeting hall of the fort to proceed with this business.[9]

Blanchot called the services of the council members "useful to their fellow citizens and necessary for the general peace."[10] Apparently this council had already served at least one term; another reference in 1798 indicates that the terms were two years in length, and that at least eight local notables served at once. There was still a third council, never called by name but alluded to in the registers; it had the specific function of setting the corvées for public works projects, and was also asked to settle a quarrel between several African parties in 1808.[11]

Although the evidence is far from complete, Senegal's isolation from France during the Revolution and First Empire seems to have stimulated the development of local assemblies under the direction of the Governor. This laid the foundations not only for municipal councils and councillors (as a further extension of the municipal powers already developing in the mayor and his two aides) but also for a colonial council. Moreover, the tradition of creating de facto local institutions was reinforced by Blanchot (assuming that the mayors who appeared at mid-century were the first development in this sphere). The two circumstances set precedents that sustained the Senegalese interest in municipal politics all through the nineteenth century.

The Senegalese tradition of local government was never fully understood in Paris, or was perhaps forgotten. After Senegal had been reoccupied by the French in 1816, Governor Jacques-François Roger was surprised that the inhabitants of Saint-Louis had their own mayor. He wrote to the Minister of Marine that he found the mayor most useful in controlling the local populace, "especially the blacks." When it became necessary to replace a senile mayor in 1823, the Saint-Louisians told Roger: "Since time immemorial we have had our own mayor; he is always locally born and is elected by the people."[12] Such democratic aberrations shocked the aristocratic Roger, who attributed them to the English occupation rather than the Revolution. Roger dispensed with elections and appointed a Creole named Pellegrin; but he had deferred to public opinion, for he admitted that Pellegrin would surely have won if elections had been held. He also changed the tradition of mayors serving for life once elected (he noted that two had been dismissed for bad behavior in the past) and made their tenure in office subject to the pleasure of the Governor. The next year, still confounded by the great power of the mayor and his aides, Roger informed Paris that he had a plan for creating a municipal council to help run Saint-Louis. He hoped to bring French merchants now active in the colony into local politics, still completely dominated by the Creoles.[13]

For the next forty years there are few references to municipal political life in Saint-Louis and Gorée, but Senegalese tradition holds that the municipal officials continued in office (though sometimes dismissed by Governors) with a de facto legal status.* This was a case of limited democracy that had become rooted among the townspeople, especially among the Creoles and assimilated Africans.

Toward the end of the Second Empire, unrest swept the commune of Saint-Louis. Two decades earlier the colony had possessed a General Council, established in 1840 to debate local affairs; but this body had been suppressed by Louis Napoleon. In 1869, the inhabitants of Saint-Louis began to campaign for the revival of the General Council. A few French merchants with interests in Senegal (principally from Bordeaux) were satisfied by the creation of chambers of commerce in Saint-Louis and Gorée. But the majority of Bordeaux merchants, the Creoles, and the assimilated Africans continued to press for a full restoration of the General Council. Several petitions were sent to the Minister of Marine in 1869, 1870, and 1872, all requesting that he take note of the colony's needs.[14] The 1872 petition contained 230 signatures, of which 79 were French names and the balance African names written in either French or Arabic script. Only seven or eight of the French names were known in Paris to be Frenchmen; the rest were considered to be Creoles. The traditional leaders of municipal affairs were clearly seeking to reassert their privileges in opposition to the new French commercial interests and the tightly controlled colonial administration. The earlier petitions had contained the names of some Bordeaux merchants who favored the reinstitution of the Council, but the 1872 petition indicated that the colored segment of the community was seeking redress virtually alone.

Luckily for the citizens of Saint-Louis, Senegal's seat in the Chamber of Deputies had been restored in 1871. (This representation, granted in 1848, had also been abolished by Louis Napoleon.) The new deputy, Lafon de Fongaufier, knew Senegal well and was sympathetic to the petitions. In 1872 a separate petition to him from the Saint-Louisians indicated that now they envisioned not only a General Council for the colony but also a revived municipal council for Saint-Louis. They rejected the idea, discussed in some quarters, that there be a quota system for whites, mulattoes, and Negroes; they favored universal suffrage for all three groups, who would choose among French, Creole, and African candidates for the Council. The

---

* For example, Durand Valantin, Senegal's first deputy to Paris, was already well established in local politics as mayor of Saint-Louis when he won election to the National Assembly in 1848. Yet in terms of statute law there was no provision for a mayor of Saint-Louis.

petition also suggested that the General Council should not simply discuss the budget but should be in full charge of expenditures; and that its members should have a deliberative voice in political matters, not just a consultative power (Senegal already had an advisory council to the governor, the Administrative Council, on which several local notables served as consultants).

The petitioners complained that given the "dictatorial powers" possessed by the central administration in Senegal only a strong local assembly could guarantee the citizens any redress. They charged that the administration was in fact trying to eliminate all African Muslims from the electoral lists. Most black Senegalese in the Four Communes were Muslims, said the petition; their right to vote and hold office should not be challenged, since they paid the same taxes as everybody else, owned property, and operated businesses.[15]

De Fongaufier pressed the Minister of Marine for a favorable decision for his constituents, arguing that Senegal's loyalty to the Republic was unquestioned. For example, the Senegalese, aware that France had heavy war debts, had voluntarily refused their annual subsidy of 300,000 francs in 1871. To finance the colony in that year, the local chamber of commerce voted new taxes that were, strictly speaking, illegal. To de Fongaufier, this showed the need for local institutions to handle such matters. He defended the Africans' right to vote and hold office:

You don't really know Senegal if you don't understand the contributions made by the African Muslims for generations in Saint-Louis and Gorée and lump these men together with Africans from the interior. They pay the same taxes as the French, for they are proud of the French status they have acquired by their devotion. . . . In fact, they pay the blood tax, which none of the other colonies pay, by fighting in our colonial armies. . . . It is not the French merchants themselves who go trading up the river, but rather natives from Saint-Louis and Gorée, to whom the largest houses of Marseille and and Bordeaux do not hesitate to consign hundreds of thousands of francs' worth of merchandise.[16]

He lauded the African Muslims' personal conduct, claiming that they never stole, committed assaults, or broke the peace. The government in Saint-Louis, he said, invariably used them as agents and judges in isolated posts in the interior. De Fongaufier then charged that a strong oligarchy of self-serving merchants wanted to deprive these African citizens of their privileges; and that since Senegal had hitherto been free of racial strife and prejudice, everything should be done to avoid its appearance there. "After experiencing arbitrary government, [the Senegalese] feel the time has come to demand the liberty and institutions given our other overseas colonies."[17]

The Ministry replied the following month that it would be premature to create a General Council in Senegal; however, the interest shown by the petitions indicated that the Senegalese should be allowed municipal institutions. The Minister said that he would personally ask the President of the Republic to give Gorée and Saint-Louis full communal status under French law.[18] While the process of lawmaking got under way in Paris, a campaign to discredit the petitioners was begun in Senegal, aided by many of the colony's officials. But the petitioners, writing de Fongaufier in May claimed they were able to survive these attacks and would, if necessary, send a delegation of notables "to visit Monsieur Thiers in person at his residence at Versailles" and present the National Assembly with another petition.[19]

Finally the report requesting the creation of the Communes was given to President Thiers, who signed the Decree of August 10, 1872, giving the Communes the rights of French municipalities. The report had noted that since Senegal had been given back its deputy in 1871, it now seemed logical to endow the colony with the local institutions necessary for managing internal affairs. The decree itself enumerated the powers and duties of the municipal councillors and mayors to be chosen in Saint-Louis and Gorée. Saint-Louis was allowed to elect a mayor, two adjoints, and fifteen municipal councillors. Gorée elected a mayor, two adjoints, and eleven councillors. Municipal terms were for six years, with elections at staggered three-year intervals. There was no salary or remuneration attached to any office. To be eligible for election, a candidate would have to know how to read and write French.[20] This provision was expected to encourage the assimilation of the African voters. Finally, the electoral list was to be drawn up on the basis of the 1849 law that regulated voting for Senegal's deputy to the National Assembly—a measure exceedingly liberal in its interpretation of who should vote.[21]

Elections were held by the end of 1872, and municipal government controlled by the local populace was once again a reality in Senegal. In 1880 Rufisque was given the same form of government, and in 1887 Dakar was separated from Gorée and made a full commune. From the beginning, the local administration of Dakar and Rufisque was controlled by the French merchants, who formed the majority of councillors and invariably chose Frenchmen as mayors. The Creole aristocracy of the colony controlled Saint-Louis and Gorée and held some positions of influence in the other two communes. By contrast, few black Africans were municipal councillors in any commune until the 1890's, when some assimilated Africans in Dakar began a campaign to win seats on the Dakar council.*

On July 17, 1898, a by-election took place in Dakar to fill three vacant seats on the municipal council. Three Africans were elected. Two days later, five French councillors resigned, protesting that the new Africans did not know French, that one was a servant, and that this election brought to five the number of "ignorant" Africans on the council. This placed the governor-general of French West Africa, who intervened, in a quandary. If new elections were held immediately to fill the five vacant seats, Africans would surely win, since this was *hivernage*, the hot season when most Frenchmen and some Creoles were vacationing in France. Governor-General Noël Ballay decided not to run the risk of adding another five Africans to the 14-man Council. Although the electoral statute required that new elections be held immediately, Ballay dissolved the council on spurious grounds and postponed the election until fall, when the French would return.[22] In October, the Frenchman Fernand Marsat was elected mayor, and his list of candidates triumphed over a coalition list of Africans and Creoles. He was forced to admit five Africans to his list to ensure victory, but these five were "yes men."[23]

Similar events took place in Saint-Louis in 1900. An African electoral committee was formed to prepare a slate of candidates for the May 6 elections. Not being able to convince enough Africans to run for office, they finally compromised by supporting a list dominated by Frenchmen and Creoles who seemed sympathetic to African interests. This list lost to the wholly French-Creole list of the incumbent mayor, Louis Descemet, who was one of the colony's most respected and powerful Creoles.

Thus municipal government was fully organized in Senegal by the turn of the century, and the Four Communes enjoyed the same privileges of self-government as cities in France. But the black Africans, who had formerly been allied with the Creoles, were largely passed over. The councils were dominated by an oligarchy composed of well-

---

* A list of Africans on municipal councils about 1892 included: Abdoulaye Gaye and Masseck Seck (Saint-Louis); Youssouf Bamar and N'Diaga N'Dir (Dakar); Abdou N'Diaye and Aly Gaye (Rufisque); and Diouga Dieng (Gorée). These men were always mentioned last in any official enumeration or publication; furthermore, they were generally known as "safe Africans" or "yes men." See municipal elections report, Saint-Louis, April 5, 1891 (ARS 20-G-7); dossier of 1892 municipal elections (FOM, Sénégal VII-61).

to-do Creoles and the French agents of firms in Bordeaux and Marseille. The Africans and the smaller French businessmen were excluded from positions of power. The mayors of Gorée and Saint-Louis were still usually Creoles, but Dakar and Rufisque were ruled by French machine-style politicians. Africans could still vote, but even this privilege was soon to be attacked.

### Representation in Paris: The Deputy

The second political institution that developed in Senegal was the idea of representing the colony in metropolitan France. This representation was proposed in 1791 by Dominique Lamiral, who had been the prime instigator of the Saint-Louis general meeting that had prepared the letters of grievance in 1789. Lamiral returned to Paris to present the letters himself, and he published them in *L'Affrique et le peuple affriquain* (1789), a book in which he also defended the slave trade as an economic necessity for Senegal. He was especially critical of the monopoly privileges enjoyed by the Senegal Company. On January 18, 1791, these privileges were abolished and freedom of commerce proclaimed for all Frenchmen. The Creoles and assimilated Africans in Saint-Louis considered this applicable to them as well, though not to their slaves and servants.[24] It seemed clear that a new regime would be instituted in Senegal as well as in France.

In March 1791 Lamiral submitted to the Assembly a document that purported to give the views of the Saint-Louisians on the political future of their colony.[25] Since the monopoly "that had poisoned our commerce" was ended, he wrote, the National Assembly must bring liberty and reason to Senegal, which needed a proper civil government to prevent anarchy and guarantee the rights of her citizens. Moreover, Senegal should have an official representative in Paris.* Lamiral's document then suggested a plan for reorganizing the colony by abolishing the post of governor and substituting a *résident de la nation*, who would be an unofficial representative of Paris. All true

---

* Lamiral's impassioned plea was typical of the Republican universalism that characterized the times: "Il nous reste encore une faveur précieuse à demander au corps législatif, c'est de voir siéger un de nos concitoyens parmi vous, Messieurs, dans ce temple majestueux où se proclament les oracles de la Liberté, et où les Droits de l'Homme ont été solennellement reconnus. Vous donnerez par là, Messieurs, un grand exemple à l'Univers. Vous réunirez dans votre sein les représentants des peuples des quatre parties du monde qui bientôt sera tout entier soumis aux lois que vous avez prononcés (*sic*) et que la nature et les sentiments seuls vous ont dictés." Quoted in Jore, p. 131.

power would lie with the municipal assemblies and the deputy in Paris. The assemblies would be modeled on those in France. The deputy would be elected by all Saint-Louis citizens, but they would choose from a list of whites who owned noncommercial property worth at least 6,000 francs.

The entire proposal, including the demands for municipal government, was referred to the Colonial Committee for study. Jean Adrien Queslin, a deputy from La Manche, headed the Committee and was favorable to the Senegalese request, but he chose to act cautiously. His report to the Assembly endorsed the idea of establishing regular municipalities at Saint-Louis and Gorée, but reserved "other questions of interior government" for further study. Apparently, the Committee had not been able to agree on Senegal's having a deputy. Lamiral nevertheless considered himself Senegal's de facto representative and signed his correspondence "Député de la Colonie près l'Assemblée Nationale," during this period. After being imprisoned for a year for "undetermined reasons," he finally took over a Paris newspaper when his mandate as deputy never materialized.[26] There is no record of the Assembly's ever acting on the Committee report. However, unofficial municipal governments continued to function in Saint-Louis and Gorée.

The idea of a Senegalese representative in Paris was forgotten for some years, and was eventually revived by Governor Roger, the ambitious parvenu of the Bourbon restoration. Hoping to keep some contact with the colony after the end of his term as commandant in 1826, Roger asked his friends to petition the Ministry of Marine to appoint him deputy from Senegal when he left for Paris.[27] He felt that since Senegal's commerce was now equal to Cayenne's, it should have a deputy on the advisory council of the Ministry, as Cayenne did; and he saw no reason why he should not hold this post. In June 1827 the Ministry received a petition from Commandant Gerbidon, who had replaced Roger: "The Committee on Commerce, the Society for Agriculture, and the notables among the Creoles and Africans of Senegal have simultaneously, in resolutions that I have the honor of sending you, expressed the desirability of having the colony represented in Paris by a deputy, who would be part of the [advisory] council to the Minister of Marine and Colonies."[28] However, before any decision was made Roger managed to become deputy from Loiret, and the project was dropped.

In 1837 the Governor of Senegal wrote to the Ministry of Marine that the French, Creoles, and Africans of Senegal were again asking that a deputy be elected to represent the colony in Paris. An 1833 law had established a new advisory council, the Conseil des Délégués des Colonies, and the Senegalese expected a place on it. But again Senegal was not included with the other colonies.[29]

The Ordinance of 1840, one of the fundamental organizing laws given the French colonies (especially Senegal), provided for the establishment of a General Council in Senegal. It also authorized a Senegalese delegate to the advisory Conseil Supérieur des Colonies in Paris, to be elected by the General Council. It would seem that the Creole Victor Calvé was the first such delegate.[30] Calvé served until January 1846, when Governor Roger (now Baron Roger) was chosen to replace him. Twenty years after his first attempt the Baron was finally a member of the advisory council, with a yearly allowance of 12,000 francs.[31]

The revolution of 1848 changed Senegal's representative from an advisory figurehead to a delegate with real power. In the spring of 1848 the Senegalese hastily sent the dynamic Creole Durand-Barthélemy Valantin to Paris to express their views before the leaders of the Second Republic. On May 10 the Minister of Marine sent Valantin a letter, addressed to the "Citoyen Commissaire de la République au Sénégal," informing him that a decree of March 5 had provided Senegal with one deputy to the new National Assembly. All indigenous peoples who could show a residence of at least five years in the "French possessions" in Senegal would be eligible to vote. These 1848 ministerial instructions, formulated in the heat of the revolution, were to be the cornerstone of African political liberties in years to come.[32]

Valantin's temporary mandate as deputy was confirmed on October 30, when the first elections for deputy took place. The voters were asked to prepare their ballots in advance, fold them, and give them to the voting committee in the voting hall. Voting continued in a leisurely fashion for four days, and each day voters from different districts were called in.* The company of native soldiers was allowed to vote on the second and third days.[33]

Valantin's opponents in Senegal's first election were both Frenchmen. The noted abolitionist Victor Schoelcher had visited Senegal just before the revolution and ran for deputy *in absentia*; he swept the voting at Gorée, but received little support elsewhere. The other

---

* One citizen named Commence, a Wolof mason, created a scene because the committee did not think he was 25 years of age and hence old enough to vote. He was finally allowed to deposit his ballot.

contender was B. du Château, the Commissioner of the Republic in Senegal (i.e. Governor). Du Château's campaign promises were extensive: to make the Senegal River navigable to Bakel in all seasons (how this was to be accomplished is not clear); to start regular steamboat service between Senegal and France; to create public schools in Gorée and Saint-Louis; to petition the National Assembly to vote an indemnity for owners of recently liberated slaves; and to organize Saint-Louis as a municipality under French law. Du Château was not personally liked and was no match for Valantin, who was supported by the Creoles, most assimilated Africans, and some recently liberated slaves who now had the vote. Valantin polled 1,000 votes out of 2,071 voting; Du Château ran second with 648 votes.[34]

Valantin came from a distinguished Creole family of Saint-Louis and was a wholesale merchant. When elected, he was serving as mayor of the city (although the post had no legal status). Apparently conservative in outlook, he took a seat to the right in the Assembly. He was reelected in 1849, this time winning 1,319 votes from a total of 2,033.[35] In this legislature he followed the conservative monarchists' line, voting for the Falloux-Parieu law on education (a church-sponsored reform bill) and for legislation restricting suffrage. In the summer of 1851, when the Assembly and Louis Napoleon came to a stalemate, Valantin decided to retire from public life.

The next deputy was John Sleight, who had been a mayoral aide during Valantin's term as mayor of Saint-Louis.[36] Like Valantin, Sleight was a wealthy Creole merchant, and he held the prized contract to furnish the French colonial troops with millet. This annoyed his fellow merchants, who complained to Paris that Sleight had too much influence with the army, and that his election was improper. Sleight thereupon signed over his army contract to Gaspard Devès, a junior partner in his firm.* Other ill-wishers complained that Sleight was not really eligible for the deputyship, since, although he had lived in Saint-Louis for many years, he had been born in Gambia of an English father. His election was finally invalidated by Paris in December 1851 on the ground that he had been a government contractor at the time of his election, which was forbidden by law.[37] Before he could be replaced, Louis Napoleon signed the Decree of

---

* Devès, a Creole, was the patriarch of the Senegalese branch of the Devès family of Bordeaux, merchants who had great influence in the colony. During the latter half of the nineteenth century Gaspard was the most important Creole merchant in Senegal; his son Justin competed with the Carpot family for control of Senegalese politics after the beginning of the twentieth century.

February 2, 1852, which suppressed all colonial representation in Paris.

For the next twenty years France seemed to completely ignore its far-off African enclave. If it had not been for the administration of Louis Faidherbe, French Senegal would have remained in total obscurity during the whole of the Second Empire. Senegal regained its deputy at the outset of the Third Republic, but by then the political makeup of the colony had changed. The Creole aristocracy had lost much of its power to the growing French community in Senegal, and could no longer elect a Valantin or a Sleight over French candidates. Power was divided in the colonial councils, but the French dominated the deputyship between 1871 and 1902.

When the Committee of National Defense called for the election of a new Assembly in September 1870, it specifically authorized elections in all the colonies that had been represented in Paris under the Second Republic. Furthermore, it was stipulated that the liberal voting requirements of March 1848 would be in force. The mayors of Saint-Louis and Gorée and the French administrative officials in Dakar and Rufisque were empowered to draw up electoral lists. Nothing resulted from this decree, and a new decree specifically applied to Senegal was issued in February 1871. The election was finally authorized.

Ten candidates were entered in the 1871 campaign, but only three were major contenders: the retired French naval officer Jean-Baptiste Lafon de Fongaufier, and the wealthy merchants Clément de Ville-Suzanne and Albert Teisseire. Gaspard Devès gave his support to Ville-Suzanne, whereas the influential Creoles Louis Descemet and Léon d'Erneville threw theirs to Teisseire. Thus the Creole vote was split, and de Fongaufier easily won the election, receiving 1,186 of the 1,980 votes cast. For the first time, the newly chartered cities of Dakar and Rufisque were eligible to vote:

|  | Saint-Louis | Gorée | Dakar | Rufisque | Total |
|---|---|---|---|---|---|
| Electors registered | 3,427 | 495 | 252 | 103 | 4,277 |
| Electors voting | 1,587 | 222 | 118 | 33 | 1,980 |

General Faidherbe, whose candidacy was sponsored by his old friends in the colony, won a token 92 votes.[38]

The election was an orderly one, but the problem of registering the many new African voters in the cities worried Governor François Valière. He wrote Paris: "The natives will be difficult to register because few of them conform to our laws of civil registry. It will be hard to know if they are eligible and of voting age." He added that he did not want any quarrels or riots to occur and intended to register any African who could provide two witnesses to swear to his status.[39]

De Fongaufier, the new deputy, joined the Union Républicaine parliamentary group in Paris and served on a number of parliamentary commissions. He also served on the General Council of Dordogne after 1871, which indicates that his principal residence was in France. De Fongaufier voted for returning the government to Paris after the war, and he favored the Wallon amendment and the other constitutional laws that actually established the form of government of the Third Republic. He opposed the withdrawal of Thiers as chief of state, as well as the formation of the de Broglie ministry.

When the Assembly's term expired in March 1876, no provision was made for keeping a deputy from Senegal. Until April 1879 the colony was once again forgotten. Then, in response to petitions from the citizens of the Four Communes, President of the Republic Jules Grévy signed a decree restoring Senegal's representation. The man most responsible for inspiring this decision was the Minister of Marine and Colonies, Admiral J. B. Jauréguibéry, who had seen service in Senegal as Faidherbe's replacement in 1862.[40]

At this point a popular businessman was elected deputy. Alfred Gasconi was born in Saint-Louis and spent most of his life in the colony.* Gasconi was reelected in 1882 and 1885, and served as Senegal's representative in Paris for a decade in all. He, too, joined the Union Républicaine in parliament. He voted for the new press laws, became the spokesman and sponsor of the legislation that authorized the construction of the Dakar–Saint-Louis railway line, and advocated an ocean telegraph cable to Senegal from the Canary Islands. Gasconi was an ardent supporter of Jules Ferry and voted for funds to finance the Tonkin expedition proposed by Ferry in 1883.

Gasconi's principal opponent during these years, and his challenger in all three elections, was the colorful Creole businessman and journalist J. J. Crespin, who increased his following at each election. It was apparent by the third election in 1885 that Gasconi was losing support in many quarters, even though the coastal railway he had sponsored was completed in that year. However, the Catholic

* My research suggests that all deputies between 1871 and 1902 were French. But H. O. Idowu, in his unpublished study of the General Council, indicates that Gasconi was actually Creole rather than French (Idowu, "Conseil Général," p. 92). Even if this is true, my evidence strongly indicates that he was aligned with the French rather than the Creole community; and for the purposes of this analysis he can be counted with the French.

clergy of Senegal entered politics the same year and openly supported Gasconi, especially in Gorée. This action won the support of many devout Creole families, since Crespin was a convinced anticlerical in persuasion.

In his three campaigns, Crespin placed his hopes on the African voters, many of whom distrusted Gasconi because he was on record as favoring military service for African citizens of the Communes.[41] (The Africans themselves did not favor military service until after 1912, when it was viewed as a further guarantee of their status as French citizens.) A letter to the editor of the Saint-Louis paper *Le Réveil* from a "Wolof citizen" complained that Gasconi was hypocritical, catering to the Africans at election time but ignoring their requests in the years following; it was also alleged that he gave special preferenec to the needs of Catholic Africans as opposed to Muslims.[42] *Le Réveil* charged Gasconi with being a pawn of the Bordeaux commercial interests, who allegedly used drastic methods to induce the voters to support him. Crespin himself openly attacked Gasconi's alleged hypocrisy. "As for your votes, I know that you will give them to your local candidate, who is related to practically all of you, rather than to M. Gasconi, who, when in France, renounces any personal connections with Senegal."[43]

Gasconi's bid for a fourth term failed in 1889, when the French businessmen decided to support a "safer" candidate and brought Rear-Admiral Aristide Vallon out of retirement to campaign for deputy. Vallon had been Governor of Senegal in 1882 and was well known to the public; with the proper kind of campaign effort (e.g., the distribution of rice and sugar to potential voters), his victory was assured. But he was a colorless nonentity who took no interest in his job and was soon known as an "absentee deputy." It became apparent to the Bordeaux merchants that he would have to be replaced at the next election.

The next deputy was Mayor Jules Couchard of Saint-Louis, a Frenchman who had replaced a long line of Creole predecessors in the municipal government. Backed by the large business interests of the colony, Couchard also received support from many Creoles and enjoyed the confidence of both urban and rural Africans. He defeated Gasconi, who was trying for a comeback, and Crespin in the heated election of 1893. Couchard was a clever politician who realized that most of Senegal's voters were Africans, who should be properly courted not only at election time, as in the past, but all during the year. Each time he returned to the colony from Paris "spontaneous" demonstrations of the Africans' affection for him took place. In 1896, for example, he was met at the Saint-Louis railway station by parading Africans, who cheered, danced, and beat drums for hours; a committee of African notables conducted an elaborate welcoming ceremony. One of the Saint-Louis newspapers observed that Couchard's reception far outshone those given for Gasconi at the height of his popularity or those received by the popular current Governor, Timothy Lamothe.[44]

Unlike his predecessors, Couchard pushed his influence beyond the confines of the Four Communes and acted as though he were deputy for the entire colony of Senegal (the Protectorate was now fully organized) rather than the areas of direct administration alone. In fact, Wolof and Serere chiefs from certain interior regions paid Couchard a handsome subsidy to take care of their interests. This would not normally have shocked the colony, which was already used to the finer arts of political corruption. But when it was charged by a French government inspector that the subsidies were being paid out of the Protectorate's budget and routed through the chiefs, an official inquiry began.[45] The investigation was clouded with innuendos, not the least being that the governor-general of French West Africa might himself have helped arrange the subsidies. The final results of the affair were never made public; but by 1898 Couchard was no longer receiving his rural payoffs and had been thoroughly discredited as a candidate for reelection.

The 1898 election brought forth a new challenger to French domination of the deputyship: the young Creole lawyer François Carpot, who had returned from studying and practicing law in France several years earlier. Carpot was opposed by another French absentee candidate, the Count of Agoult, a former naval lieutenant with some Senegalese service. The most important families of Senegal's Creole aristocracy backed Carpot wholeheartedly. But once again the Bordeaux merchants triumphed, and d'Agoult won a narrow victory with 2,895 votes to Carpot's 2,511.[46] Nevertheless, the Creoles were on the upswing. In local politics, they dominated Saint-Louis and Gorée, and were influential at Rufisque. Because of their persistence and their interest in the colony's affairs, they were also the commanding group in the General Council. They now sought the deputyship as a rightful symbol of their past leadership.

Four years later, in 1902, Carpot won the deputyship and ushered in a new age of politics in which Senegal's deputy became the most important political figure in the colony. During the French preponderance of 1871–1902, the deputy had usually been absent from Senegal—no more than a convenient means of contact with Paris. Lafon de Fongaufier was sincerely interested in Senegal and was instrumental in having the municipalities created in 1872, but his influence inside Senegal was minimal. Vallon and d'Agoult were weak deputies who are hardly remembered in Senegal today. Gasconi and Couchard both enjoyed great popularity when first elected, but failed to transcend petty machine politics in their roles as deputies. Both were influential in local politics, however, because of their former service on the municipal and general councils. Couchard, especially, had an ambitious conception of his duties, though he achieved nothing more than a scandal. Carpot, during his twelve years as deputy, finally established the deputy's preeminence in Senegal's internal politics. He was to vindicate the hopes of Lamiral, who had advocated a deputy for Senegal in 1791.

### The General Council

The third institution of modern politics established in Senegal was the Conseil Général (General Council), which was modeled after the councils of the same name attached to each department in metropolitan France.* Owing to its position in the colony and the men who sat in it, Senegal's Council soon became far more important than any typical council in the mother country. From about 1880 to 1910, it was the prime force in Senegalese local politics, mostly because of its power in budgetary affairs and its members' assertiveness. It became the major political arena for Senegal's Creole aristocracy, who soon regarded the Council as their special preserve. The Council always had a good many French members; but since many of these took their responsibilities lightly (French members were often in France on business while the Council was sitting), the Creoles maintained their leadership. The Creoles' greatest rivals were the French mercantile agents from Bordeaux and Marseille, who expected to sit on the Council almost as a matter of right. These agents, however, were often transferred from town to town or were active in colonial service for only a few years.

A few Africans sat on almost every Council, but until the twentieth century they were of the same cut as the Africans on municipal

---

* Again, I should acknowledge my debt to the Nigerian scholar, Dr. H. O. Idowu, whose study on the General Council I saw just before publication. This study is based upon extensive archival research; it is especially valuable for the 1879–1900 period and saved me from error on several crucial points.

councils: "yes men" who could be counted on to vote with their Creole or French patrons. There were, of course, exceptions from time to time; but on the whole the Council, like the other political institutions of the colony, was dominated by Creoles and Frenchmen.*

The institution of colonial councils in France's empire dated from 1759, when the Crown authorized the creation of local councils for agriculture and commerce. Senegal had no such council; but, as we have seen, the colony developed several ex officio councils on its own during the late 1700's. There was no official notice of these ad hoc councils in France, for in 1803, when Napoleon revived the colonial councils of agriculture, Senegal was not included in his decree. In 1819, Louis XVIII authorized "colonial consulting committees" to replace the agricultural committees. Senegal, however, did not receive its committee until sometime in 1822, after the Saint-Louis merchants had petitioned the Ministry of Marine for permission to organize a regular chamber of commerce. Baron Roger, Governor of Senegal at the time, opposed this idea because he thought that a chamber of commerce would be detrimental to small traders and would also serve as a rallying point for malcontents hostile to Bourbon authority. The Ministry agreed, and instead directed the colony to organize a consulting committee of seven members appointed by the Governor. The committee kept the Governor informed of local affairs and gave opinions on specific economic questions, but it had no executive powers.[47]

Senegal was again overlooked in 1827, when the Ministry transformed the colonial consulting committees into general councils (of the French metropolitan pattern) in Guadeloupe, Martinique, Guiana (Cayenne), and Réunion. At the same time, an advisory council was created in Paris to advise the Ministry on colonial matters.[48] In 1834 the Ministry requested the Governor of Senegal's opinion on whether Senegal was ready for a general council, but no action was taken on his report.[49] Meanwhile, the Senegalese did have limited representation on the private council that advised the Governor (known as the Conseil du Gouvernement from 1822 to 1830 and the Conseil Privé from then until 1840).[50] Most members of this body were French ad-

* Idowu ("Conseil Général," p. 153) lists the following Africans who served on the General Council from 1879 to 1920: Ravane M'Boye (5 years), Pierre Chimère (9 years); Abdoulaye Seck (12 years); Yatma Sène (15 years); Bacre-Waly (18 years); and Galandou Diouf, who served from 1909 to 1920, with time out for military service during 1916–18.

ministrative officials, but one *habitant* and one *notable* were included. These representatives were traditionally citizens of Saint-Louis, but in 1837 the citizens of Gorée objected and demanded the right to have at least one Gorean on the council.[51]

A significant change occurred on September 7, 1840, when a royal ordinance of Louis Philippe gave Senegal a Conseil Général like those of the other colonies. First of all, the Governor of Senegal was to draw up a list of 40 to 60 leading citizens of Saint-Louis, who were to elect ten delegates for the Council. Eight of these were to be wholesale businessmen, and two small entrepreneurs; Frenchmen, Creoles, and Africans were all eligible. The Council was to serve a five-year term, meeting annually to advise the Governor on budgetary matters, economic policy, and general administrative needs. It was stipulated that the Council, during its first session, should name a delegate to the Minister's advisory council in Paris.[52] (The man chosen was Victor Calvé.)

Gorée was dealt with separately, in keeping with the ambivalent feeling shown toward the island city during these years, and was given a lesser council to take care of its needs (a *conseil d'arrondissement*). This body was selected from a group of 15–25 nominees, who chose five councilmen. The term of office was five years, as in Saint-Louis, but there was no provision for a delegate to Paris.[53]

Both of the new Senegalese councils were appointive: the governor invariably drew up a list of "safe" notables who tended to choose councilmen who would safeguard their vested interests. After the Revolution of 1848, the two councils were disbanded. In 1853, there was an unsuccessful effort to set up chambers of commerce in Saint-Louis and Gorée, but conciliar government in Senegal had to wait until the events of 1869–71 spurred the local citizens to petition the Ministry for their own Council. The response to these requests, as we have seen, was merely to create municipal councils in 1872.

A General Council was finally set up in 1879, the same year that the Ministry finally gave Senegal a permanent deputy in the Chamber. The Decree of February 4, 1879, created a Council composed of sixteen members, to be elected by popular suffrage in the Four Communes from the same lists that supplied candidates for the deputyship and the municipal offices.[54] Frenchmen, Creoles, and Africans were all elegible to vote and stand for election. At the outset, Saint-Louis had the right to elect ten councillors, whereas Gorée was authorized six; this representation was changed when Dakar and Rufisque legally became communes. Many members of the General

Council also served on the municipal boards, since the decree had no restriction on this practice. Only representatives from the direct rule areas were sanctioned, and the Council had no delegates from the interior.*

The Council's powers, though limited, were broad enough to make it more than a debating society on local questions (which it also was). Its basic powers were four: (1) to advise the Governor on various matters; (2) to debate a variety of local questions; (3) to legislate on certain subjects; (4) to approve part of the colonial budget.[55]

In exercising its advisory function, the Council discussed specific questions listed by the Governor—e.g., the creation of new communes-mixtes, the problems of local administration, or the treatment of visitors to the colony. The fixed list of questions, however, did not limit the Council's voice in public affairs. The Council's *voeux* (resolutions) had great moral authority, and were usually carefully noted in Saint-Louis, Dakar, and Paris. All sessions of the Council were recorded and available to the general public, either in local newspapers or in annual summaries.

Even when it could not propound formal legislation, the Council was allowed to deliberate certain specific questions on its own initiative. The most important of these questions was the handling of taxation, surely one of the critical matters in a colonial administration. Because the Council could initiate taxation schemes, the citizens of Senegal had a qualified but realistic measure of control over the French administrators; and this control was increased by the tax-assessing powers of the four municipal councils. The Council could also deliberate the conditions and rates necessary for taxing public works, the administration of market centers in the direct rule areas that did not come under the jurisdiction of the Four Communes, the proper tolls for public ferries at river crossings, the acquisition of land for public use, and a host of lesser matters.

The Council was empowered to *statuer* (legislate) on about a dozen different matters. These included the disposition of public property or gifts to the colony, the priority for constructing public roads, the contribution of the colonial budget to public works undertaken by

* This separation was given legal status in 1892, when the Protectorate's budget was separated from that of the direct rule areas. After this, the Council had no say in allocating the funds of the Protectorate. The Councilmen regarded this arrangement as an insulting invasion of their authority, and were even more annoyed when additional funds were diverted by the creation of a separate budget for French West Africa. See Buell, I, 978. The development of Council politics is covered in ARS, Series 4-E-1 through 4-E-13.

the French administration, and other similar matters. After 1895, however, these decisions were subject to veto by the Governor General of French West Africa for two months; if not rejected within that time, they became the law of Senegal. In practice, few measures were vetoed. The Council's recommendations in all these areas gained legal status only after the Governor had approved them. On the other hand, a conciliar resolution on an authorized subject of debate could only be annulled by specific decree of the Governor. Although the ultimate authority in much of this quasi-legislative process remained with the Governor, the Council could bring enormous public pressure to bear on the administration.

The Council's most important area of authority was the colonial budget, which the Governor of Senegal submitted to it for approval or rejection. Each budget had two categories of expenditure: mandatory and optional. The mandatory expenditures, which were beyond the control of the Council, included the payment of state-incurred debts, the operating expenses of the Governor and his staff, funds for the public services of the colony (public works, public health, etc.), and secret funds disbursed by the Governor (for police work and surveillance). Thus the Governor retained complete control of the fundamental services necessary to support the colonial administration. These mandatory expenditures could not be altered by the Council, but anything classified as an optional expense was fair game. Here is where the power of the Council lay. Most new construction projects in the colony were considered optional, as were certain furnishings and services for governmental offices, books for libraries, and many "nonessential" public services. Technically, the Council was not allowed to debate the governor's proposed budget for optional funds, but had to put it to a vote as one lump expenditure. However, the councillors could use their deliberative authority to formulate a resolution on the tax rate for the coming year, discussing the pros and cons of possible optional expenses in the process; the resolution could freely mention particular expenses and propose or discourage taxes to provide revenue for them. The actual budget might receive a simple vote without discussion, but the general public would know the Council's reasons for accepting or rejecting it.

The General Council members, whether Creole, French, or African, became adept politicians by comparison with the French colonial officers they had to deal with. A Carpot with twenty years of legislative experience or a Guillabert with thirty years in politics would be pitted against a new French Governor who had given orders

and directed a bureaucracy but was totally unprepared for the subtleties of republican politics. And the politics of the Third French
Republic, a veritable archetype of parliamentary intricacy, were the
model for the Senegalese councillors.

Knowledgeable observers who saw the General Council (and its
later successor, the Colonial Council) in action were impressed with
its political capabilities. Raymond Buell, who visited Senegal in the
mid-1920's, wrote: "The members of the Colonial Council of Senegal
have more power than the unofficial members of any other consultative assembly in Africa, including the legislative councils found in
British territory. They can block the imposition of new taxes and
withhold about half the expenditures of the government."[56] Legislative councils developed in the mid-nineteenth century in Sierra Leone
and Gold Coast, and later in Nigeria. But until the 1920's, these councils included only a few appointed African members with advisory
powers.[57] Not until after World War II did any of these bodies gain
the kind of power that Senegal's council possessed from 1879 on.

The French as a group were unenthusiastic about local politics,
despite the many political institutions created in Senegal during the
first years of the Third Republic. Many administrators were simply
not interested in local political events as long as these did not interfere with their colonial positions. But there were a few Governors and
administrators who thought that the only legitimate rationale of empire was the assimilationist-republican ideal: to bring French institutions to the uncivilized world; to offer Creoles and Africans the key
to assimilation; to make them new citizens of the Republic. The
permanent establishment of local political institutions in Senegal
during the 1870's, however, was chiefly intended to benefit the new
French *émigrés* who sought the wealth of empire in Senegal and to
insure that their voices would be heard in Paris. The generalized
idealism of assimilation and the self-serving pragmatism of commercial empire—these were the two cornerstones of French imperial policy. That both could not be equally served was not apparent until
World War I, when the political blueprint was involuntarily
changed.

In the 1880's, a handsome new building to house the Council was
built on the banks of the Senegal. Its rear entrance fronted the river,
the highway to the interior and the people; its front facade was
turned towards the residence of the governor and the seat of colonial administration. The Council now met in its own hall—imposing,
dignified, and testifying the Council's importance to all Senegal. This

new splendor was essentially the doing of the Creoles, who considered the General Council a sort of political club for their own group. The membership lists of that body from 1880 to 1900 are almost a roll call of the great Creole families: Descemet, Guillabert, d'Erneville, Devès, Crespin, Patterson, Valantin, Pellegrin, and Carpot. Many of these had several members in the Council over the years—the Devès brothers, the Carpot brothers, and the Crespin cousins. The Creoles considered themselves an elite by virtue of marriage, temperament, education, economic power, and race; moreover, they were all Catholic Christians, whereas the great majority of Africans were Muslims. This small, inbred Creole community constantly strove to retain its hold on the reins of power despite its diminishing numbers and its steady loss of ground to Senegal's expanding French community.

The first session of the Council, on November 24, 1879, was presided over by Louis Descemet, later Mayor of Saint-Louis. He welcomed Governor Louis Brière de l'Isle, who announced that Senegal was now entering a new era with a representative institution elected by popular suffrage; and that the future was indeed bright, since the Minister of Marine and Colonies, Admiral Jauréguibéry, had taken a personal interest in Senegal and in African development. Descemet was elected president of the Council and occupied the post for the next fourteen years. The two d'Erneville brothers then served in succession. Théodore Carpot became president for twelve years; he was replaced by Justin Devès, and then by Louis Guillabert, who was president when the General Council was modified into the Colonial Council in 1920. In other words, the management of the General Council was exclusively in Creole hands throughout its 41-year existence. Frenchmen such as Valmy Lavie, Le Bègue de Germiny, Maurice Escarpit, and François Vézia were important Council members; but most Frenchmen did not stay in Senegal long enough or lacked the Creoles' tenacious desire to dominate the Council.[58]

The minutes of the Council sessions reveal the Creoles' flair for politics, devotion to political questions, hostility to the French administration, and ingenuity in framing proposals to benefit their constituents. The Governor of Senegal often complained to the Paris colonial offices that the Creoles thought only of their own interests and their own part of Senegal. This was one reason for the 1892 decision to separate the Protectorate's budget from that of the direct rule areas. After this, the latent rivalry between the north and the south of Senegal became overt (that is, a rivalry between the first

and second arrondissements). Saint-Louis, in the north, was the traditional economic and political center of the colony; in the south,
Dakar and Rufisque were yearly becoming more important and openly challenged the northern leadership. Thus many conflicting forces
were at work in the Council by the turn of the century: Creole versus
French, Saint-Louis versus Dakar and Rufisque, local citizens versus
imported professional administrators. It made for a brisk political
climate, especially at election time.

◇◇◇◇◇◇◇◇◇◇◇◇◇◇◇◇◇◇◇◇◇◇◇◇◇◇◇◇◇◇◇◇◇◇◇◇◇◇◇◇◇◇◇◇◇◇◇◇◇

CHAPTER 3

# The Structure of French Rule

FRENCH COLONIAL rule spread over most of Senegal after 1850, completely eliminating the political sovereignty of traditional states.
Some traditional rulers (such as the Bourba of Djolof) became French-
supported chiefs; other traditional chiefs (such as the Bours of Saloum) survived but had no legal authority.[1] French administrators
transformed the Protectorate into an adjunct of the central administration. Some chiefs were kept in place at middle and lower levels,
but they increasingly became dependent on French orders and salaries. In the urban areas of direct rule, the style of government was
scarcely different from that of metropolitan France: decrees, arrêtés,
and informal administrative decisions regulated matters over which
the local elective institutions had no jurisdiction.

In Senegal, as in other French colonies, the highest law was derived from decrees prepared in Paris by the Ministry of Colonies and
signed by the President of the Republic. To be sure, laws enacted
by the Chamber of Deputies stood above presidential decrees; but
few laws of this kind were made since the Chamber preferred to let
the Ministry handle all colonial problems. Decrees could also be issued by the Governor-General of French West Africa, who had the
additional power of promulgating certain decrees issued in metropolitan France or letting them hang in abeyance. Individual governors
of colonies were allowed to issue arrêtés and decrees on matters not
handled by superior authority. The local government in Senegal,
then, although possessing a number of exclusive powers, was hemmed
in by the complexities of the French legal and administrative system
on several different levels. The local citizens were very much aware
that they were only one colony in a vast intercontinental empire.

The legal and institutional structure of the French empire in Africa
has always received a great deal of scholarly attention. I will give only
a brief account of colonial institutions at this point, since the political history of the Four Communes essentially concerns matters rarely
deemed important by the colonial mind, which was far more occu-

pied with building political systems, constructing rationales for the domination of peoples, and training new proconsuls of empire.*

It is perhaps understandable that most Frenchmen were not interested in traditional Africa *per se*, however much they might be attracted by Africa's exoticism and chances for adventure. Interest in African society, culture, and peoples for their inherent worth had to await such administrator-scholars as Maurice Delafosse, who showed the way by learning African languages, studying African ethnography, and pioneering in African traditional history. It is surprising, however, that so few Frenchmen were interested in the European-inspired political institutions and movements that developed in urban Senegal. To most governors and officials, these were a nuisance, tolerated because they might be educational—that is, they might help "civilize the natives." For many career men, the intricate organization and benefits of the colonial service were the stuff of empire. Even Robert Delavignette, certainly one of the most enlightened, humane, and African-oriented French governors of the twentieth century, called his book on West Africa *Les vrais chefs de l'empire* (*The True Chiefs of Empire*) and devoted it to an analysis and glorification of the colonial administrator who carried the white man's burden in the bush.

Although most administrators were indifferent to local affairs in the Communes, the urban citizens of Senegal were keenly interested in the politics and business of empire. Politics hinged on personalities, and consequently it was important to know who the new governor would be in Saint-Louis. Could he be trusted? Was he sympathetic or antagonistic toward local questions? What did the Governor-General in Dakar think? Who was the new Minister of Colonies? What views did his *directeur du cabinet*, who really ran the Ministry, have toward Senegal's deputy and General Council? Who was president of the Committee on Colonies in the Chamber of Deputies? These questions were constantly in the minds of informed citizens in Saint-Louis and Dakar.[2]

It soon became apparent that the Third Republic, republican and democratic in France, intended to remain imperial and autocratic in

---

* During the colonial period the literature made almost no mention of local political institutions. If they were mentioned, it was usually to indicate their origins during the beginning of the Third Republic, which is, as we have seen, false; no serious analysis appeared until Raymond Leslie Buell visited French West Africa in 1926–27. One of the most enlightened Frenchmen was Marcel Olivier, but he gave local government only 7 out of 483 pages in his study of Senegal's political and economic life.

the colonies despite its apparent liberality in urban Senegal. In fact, the basic "constitution" that still regulated colonial law was the Sénatus-Consulte of 1854, which held that the head of state could make all colonial laws by decree. The new regime simply did as most French regimes have done: kept all laws to date on the books as valid until changed. Owing to this autocratic system, the Senegalese, to survive politically, had to know everything that was happening in the French government and colonial empire—hence the Saint-Louis and Dakar newspapers often ran stories about policies in Indochina, incidents in Madagascar, riots in Guadeloupe, repression in Martinique, and the stability of the franc in Paris. Given enough information, unofficial pressure groups could sometimes accomplish something. The urban Senegalese understood very well the way their local institutions meshed with the apparatus of colonial administration in both the areas of direct rule and the Protectorate. Because the federal capital of French West Africa was in Dakar, they could perceive the lines of authority running to Paris more clearly than was possible for Africans in the Ivory Coast or Dahomey. And they could perceive from afar the political maneuvering in Paris that determined overall French colonial policy. Let us now consider each of these relationships from the point of view of the Senegalese.

## The Organization of Senegal

The structure of French rule took shape under Faidherbe and was completed by the time the Wolof state of Baol was annexed in 1894.[3] The urban dwellers along the coast were under direct rule, and the traditionally oriented rural peoples in the Protectorate were rapidly coming under a modified form of administration not unlike the British system of indirect rule. At the top of the pyramid was the Governor of Senegal, who in 1895 was also named chief executive of French West Africa. In 1902 these offices were separated, and henceforth the commander on the Senegal, whom the Wolofs had called Borom N'Dar ("ruler of Saint-Louis"), governed only Senegal. In practice, he governed only the Protectorate, since his relationship to the direct rule areas was more like that of a provincial prefect in France.[4] However, the Governor always enjoyed great prestige because he represented an authority and tradition that was traced back through such noted Governors as Faidherbe, Roger, and Blanchot. To the older Senegalese, he was the incarnation of French authority.

The Governor was aided by a secretary-general, who often filled in when the Governor was on leave or traveling in the interior. Various bureaus and departments, such as the Office of Native Affairs, reported directly to the Governor. The directors of these bureaus constituted what was in essence a cabinet; and with several other officials they formed the Governor's privy council, which dated from the same 1840 royal ordinance that gave Senegal its first General Council.[5] By 1907, there were two councils to advise the Governor: the Conseil d'Administration for the Protectorate, and the Conseil Privé for the direct rule areas. After the administrative reorganization of 1920, only the Conseil Privé was retained, and it then became the Governor's Executive Committee.

Senegal had financial and administrative autonomy even after becoming part of the West African federation. It could levy and collect its own taxes, determine its own budget, and issue decrees for its particular needs. All decrees had to be issued in the name of the Governor, who was also empowered to mete out discipline, settle disputes, or dismiss any employee from the colonial service. There was one important restriction on the governorship, however: the Governor of Senegal could not communicate with Paris directly on any subject, but had to send all reports, letters, or proposed budgets through the Governor-General at Dakar. As a result, the authorities in Paris had much less contact with Senegal's problems (especially those of the areas under direct rule), since a good deal of information was filtered out in the process.[6] (Furthermore, this circumstance enhanced the power of Senegal's deputy, who had direct access to Paris.)

Orders from the central administration in Saint-Louis went out to the different regions, or *cercles*, into which the colony was organized. The administrator of a cercle was called a *commandant de cercle*; under him were lesser functionaries who headed *subdivisions*, and under them the heads of *cantons*. At the subdivision and canton level, the central government often appointed a local chief to help the French administrator. As time went on, subdivision (i.e. paramount) chiefs were either stripped of authority or simply not replaced when they died. Below the cantons were villages, which were almost always administered by African chiefs or headmen. A town of any great size, however, usually had a French official in charge. The traditional rulers and nobles of Senegal had little power under the French. The most important African states were broken up and their rulers dethroned. African commoners who had worked for the French as interpreters, messengers, or filing clerks were occasionally appointed as chiefs over a village or canton because they had the ear and confidence of the local French administrator. Since these men usually knew rudimentary French and had some schooling, they could be relied on to behave as loyal French bureaucrats.[7]

A village chief was responsible for collecting taxes (from which he got a healthy rebate), recruiting corvée labor for the colony, judging local disputes, arresting offenders against French and customary law, and a variety of other tasks. He was often aided by a council of elders and notables. Immediately above the village chief was the *chef de canton*, who administered several villages or rural areas and was responsible for keeping the tax rolls, helping the French conduct the census, and deciding who would be liable for military conscription in his canton. He was assisted by a council of notables and village or regional chiefs. In some parts of French West Africa there were paramount chiefs above the canton chiefs; but in Senegal there were few paramount chiefs after 1900.

The French retained the institution of local chiefship only because they found it essential for the smooth functioning of the colony. Where a French official might bog down in his dealings with the Africans, a traditional authority could accomplish a great deal. Moreover, the great moral authority of a respected local chief soon associated itself with his French superior as well. But most chiefs were well aware that all their real power derived from the French administration. The influence of the chiefs seemed to increase in 1920, when cantonal chiefs from the Protectorate were brought to Saint-Louis to sit on the new Colonial Council.[8] But the chiefs, unlike the urban members of the Council, were still appointed by the French; and their role in the Council remained largely advisory, since they were unwilling to risk their pay and status.

The lines of authority in the direct rule areas were diverse: if an African lived in a full commune, he was under French municipal rule, if he lived in the *communes-mixtes,* he was under a mixed municipal and colonial system. The African who resided in neither simply came under indirect rule; his local chief was responsible to a French administrator, or, in many cases, his local administrator was his immediate ruler.

The distinction between urban and rural areas was further enhanced by the judicial system that evolved in Senegal.[9] Simply stated, there were three different judicial procedures to which an African might have recourse. First, people in the rural areas were subject to native law and native tribunals; these were presided over by the provincial administrator, who was aided by two local notables versed in customary law. French law was used as a guide, but the custom of the region and the temperament of the administrator were the controlling factors.* Second, the Africans who were assimilated legally as French citizens or who were citizens of the Four Communes had access to a system of French law, codes, and courts for both civil and criminal affairs.† Third, for Muslim citizens of the Four Communes Muslim tribunals and courts were available to settle questions of marriage, inheritance, and a few other civil matters.

## Senegal and French West Africa

In the late nineteenth century Paris decided that an overall commander was needed to establish a unified policy and purpose for the West African territories that France had conquered between 1880 and 1895. In 1895 the Minister of Colonies decided to appoint the Governor of Senegal to serve concurrently as Governor-General of French West Africa, a new federation including Senegal, Ivory Coast, Dahomey, Guinea, the French Soudan, and eventually Mauritania, Niger, and Upper Volta. The new post was given authority but not the means by which to operate, and for the next seven years the Governor of Senegal carried out his extra duties mostly in his spare time. By 1902 it was evident that the administration of French West Africa should be a full-time job, and the entirely separate post of Governor-General was created. All other heads of colonies (including Senegal) would now be technically Lieutenant-Governors.

The Governor-General received his own staff and cabinet, which were soon moved from Saint-Louis to Dakar. And in 1904 French West Africa was given a separate budget to insure its autonomy. Customs receipts from all the colonies were channeled to Dakar to finance the Government-General, leaving each colony with only its own revenues from head taxes, municipal taxes, port taxes, etc. The General

---

* Lamine Guèye has commented: "A ces tribunaux, il était permis, en matière répressive, de prononcer toutes sortes de condamnations, y compris la peine du mort, sans être tenus de s'appuyer sur un texte pré-existant, ni pour caracteriser l'infraction, ni pour déterminer la sentence. Leurs justiciables, à la différence de ceux qui relevaient des tribunaux français, n'avaient pas le droit de se faire assister d'un avocat, pas plus qu'il leur était permis de se pourvoir en cassation." Guèye, *Itinéraire africain*, p. 26.

† The Decree of May 25, 1912, set out, *inter alia*, the following requirements for citizenship, which were so demanding that few Africans down to 1940 bothered to apply for naturalization. It was necessary to occupy a position in a French office, public or private, for at least ten years with merit; to read and write French; and to give evidence of a means of existence and a good character. Applications had to be approved by local administrators, the Governor, the Governor-General, the Minister of Colonies, the Minister of Justice, and the President of the French Republic. See Buell's discussion of naturalization in French West Africa, I, 946–47.

Council of Senegal was especially outraged at this, inasmuch as Senegal contributed about three-fourths of the funds collected by federal customs and now had no control over them. The General Council brought suit in the Council of State in Paris to set aside the decision, but lost in a final judgment.[10]

Under the federal system, the Government-General in Dakar decided budgetary requests, conferred with Paris and the various departmental services, and had the right to appoint civil-service employees in the regional services. Moreover, all correspondence between the colonies and Paris had to be routed through Dakar. The Decree of October 18, 1904, which served as a constitution for the federation, gave full legal and executive powers for the Third Republic in West Africa to the Governor-General. He was to be in charge of military action in the colonies, formulate general policy, and carry out the will of Paris. His chief assistant in these tasks was the Secretary-General, who supervised finance, political and administrative affairs, economic services, and the colonial inspectors-general. The Governor-General was advised by a Conseil du Gouvernement, which met annually in Dakar and included the colonial governors, the French military commanders, and certain senior officials. There were also several nonadministrative members: Senegal's deputy, the presidents of the Senegal General Council and the Dakar chamber of commerce, and delegates from the various colonies. The Council was strictly advisory and exercised little practical influence, usually being asked only to confirm what the Governor-General had already decided.

The Governor-General derived great power from one of his prerogatives: the right to decide which general decrees issued in the metropole should be applied in Africa. Laws providing for labor organizations, for example, were theoretically available to Africans before 1914, but the decrees were not promulgated in French West Africa until 1936. Similarly, he could amplify or modify certain decrees by adding amendments in the *Journal Officiel* of French West Africa, which published relevant decrees from France. The Governor-General also had to approve many of the orders given by the Governors in their own colonies. As a result, his secretariat built up a strong centralizing influence. (This was somewhat curtailed in 1917, when Governor-General Van Vollenhoven restored the right of the Governors to direct their own colonial services, which had been reporting directly to the Dakar secretariat.[11] In each colony only the Governor now had the right to correspond with Dakar.) The Government-General also controlled three general inspectorships, which kept track of public works, education, and public health services in the various colonies.

After 1923, the economic affairs of the federation were partly handled from Paris by the Agence Economique, especially created for that purpose. The Agence issued bulletins on commerce in the colonies and served as a liaison between the home administration, French businessmen, and the Agence Générale des Colonies in Paris, which handled the colonies' business affairs.[12] The budgets for the colonies were submitted to the Minister of Colonies, who could only approve or reject *en bloc* what the Governor-General had requested. Dakar could create state monopolies in trade and industry if it so chose.

From the vantage point of imperialism, France was fortunate in having the services of several able Governors-General during the first decades of the century. The first man to run West Africa effectively was the third Governor-General, Ernest Roume. Roume was a young administrator who had been trained as a *maître des requêtes* for the Council of State in Paris; by 1895 he was Director of Asian Affairs at the Ministry of Colonies, and in 1902 he was named Governor-General. He brought a passion for centralization, order, and specifically defined powers to West Africa. His excellent qualities as a bureaucrat, however, were not appreciated by many. As *Le Soir* observed: "Il fallait un Africain d'expérience, répétaient les coloniaux, mais on a choisi un Indo-Chinois de Paris."[13] Roume, in fact, had never previously visited West Africa. He set out to concentrate complete control of the federation in the person of the Governor-General; and to increase the prestige of the office he built a 3,000,000-franc gubernatorial palace on Cape Verde overlooking the Atlantic. He also built up the staff necessary for a centralized operation, for which he was criticized by veteran colonialists used to running the empire on a more informal basis.

Roume's administration was proof that armed conquest and military rule were at an end, and that the age of the professionally trained administrator had arrived. The Ecole Coloniale, founded in Paris in 1889, was now graduating dozens of trained administrators and magistrates every year. These were the young men whom Roume expected to staff his new administrative creations.

Roume was replaced in 1908 by William Ponty, one of the most energetic and respected colonial figures in French African history. Ponty got his early African training in the French Soudan, where he worked his way up from second-class administrator in 1890 to Governor in 1904. When named to the Dakar post, he was well known for his just rule in the Soudan and his liberal attitude toward Africans.[14] *La Démocratie*, the voice of the Africans in Dakar, observed that only Ponty, with his vast practical experience, was capable of filling Roume's shoes.[15] Roume had seemed something of an aristocrat—cold, aloof, and surrounded by bureaucrats and colonial big business.[16] Ponty, by contrast, was sincerely interested in Africans, both urban and rural, and he was the first Governor-General to make a personal impression on France's new African charges. For example, when he sailed to France to take a wife in 1910, many Senegalese speculated about the new "first lady" who would occupy the palace at Dakar. Ponty's attachment to his job and to Africa was perhaps too strong: he died in 1915 at the age of 49 after refusing to leave his post and return to France for proper medical treatment.

The most famous Governor-General was the mercurial Joost Van Vollenhoven, who held the post for only six months, in 1917, but who in that time deeply impressed his subordinates and many Africans. Van Vollenhoven seemed destined for colonial leadership from the first. Born of a Dutch family in Algeria, he advanced quickly through the colonial grades in West Africa, became the youngest Governor-General ever appointed for Indochina, and was finally appointed to Dakar. He was filled with ideas for reform, which he poured out in endless circulars and memoranda;[17] and he even assembled a "brain trust" under Maurice Delafosse to generate new ideas for French rule in West Africa. However, when the Clemenceau war government decided to recruit more Africans for service in the French Army, Van Vollenhoven put his foot down. Unalterably opposed to further conscription, he resigned, went off to war himself, and died on the field of battle soon thereafter; his loss was mourned by many in Senegal, French and African alike.*

These three—Roume, Ponty, and Van Vollenhoven—were important administrators for the crucial period of Senegal's political history, for varying reasons. Any Governor-General exercised great influence on local politics in Senegal, however, because the citizens of the Communes knew that they could appeal to him whenever they were at odds with the Governor of Senegal. There was constant rivalry between Saint-Louis and Dakar. The Governor resented inter-

---

* It should also be noted that Van Vollenhoven was not pleased with the appointment of Blaise Diagne, deputy from Senegal, as high commissioner for recruiting. Van Vollenhoven was hostile to the idea of any Governor-General sharing power with others. See p. 193.

ference by the Governor-General, but the latter often thought the former was not doing his job properly. The Governor of Senegal also had the misfortune of being in the same colony as the Governor-General, whereas the other governors were far away. In practice, then, the Governor-General constantly intervened in Senegalese local politics when in theory he should have remained aloof and operated only through his subordinate in Saint-Louis.

### Senegal and the Home Government

After 1902 Senegal's official relations with the Ministry of Colonies in Paris were handled exclusively by the Governor-General. But Senegal also had a deputy in Paris, and he could therefore bring pressure to bear on the Ministry in a manner not available to other French possessions south of the Sahara. Moreover, the members of both the General Council and the municipal councils in Senegal did not hesitate to send unofficial petitions, delegations, and complaints to the Ministry with a persistence that would have been unthinkable in other colonies. In short, even though all contact with Paris was supposed to be channeled through Saint-Louis and then Dakar, the Senegalese found numerous ways to circumvent the barriers that were intended to protect the Ministry from local details. And after Blaise Diagne became deputy in 1914, he successively became commissioner for recruiting African troops, president of the Chamber's Colonial Committee, and Undersecretary of State for Colonies. Through him, Senegal had real power to influence colonial affairs and policy.

The same influence existed outside governmental circles. The giant French commercial interests that operated in the colonies were determined that their views should get a fair hearing from the Ministry. Agents from Bordeaux or Marseille who had complaints in Senegal simply made their grievances known to their home offices, who then informed the proper bureaus in the Ministry or worked through colonial leagues and lobbying organizations (e.g., the Union Coloniale or the Comité de l'Afrique Française). Small businessmen or Africans who felt their rights in jeopardy could turn to the famous Ligue des Droits de l'Homme, which was a vigilant defender of French civil liberties and was especially interested in colonial matters. And by the 1920's, the local political organizations in Senegal had established contact with metropolitan political parties (notably the Socialist Party). In sum, Senegal had ties with France that no other colony in Black Africa could maintain.

Although France had the second largest overseas empire in the world, the Ministry of Colonies had for years been a section of the Ministry of Marine (and on occasions the Ministry of Commerce); but in 1894 it was established as an independent ministry. Its creation was a victory for the colonial movement set in motion by Jules Ferry a decade earlier and now led by Eugène Etienne. That the new ministry did not administer Algeria (under the Ministry of the Interior) or later Morocco and Tunisia (under the Quai d'Orsay) did not seem to trouble the official French mind, which accepted the division of French Africa into three sections as normal and convenient. From a legal (and European) point of view this made sense: Tunisia and Morocco were protectorates; Algeria was considered part of metropolitan France and was divided into departments; and everything south of the Sahara was part of the colonial empire.

At first the Ministry was divided into geographical bureaus, each dealing with all the problems of a particular colony. But this arrangement seemed to create overspecialization and an excessive concern for petty details. In 1920, therefore, the Ministry's bureaus were rearranged according to administrative functions—political affairs, economic affairs, military affairs, personnel, public health, and so forth. The permanent bureaucracy of these departments effectively controlled the Ministry, since colonial management was a mysterious art about which most Frenchmen, and perhaps most of all the various French politicians who held the post of Minister, knew little or cared nothing. An English writer on French colonial policy observed: "The Ministry in the Rue Oudinot reduces itself to the permanent *bureaux*, with more or less surface concessions to the idiosyncrasies of the politician or party in power for the moment. The permanent officials are everything, the Minister, unless of an outstanding personality, a subsidiary, both to the other ministers and to his own officials."[18]

The government made numerous unsuccessful efforts to reform the Ministry and let specialized commissions handle specific areas of colonial policy. But the only such commission actually established was the Conseil Supérieur des Colonies, a relic from the days of Louis XVIII. This body was reorganized in 1925 and included delegates from all the colonies as well as the deputy from Senegal. However, it was purely advisory, cumbersome, and of little political consequence.[19]

The Ministry was responsible for and had direct control of the corps of administrators, the upper echelon of the colonial service. The administrators usually spent three years at the Ecole Coloniale and were then sent out to the colonies for field training; their terms of service were fixed by presidential decree. These men were the career executives usually chosen as governors of colonies, although a few governors were either political appointees or came from other services. Because the administrators all belonged to the same corps, they were easily transferred between the various colonies in West and Equatorial Africa.

Below the trained administrators was the colonial civil service, a collection of poorly paid clerks and specialists from various backgrounds. Civil servants could not easily be transferred between colonies, and had their terms of service fixed by local administrative orders.[20] They were therefore at the mercy of colonial budgetary needs, and it was not unusual for the wives of junior civil servants to work in local small businesses so that their families could survive economically. Many Frenchmen came to the colonies as civil servants and later left the colonial service to set up small businesses of their own in Africa. They were naturally fearful of African assimilation, since educated Africans could do their jobs more cheaply (receiving no bonuses, European vacations, or the like). Consequently, the lower ranks of the colonial service had little sympathy for Africans in Senegal. But at the same time, they were the very Frenchmen that Africans saw the most of after 1900. The same was true of the commercial world: it was the *petit colon*, with his dreams of making a quick fortune in the colonies, who was most in contact with the Africans. These men, too, dreaded the increasing role of Africans in business and commercial affairs.

So far, we have examined the structure of official administrative rule. Economic matters, by contrast, were largely private affairs in Senegal. (This was not always true elsewhere; in the French Soudan, for example, the government-financed Office du Niger struggled to develop the middle Niger.) It should be emphasized that the great merchants and agents of Bordeaux, Paris, and Marseille were just as important in the everyday life of the native Senegalese as the civil servants, administrators, and governors.

### Assimilation, Association, and Colonial Theory

France's vacillation between policies of assimilation and association has provided jurists, political scientists, and sociologists with much food for thought. Remarkably few observers, however, have been concerned with the actual effects of French policy in a given colony; most have preferred to discuss the entire empire, a particular group of colonies, or abstract theories of colonial rule.[21] Crowder's study of Senegal and Amon d'Aby's of the Ivory Coast are rare attempts to examine the reality of French colonial policy as it was applied in practice.[22] Colonial theory was especially important in Senegal because it was France's oldest African possession and in a very real sense a "pilot" colony; with its combination of direct and indirect rule in urban and rural areas, Senegal provided an ideal setting for testing the theories evolved in Paris.

Senegal, however, seemed to justify the caveat that in formulating colonial policy one could not simply brush aside the past. The Four Communes' political history and traditional association with France had produced definite attitudes about political participation among the urban Senegalese, who believed they had a vested interest in the status quo. In the past, France had given them certain rights and institutions, and these were not to be swept away by a few theorists. To theoretically oriented jurists, even in France, the Senegalese experience was an anomaly in the light of later colonial doctrine. For these reasons, the development of political rights in Senegal was not influenced exclusively by colonial theory or policy but also by the attitudes of administrators in the field, French businessmen, and Creoles—and especially by Africans of the urban class, who, as members of an expanding political elite, aspired to the benefits of full French citizenship.

The French theory of colonial assimilation, which derived from Roman precedents, was given its classical formulation during the French Revolution. The Rights of Man were held to be applicable everywhere, since it was thought that if men were given the opportunity they would become civilized, rational, and free. The implicit assumption here was that non-European peoples (especially Africans) could find freedom, civilization, and dignity only by accepting European culture. The Revolutionary fathers agreed with Helvétius that all humans were essentially equal but that education was needed to correct the inequalities caused by environmental differences.[23] "Thus the French, when confronted with people they considered barbarians, believed it their mission to convert them into Frenchmen. This implied a fundamental acceptance of their potential human equality, but a total dismissal of African culture."[24] Thus assimilation was revolutionary and egalitarian on the one hand but conservative and elitist on the other. The democratic assimilation policy of the Revolution and its lingering influence in later French regimes gave Senegal its political rights and institutions. But it was the assimilation practiced by the autocratic New Empire—and attacked as elitist and conservative by later theorists—that guaranteed the survival of political rights among urban Africans.

Legally, Senegal gained nothing from the Revolution of 1789. Other colonies received deputies, whereas Senegal did not; and other colonies had legal municipal institutions, whereas the councils in Saint-Louis and Gorée were only de facto bodies. Nor did unassimilated Africans in the Communes qualify as French citizens, even though citizenship was theoretically available to all free men on French soil. Rather, the precedent of granting democratic freedoms and institutions elsewhere benefited Senegal when the doctrine of assimilation was put into practice. Senegal won the permanent establishment of its three democratic political institutions because it was presumed that assimilation would continue there; after all, Senegal was one of France's oldest colonies.

The important organizational acts and decrees of the nineteenth century were all prompted by the assimilationist philosophy. Deschamps has suggested that the high tide of assimilation came during the early years of the Third Republic, when liberal republicans were in office.[25] This was certainly true in Senegal: 1871 saw the deputyship reestablished, and in 1879 the General Council was organized. Senegal was not suitable for European colonization and hence could not be assimilated directly, as Algeria could; but it nevertheless enjoyed special privileges that its younger sister colonies in tropical Africa would never possess until after World War II. Raymond F. Betts has summarized French policy as follows:

It was during the early years of the Third Republic that assimilation became the central doctrine of French colonial policy, whenever that policy was considered ideologically. In a rash of laws and decrees the idea seemed to be realized. The colonies which existed in 1848 were again given the right to send representatives to parliament. Everywhere the French penal code was to be applied; the commune was adopted as the basis of local overseas government. Two extraparliamentary commissions in 1879 and 1882, charged with the task of studying the possibilities of change in colonial administration, favored assimilation.[26]

Even during the ascendancy of the assimilationist doctrine, however, another school of thought was developing. This second viewpoint, generally termed the doctrine of association, had its roots in the fact that France's colonial empire was composed largely of non-European peoples. Was it rational to assume that all men were fit to receive French law and culture, or were there differing levels of civilization? Frenchmen familiar with Indochina argued that Asian civilization did not need to be assimilated; those who had served in the interior of Africa said that African civilization could not be assimilated. Gustave Le Bon, in his influential work *L'Homme et les sociétés: Leurs origines et leur histoire*, contended that there were basic inequalities in human races and societies. Evolutionary theorists pointed to Black Africa as an example of how some societies had not evolved beyond the primitive (perpetrating a stereotype of static, backward African society that is only now being corrected by African anthropologists and historians). How, they said, could simple tribesmen from Gabon or Ivory Coast possibly be assimilated by French culture, which was, of course, at the highest stage of social evolution.[27]

The associationist viewpoint was in the minority at an informal 1889 congress of persons and groups interested in the colonies. At the Colonial Congress of 1900, however, serious doubts and reservations were expressed about assimilation; it was evident that the alternative view was gaining ground. And at the Colonial Congress of 1906, most of the participants were in favor of association and hostile to assimilation.[28] By this time, the doctrine of association had vigorous champions among the more important colonial theorists (most notably Jules Harmand and Paul Chailly-Bert). The shift toward an associationist viewpoint was both a blessing and a curse for Africans. The policy of association demanded a respect for "native institutions," but this respect too often took the form of paternalistic condescension. The Senegalese tradition of urban enclaves in which a native elite could be gradually assimilated to French culture was now condemned as anachronistic. Critics of the old policies saw no reason to give a few Africans in the Communes special consideration. There was, after all, no reason to suppose that Africans were even suited to assimilation. The same arguments were applied to all the colonies; and the assimilationist doctrine was rejected as valueless, if not actually harmful.[29]

Although the new generation of colonial thinkers was willing to respect native institutions, French associationist rule was not the same as British indirect rule. Association rarely involved a coexisting native authority in the same region (there were some exceptions, such as the Mossi of Upper Volta), since French authority had to be unquestioned.[30] French rule in Africa was basically direct rule (with African chiefs serving as auxiliaries), and its pattern was derived from the circumstances of French military conquest.[31] Associationists held that new legislation for the colonies should be flexible and adapted to

local needs, and that local authorities should be allowed enough lati-
tude to cope with differing customs. But L. Gray Cowan, studying
local government in French West Africa, found that the methods of
direct rule "were scarcely disturbed by the concept of association."[32]

Two of the earliest Governors-General, Ponty and Van Vollenhoven, pleaded for a greater employment of Africans in local rule,
for both were convinced associationists who wanted to preserve much
of the indigenous African society.[33] But many French administrators
were still imbued with the assimilationist ethic, even after Maurice
Delafosse had popularized African ethnography, languages, and history, inspiring a generation of administrators to write studies of the
peoples who surrounded them. Writing from the perspective of the
1950's, Cowan observed: "Where native institutions showed that they
were capable of adaptation to French administrative standards, they
were permitted to exist; but where they failed to meet this test, they
were ruthlessly discarded as rapidly as possible. The tendency was
to substitute institutions based on the French model as soon as the
population was considered ready to accept them."[34] In the final
analysis, association proved to be only one stage of assimilation.

In Senegal, the doctrine of assimilation was attacked at the precise
moment that Africans were beginning to awaken to the political
potential of the institutions given them by this doctrine. The struggle to retain the old political rights and institutions was the main
fact of political life in the Four Communes from 1895 to 1915. Assimilation had provided the rationale for these rights and institutions;
association furnished the argument for taking them away.

## CHAPTER 4

# The Political Rights of the African Electorate

SEVERAL PROJECTS, decrees, and resolutions for the extension of political rights overseas were brought before the Constituent and National Assemblies in the early years of the French Revolution. After discarding many of these proposals, the Assembly in 1792 decreed that among people of color only mulattoes and free Negroes born of freed parents should be endowed with political rights in the colonies. As the Revolution progressed, sentiments became more liberal, and in August 1794 the old qualifications were removed: the Convention abolished slavery in French colonies and decreed that all men living in the colonies, whatever their race, would henceforth enjoy all the rights of French citizens.[1] This democratic gesture set a precedent referred to by liberals during the entire nineteenth century, but its practical consequences were short-lived. Riots and rebellion broke out in Haiti, and in 1802 Bonaparte suspended the 1794 decree and reestablished slavery.

In 1833 the Orleanist Assembly issued a law providing that any freeborn person or liberated slave in a French colony was to have full political and civil rights under the French codes. This confirmed the view of Senegal's urban inhabitants that they were citizens. A local arrêté of November 5, 1830 had stated: "This territory, in the application of the Civil Code, is to be considered an integral part of the mother country; each person born free and living in Senegal or its dependencies will have the rights of a French citizen as guaranteed by the Civil Code."[2] There was no question about the political rights of Frenchmen, Creoles, and the few assimilated Africans. But 1848 provided a new problem: What were the rights of a freed slave? The Second Republic permanently abolished slavery in all of France's colonies. Thousands of Africans in the Four Communes gained a new status, and hundreds more flocked to the cities after hearing of the new law.

For Senegal, the key decision came in the voting instructions issued on March 27, 1848. These specifically declared that a Senegalese no longer had to furnish proof of French naturalization in order to vote, provided he could prove five years' residence in the Communes. Almost immediately an estimated 12,000 Africans, many of them freed slaves or former servants, sought to qualify as voters. About 4,500 citizens were registered in the first election for deputy, but no more than about 1,800 actually voted (see Table 2). The first deputy, Durand Valantin, was reelected by about the same number of votes in 1849, an indication that the electorate had been stabilized. During the rest of the nineteenth century the number of registered voters slowly increased, and the majority remained African. By 1906, there were over 10,000 eligible voters on the rolls. The French authorities considered this registration far too great; and the Governor of Senegal, alarmed, decided to strike some 2,000 African voters from the lists.

This affront to electoral justice was only part of an offensive against the African voters that had begun just after the turn of the century. The new generation of French administrators had little use for the doctrine of assimilation and was unaccustomed to the idea of Africans voting in elections. The immediate cause of the colonial administration's hostility to the African electorate, however, was the report made by a French inspector-general from Paris, M. Verrier, who visited Senegal in 1905 in answer to complaints from a number of French officials.

Verrier intended to see how voter registration lists were drawn up and to ferret out abuses and fraud. After finding that the irregularities described by his informants did exist in all the Communes, he discovered that the registration of voters everywhere in Senegal was

TABLE 2

*Registered Voters in Senegalese Elections, 1848–1919*

| Year | Voters | Year | Voters |
|------|--------|------|--------|
| 1848 | 4,706  | 1893 | 9,380  |
| 1849 | 4,991  | 1902 | 9,556  |
| 1871 | 4,277  | 1906 | 10,900 |
| 1881 | 6,681  | 1910 | 8,018[a] |
| 1885 | 7,552  | 1914 | 8,677  |
| 1889 | 9,471  | 1919 | 16,013[b] |

SOURCE: *Tableaux des élections de la Chambre des Députés*, Archives de l'Assemblée National, Paris.
 [a] Reflects the cutback in voting lists following the Verrier investigation in 1907.
 [b] This expansion reflects the *jugements supplétifs* and the Diagne citizenship laws, 1916–19.

still governed by the voting instructions of 1848. Although these instructions had obviously been a temporary stopgap, he said, each succeeding Governor had simply followed the same procedure in establishing voters' eligibility. Verrier was shocked. In all other French colonies the right to vote depended on proving one's French citizenship; in Senegal, he claimed, most of those voting would not be able to do so. Time had stood still in Senegal while more recent and stringent voting requirements had been put into effect in other colonies. The whole might well be a deliberate plot, and was certainly administrative negligence of the worst kind.[3] Verrier found the situation intolerable. He was particularly incensed at the idea that residence in one of the Communes could make an African into a French citizen. "Because the 1848 instructions, the only authority for Senegal's elections, held that proof of naturalization was not necessary, it was concluded in practice that all natives registered on the electoral lists were by this fact French citizens. What a strange application of principle—to make French nationality the consequence of electoral rights when in fact it is the *sine qua non* for electoral rights."[4]

Senegalese tradition held that all Africans born in the Four Communes, or of parents from the Communes, were French citizens, but that those born in the Protectorate were simple French subjects. How could birth in a specific urban area confer citizenship when there were no texts, laws, or decrees actually defining citizenship for the Senegalese?[5] The Africans were judged in Muslim courts, and their language and customs were not French. How could these people be considered French citizens? To Verrier, the answer was clear: the Africans were not citizens and therefore had no voting rights. He recommended reducing the number of voters in Senegal from 9,441 to 898, leaving only white Frenchmen and "those who were assimilated" on the lists. He also warned: "If ever the great majority of voters were to act as one we would see the General Council and Municipal Councils composed exclusively of native Muslims who retain their customary law while having civil jurisdiction over [our] special tribunals. In the future, the deputy from Senegal could conceivably not even be a French citizen!"[6]

Verrier's report caused great uneasiness both in Senegal and in Paris. Governor-General Roume expressed his own views on the matter in a letter to the Minister of Colonies. Roume agreed that historical accident had been responsible for the retention of the 1848 voting instructions: officials, from governors through clerks, had simply con-

cluded that the Africans, because they were registered on the early
lists, must have political rights. However, there was no easy way to
reform the electoral lists. Verrier had proposed to restrict the franchise to Frenchmen and "assimilated" Africans. But what did this
really mean? No official texts defined an *assimilé*. Roume agreed with
Verrier's analysis but disagreed with his solution on the ground that
disenfranchising all the Africans on the lists "would be revolutionary."

Roume also feared that cutting the electorate to 898 would allow
Senegal to be dominated by a handful of local traders, "as is the case
in Indochina." He preferred to leave the situation as it was, fearing
that Verrier's solution would be just as illogical as the system it replaced. However, he recommended that the Council of State in Paris
look into the matter again, as it had done in 1902.[7] Roume's personal
intervention may have saved the Africans from a hasty ministerial decision, but it did nothing to solve the problem. For the next eight
years, a series of court cases, interventions in parliament, decrees,
suits, and judgments in both French and native tribunals centered
on two questions: Did Africans have voting rights? If so, were they
French citizens?

To a colonial administrator who believed in association, this mix-
up was one further proof that assimilation was outmoded. Administrators in rural Senegal, in particular, let it be known that they could
see no reason why Africans in the cities should be treated any differently from those in the countryside. They sincerely believed that it
was an injustice to give a small native elite special privileges, and
that the urban Africans "set a bad example" for the French charges
in the bush. At that time, in fact, the citizens of the Four Communes
were often met with in the Protectorate. While rural Africans were
emigrating to the cities, the urban Senegalese roamed the interior to
trade in peanuts or to serve as agents for the large French companies.
These adventurers maintained that they were entitled to all the privileges of French citizenship wherever they went in Africa. The French
administrators in the bush denied this on principle. Besides, how
could one tell a genuine originaire of the Communes from a rural
African?

One of the most important legal cases arose in 1907. Aly Seck, an
African, was sentenced to two years' imprisonment by the French administrator of Kaolack in Saloum. Seck appealed his sentence, maintaining that he was an originaire and therefore exempt from the Protectorate's native tribunals. The administrator challenged Seck to

prove that he was French and hence subject instead to French law and courts. Georges Crespin, Seck's Creole lawyer, argued that Seck was registered on the Saint-Louis voting lists and should be brought to the capital for trial. When it was finally shown that Seck had actually been born at Gandiole, a small village near Saint-Louis but technically not part of the commune, his case was lost. The Court of Appeal in Paris ruled that only natives of the Four Communes (*originaires des quatre communes de plein exercice*) could register.[8] This decision excluded Africans from other urban areas under direct rule, as well as Africans in the Protectorate.

The Governor of Senegal, Camille Guy, was still convinced that something should be done to reduce the voting lists. In 1907 he ordered Africans who could not prove they had been naturalized as French citizens to be struck from the Dakar registers. Dakar's municipal council, which was in charge of formulating the lists, rejected the demand. The next year the French tribunal at Dakar decided the question in favor of the Governor; but its decision was reversed by the Court of Appeal, which recognized the electoral rights of all originaires. And in 1909 the Court specifically stated that the originaires had full political rights only in the Communes; elsewhere, they were subject to their own "special statute" for civil matters unless they had been naturalized as French citizens.[9]

What was this special statute? In 1857, Faidherbe, because there were so many Muslims in Saint-Louis, decided to legalize the de facto Muslim courts by creating a Muslim tribunal in which Africans would be permitted to seek justice for civil matters such as divorce, inheritance, and property settlement. Various courts later held that this 1857 statute had replaced the French codes set up by the 1830 arrêté, and that since 1857 native Africans in the Communes had been subject only to the Muslim tribunal.[10] Moreover, in 1905–7 more Muslim tribunals were created in Dakar and Rufisque to handle disputes in the newer Communes. As a result of the 1909 decision in the Dakar electoral list cases, Africans' political rights were relegated to a quasi-legal limbo. They had to work through the Muslim courts, and they had full rights only within the Four Communes.

In 1910, a court decision enfranchised Frenchmen and Creoles living in the Protectorate, who had previously been unable to vote in the colony's elections. Africans, even originaires, were prohibited from voting outside the Communes. Matters came to a head in 1912, when it was decreed that all Africans would henceforth be judged by the native tribunals unless they could prove they were under

French law (or Muslim law in the Four Communes). This Decree of August 16, 1912 became infamous in the African community. The minute an originaire stepped outside the Four Communes, he would have no recourse to French or Muslim courts, but would be liable to summary administrative justice like all other French subjects in the Protectorate: he could be detained without a charge, tried without a lawyer, and sentenced to prison with little hope of appeal; he would be subject to the body of colonial law called the *indigénat*. The decree quickly became a landmark in Senegalese political history, for it threatened the rights that the urban Africans had acquired over more than a century.*

### The African Electorate

In Senegal there were three groups involved in political activity: French, Creoles, and urban Africans. Each group was committed to a policy that reflected the particular political goals and ambitions characteristic of its members; and each was conscious of its social and political differences from the other two groups. We are only briefly concerned here with the French and Creoles (who will be discussed at length later).[11]

There was never any question about political rights for Frenchmen living or working in the colony. They had full voting and civil rights, although they could only vote within the direct rule areas until the 1910 decree extended their political rights to all of Senegal. The French were a small community divided into three major categories: government officials and civil servants; wholesale businessmen and their agents; and small businessmen, clerks, and petits colons. Administrative personnel could vote but were legally forbidden to participate in campaigns. In practice, this prohibition was openly flaunted, and many functionaries campaigned actively for their candidates. The French, though the smallest group, held the major positions of political and economic power in the colony.

The Senegalese Creoles made up a second group. They were highly conscious of their status because it was based primarily on race. They had usually dominated municipal politics, and sought especially to control the General Council. Because they professed Christianity and were close to the French in education, taste, and style of life, they had

---

* Idowu emphasizes the impact of the 1912 decree: "It put the Senegalese [Africans] on the verge of revolt." Idowu, "Conseil Général," p. 425. See also Guèye, *De la situation politique*, p. 50, for a Senegalese assessment of the decree by a contemporary observer.

been associated with the French elite group since 1790, when the Frenchman Lamiral and the Creole Cornier had joined forces to draft Saint-Louis's petition to the Estates-General in Paris. The Creole community was small, based primarily in Saint-Louis and Gorée, and well defined in its attitudes and outlook. There had never been any attempt to deprive the Creoles of civil or political rights, inasmuch as they were considered the finest result of assimilation; however, their status was in some ways unclear, since no legal text had defined an assimilé. They were second to the French in economic power and sought an equal share of local political control.

By far the largest group was the African elite, which had been created by the French policy of assimilation. When politics first began in Saint-Louis and Gorée, in the late eighteenth century, urban Africans developed an interest in who would become mayors and counsellors. This interest grew in the years that followed, especially after the 1848 decree authorized this urban class to vote for the colony's deputy. From 1848 to 1912, courts, decrees, and orders continually sought to define who among the African urban class would be eligible to vote in municipal, General Council, and parliamentary elections. Gradually, an African political elite, definable in terms of law, was created in the Four Communes. This group did not by any means include all the municipal inhabitants. Thousands of Africans from the Protectorate, other French colonies, Gambia, Portuguese Guinea, or the Cape Verde Islands were assimilated to urban values and became members of the urban work force.[12] But they did not become members of the elite group, which was eventually restricted by law to those who had been born or could show long residence in the Communes.

These native communards, popularly called originaires, were mostly Muslim, though a few were Christians and animists. Ethnically, Wolofs were predominant, followed by Lebous and Toucouleurs. However, it is difficult to reconstruct the exact ethnic composition of either the urban population or the political elite. It may be assumed, in the absence of precise records that the same pattern was common to both until about 1900; after that, migrations from the interior and from other colonies changed the urban milieu, but the elite remained fairly constant. The Wolof influence was paramount in every way, even in Rufisque and Dakar, where Lebous were in the majority. The Toucouleur influence in Saint-Louis was attenuated by intermarriage and acclimatization to Wolof culture; it became stronger in Dakar because the Toucouleurs who migrated there in later years tended to retain their cultural identity. The Lebous abstained from active political leadership until the 1920's, although they had become voters when Dakar and Rufisque became communes. The urban population also included a few Sereres, a few Fulbe, and a scattering of peoples from the Casamance; but these were rarely members of the political elite.

There were no class or caste restrictions on membership in the political elite; that is, members of the artisan caste and former slaves could become originaire voters regardless of their ancestry or occupation. After 1900, however, when Africans were candidates for political office, it was rare to find lower-caste names among the candidates. The Communes, in many respects, still retained traditional attitudes toward caste, especially concerning African political candidates.* It was nevertheless possible for a person of any traditional social rank to enter politics and stand for election on personal merit, but successful candidates were most often from the upper status groups.[13] Tribal or ethnic groupings, save for the Lebous, were politically unimportant; this was basically owing to the strong influence of Wolof culture, which permeated the urban areas.[14]

The African political elite was in an enviable position in some respects. It included the majority of voters in the Communes, and its votes invariably decided each campaign. No possible combination of French and Creoles could defeat it as long as it stayed united. But from 1848 to 1914 the Africans had no organization and no unity. The French and Creoles were well aware of this and had long ago realized that the African electorate should be assiduously cultivated and carefully divided before each election.

When the Africans awoke to politics after 1900, the originaires were also courted by other urban Africans who wanted to enter the magic circle, as well as by rural Africans who continued to be simple French subjects. In addition, the important minority groups in Senegal who had no political voice—Moroccans, Moors, Lebanese, Cape Verdeans, and a host of Africans from other colonies—all paid hom-

---

* For example, Amadou N'Diaye Duguay-Clédor, president of the General Council in 1925–35, suffered political humiliation because of a Bambara ancestor who had supposedly been brought to Saint-Louis as a slave. Even as late as the 1950's, when all Senegal could vote in elections, the Communes were still highly sensitive to class. Assane Seck, a Senegalese geographer at the University of Dakar, made his debut in politics on a ticket sponsored by Lamine Guèye in Rufisque. When presented to the crowd, he was booed and jeered, ostensibly because Seck was a common lower-caste name. The day was saved when an elderly man got up and said: "Let him speak. He is related to Ibra Seck, who was our mayor of Rufisque in 1928." Thus sanctioned by an accepted precedent, Assane Seck was allowed to make his speech. (Personal communication from M. Assane Seck, Dakar.)

age to the originaires.[15] The African political elite occupied the middle ground between the French and Creole elites and the mass of urban and rural Africans and foreigners who had no political or civil rights whatever. This is why the originaires' political power was so much greater than their numbers. He who controlled the African elite controlled local politics in Senegal.

Before the 1900's, most originaires were content to follow French and Creole leaders. There was a lack of effective leadership until 1909 when Galandou Diouf, a Wolof from Saint-Louis, was elected by the Lebous of Rufisque as a representative to the General Council. Diouf was not the first African to sit on the Council, but he was the first to openly criticize the Creoles, the French, and the colonial administration.[16] His election symbolized the beginning of a new era for an elite that had been dispossessed of its inherent political power since its creation by French law and the assimilation policy. Now the originaires consciously sought the leadership needed to bring them to power.

Below the African elite on the political scale were the African *sujets* who made up the bulk of Senegal's population. These people did not receive political rights until after World War II, when the French overseas empire underwent great changes. However, it should not be supposed that they were uninterested or without influence in the politics of the Communes before that time. After the reform of 1920, they had traditional chiefs sitting in the Colonial Council at Saint-Louis—men under French tutelage but nevertheless interested participants in the modern political process. Originaires continually moved into the interior, and by 1914 election campaigns were carried far into the bush to reach them. With great interest and no little envy, the other Africans watched the rallies, speeches, and campaigning that took place in rural towns or villages nearly every year.

These same rural Africans were soon to serve in World War I, returning home as far different men. Even before this, life in the Protectorate was far from static. Senegal's economic boom in peanuts led to a redistribution of population as farmers rushed southward and westward to find more suitable and productive fields. Interior towns like Thiès, Kaolack, and Ziguinchor soon passed Gorée and Rufisque in population and commercial importance. These cities became communes-mixtes, and their inhabitants obtained a kind of second-class citizenship with a limited, local municipal franchise.

There were also many rural Africans who flocked to the Communes in search of jobs, adventure, and citizenship. There were often complications in drawing up electoral lists for coming elections, for these newcomers tried every possible means to get themselves registered as originaires. Moreover, their lack of a franchise did not keep them from participating in politics vicariously: they attended committee meetings, cheered at rallies, carried placards, and put up posters. The French disliked these noncitizens for an obvious reason: they were hard to control. As demonstrators, they occasionally broke up campaign meetings with rocks and bottles (in favor of rival candidates or out of sheer frustration). In sum, they formed the heart of the mass crowd that has been important in the history of urban politics the world over. Yet they, like the rural Africans and foreign minorities, could never vote. That right was reserved by official fiat for certain Africans born or bred on the historic soil at the mouth of the Senegal, on an offshore island, and on Cape Verde—for the originaires of the Four Communes.[17]

In 1848 most Africans living in the Communes had been registered as voters. This began to change after 1872 as the total population of the Communes climbed much higher than the total number of Africans in the elite.* The originaires became aware of themselves as an elite, and they tried to perpetuate their status by seeing to it that only their friends were admitted to the electoral lists. They were becoming conscious of their unique place in Senegal's political and economic world—as middlemen between big business and small enterprise in the bush, and as mediators between the French and Creole elites and the African masses. The privileges of the urban elite were jealously defended in the face of rural envy; and by 1900 there was a sharp division between Communal and interior interests.

Most of all, many originaires had a sense of historic mission. They remembered the founding of Saint-Louis and were proud of the fact that their ancestors had been the first French auxiliaries. The fathers, uncles, and grandfathers of the Communes' citizens had stood beside the French in many campaigns throughout Africa and had received the highest praise for their skill and courage. The originaires were also conscious of their economic ties with Europe, which dated back to the Portuguese presence, at Gorée and Rufisque long before the French arrived. The history of coastal Senegal and its colonial past was as important to the urban elite as the history of Tekrour, the

---

* In 1878–79 there were 5,000 originaires qualified to vote out of 30,000 Africans living in the Four Communes; there were 7,000 out of 65,000 in 1910, and 18,000 out of 66,000 in 1922. (See ARS, 27–G–237–108; the total number of Africans is only an approximation.) The relative increase of originaires in 1922 was a result of the *jugements supplétifs* and Blaise Diagne's citizenship laws.

Wolof empire, and Al-Hajj Umar or Lat-Dior was to the interior peoples. Even certain stubborn Lebous of Cape Verde eventually took pride in their early treaties with the French.[18]

Perhaps the greatest unifying force affecting the political elite was a common adherence to Islam. The coastal towns of Senegal had been convenient fields for spreading the Prophet's word, and by 1850 Saint-Louis's African population was predominantly Muslim. A dynamic faith, shared convictions, and a respect for Islamic traditions helped the originaires make a common front in the face of French assimilation; but under the surface, the rivalries between the various Islamic brotherhoods continued. Even sects from the interior, such as the powerful Mourides, recruited talibés in the towns.

The African political elite was not, of course, a monolithic block. Saint-Louisians considered themselves superior to all others—better educated, more cosmopolitan, and more discerning in their European-oriented tastes. The people of Gorée took a similar view of themselves, emphasizing their loyalty to the Catholic Church and their connections with the Creoles. There were tribal divisions as well: the Lebous of Dakar and Rufisque had their own rich tradition of the "Lebou Republic"; the Toucouleurs possessed a great Islamic tradition dating from the empire of Tekrour; and the Wolofs lauded their own widespread language and culture, as well as Wolof heroes like N'Diadiane N'Diaye. But these and other differences fell by the wayside when the elite's liberties and special privileges were threatened.

The real political task for the French in Senegal should have been coming to terms with this African political elite, which had appeared almost by historic accident.[19] But as the new century began, the French were still preoccupied with a nineteenth-century problem: the attempt of the Creole elite to dominate local politics. Sharing power with the French did not appeal to the younger Creoles, who wanted to control local government themselves. The Creole's bid for greater power came just as the African elite had become conscious of its own political potential under assimilation; at the same time, the French were seeking to implement their new policy of association. The resulting conflict between the three groups, which continued until the eve of World War I, was the immediate background for modern Senegalese politics.

# PART II

# The Emergence of Black Politics
## 1900–1920

CHAPTER 5

# The French Attempt to Dominate
# Local Politics

THE MOST important forces in Senegalese local government at the turn of the century were the French and Creole political elites. The center of power in the French group was undoubtedly the community of Bordeaux merchants, who dominated Senegal's economic life. The Creole group was led by a number of talented men, but those from the Carpot and Devès families were perhaps the most ambitious and politically astute. Together, the two groups formed an oligarchy that totally dominated business and politics in the colony, confining Africans to minor roles in both spheres. Control of the Protectorate's budget had been taken away from Senegal's General Council in 1892; but the oligarchy still controlled politics in the direct rule areas, which included the most important urban centers, ports, railways, and markets. Similarly, although the creation of the Government-General of French West Africa in 1904 considerably reduced Senegal's revenues, the oligarchy was powerful enough to influence fiscal policy not only in the direct rule areas but in the Protectorate and in all of French West Africa. Bordeaux and Marseille merchants led the economic penetration of the West African hinterland; the Creoles furnished army commanders, bureaucrats, and a strong coterie of merchants.

In all of this, the French clearly had the upper hand. Rivalry rather than cooperation usually marked the French-Creole relationship, and the colonial oligarchy was strictly a *mariage de raison*. The Creoles had controlled municipal government in Senegal since the eighteenth century, and they had seized the leadership of the General Council when it was first established. But their economic activities, once very important, had been impaired by the arrival of French merchants during the nineteenth century (especially after the establishment of the Third Republic).[1] True, many commercial agents and senior clerks in the colonial administration were Creoles; and at first their services had been indispensable, since they knew the country

and the Africans as no foreigner could. But as more Frenchmen settled in Senegal and brought in their families, the Creoles' importance
diminished. The newly arrived Frenchmen, some of them color-conscious, resented the idea that Creoles should play an important role
in politics, administration, and commerce. The alliance between the
two groups, therefore, was an uneasy one, based on mutual respect,
suspicion, and a tacit agreement that black Africans had no place in
the halls of leadership.

### Bordeaux and the Senegalese Economy

The heart of the French elite in Senegal was the community of Bordeaux merchants, agents, and clerks that dominated the economic
life of the entire colony. Creole businessmen, petits colons, African
merchants, and newly arrived Lebanese entrepreneurs were all subject to decisions made on the banks of the Gironde. The merchants
of Bordeaux dominated Senegal's trade, and they determined her
economic policy by influencing local politics through the councils
and colonial politics in France through the Chamber and the Ministry of Colonies. They were often at odds with the colonial administration, which from their point of view was too inflexible and bu-
reaucratic.

The Bordeaux traders carried European goods to the Africans and
peanuts to the Europeans—both at a healthy profit. They bought and
sold peanuts and consumer goods both wholesale and retail, and they
transported most of these in their own ships. Many of the French
firms were owned or dominated by a single family, so that dynastic
rule in Bordeaux was as common as dynastic rule among the Creoles.
In fact, some powerful Bordeaux families (such as the Devès), inter-
marrying with Africans during their early years in Senegal, had produced Creole branches and were therefore represented in both
camps.[2]

The economic history of Senegal has yet to be written, but the
broad outlines can be briefly described.[3] Chartered companies controlled both commerce and colonial administration until 1763, when
the French crown took an interest in creating a royal colony. During
the British occupation of Senegambia and the uncertain years of the
French Revolution, local commerce flowered and Creole and African traders became important. When the First Empire had fallen,
however, private merchant houses in Bordeaux and Marseille soon
decided to revive the African trade. At first, this trade was confined
to gum arabic, cotton, rubber, gold, indigo, and hides. But after the

1840's peanuts and peanut oil were Senegal's major export commodity. The difference was important: the old trade had centered on the Senegal river, whereas the production and marketing of the commercial peanut crop affected all of western Senegal.

The growth of peanut exports went hand in hand with the expansion of French merchants into Senegal. These men had the organization, capital, and know-how to organize the peanut market on a scale out of reach of the Creoles. The creation of new business operations in Senegal increased from the time of Faidherbe on, and the armies conquering the interior were immediately followed by the peanut trader. The Senegalese peasant, reluctant to grow cotton, indigo, and a host of other French-sponsored crops, was attracted by the simplicity and steady profits of peanut culture. By 1900 the pattern of cooperation between peasant, Creole or African agent, and Bordeaux merchant was established. The most notable changes in this commerce after 1900 were the increase in peanut production, the development of a better transport net in the interior, and the rise of the Lebanese business community at the expense of the Creoles. For some time, Senegal's economy was dependent on fluctuations in the world market prices for peanuts, but this difficulty was removed when tariff preferences with France were negotiated in the 1930's.

Senegal did not produce its export crops on large plantations owned by European firms, as certain colonies of French Equatorial Africa did. Most of the crop came from the individual plots of African peasants, who sold their peanuts to Lebanese, Moorish, and French agents for transport to the coast.* The Lebanese and Moors, in general, traded in inland regions too difficult or unprofitable for the French to reach. Once the peanuts reached coastal markets the Bordeaux companies took over and collected them at Rufisque or Kaolack for shipment to Europe.

Almost the only Africans involved in the wholesale marketing of peanuts were those theoretically connected with the directorships of the native provident societies (*sociétés de prévoyance*) that developed in Senegal after 1910 and eventually spread throughout French West Africa. These societies, directed by French administrators or trusted local chiefs, provided seed at planting time and stockpiled food sup-

---

* An African planting bourgeoisie never developed in Senegal, as it did in Ivory Coast and Gold Coast. The wealthy marabouts of the interior, however, especially those of the Mouride brotherhood, became shrewd businessmen. A few of them actually did run large plantations, with talibés furnishing the labor; others grew rich on donations from talibés and were really more merchants than farmers. These enterprises are described in Sy, pp. 70–79.

plies to help African farmers through the "hungry season" just before the harvest. As they grew in power, they were attacked by the
big French companies, who correctly regarded them as a threat to
French domination of the market.[4] The threat was never great, however; most Africans involved in the peanut trade were simply peasants
who spent the entire year growing peanuts for sale and millet for
food.

As word of the new cash crop and its profits spread, migrant workers (navetanes) flocked to Senegal from the neighboring French colonies of Guinea, Upper Volta, and Soudan. Some 60–80 thousand
might arrive during the growing season. The navetanes hired themselves for at least four days a week to Serere or Wolof farmers; the
rest of their time was usually spent working for their own profit on
small plots given them as part of the bargain. This practice had unpleasant side effects. The extra labor that Senegal needed during the
peanut season was supplied; but the navetanes, who rarely stayed
through the winter, grew their own peanuts by slash-and-burn agricultural methods. Senegal, once a lightly wooded country, now began
to suffer from deforestation and erosion.

The harvest began in early November and lasted until the end of
January. But la traite—that is, the marketing of the peanuts through
agents to wholesalers—lasted until May. The peanuts were stockpiled
in enormous hills (sécos) at the main trading centers and then shipped
to Rufisque or Kaolack, where even larger sécos awaited shipment
to France. The aroma of peanuts was everywhere during the traite.
Many Africans never saw the great commercial centers, especially
if they lived in the interior. They sold their harvest directly to Moors,
who carried the peanuts to market on camels or donkeys. After World
War I, when Senegal had better roads and some motor transport,
the Moors were replaced by Lebanese traders.[5] Some Africans did
bring their own harvest to market, since the major areas of peanut
culture bordered the Dakar-Bamako railway line. The market fluc-
tuated wildly, and these men would seldom market all their peanuts
at once, unless they had serious debts to pay. Peanuts could be stored
for months, and prices often doubled or tripled by the end of the
traite. In bad years, however, prices would drop rapidly, leaving the
speculators deeply in debt. Inevitably, credit played an important
role in peanut production.

Few Africans had enough capital to finance their peanut plantings
each year, and still support their families. The usual practice was
to buy food, cloth, and other necessities on credit during the growing

season. When harvesttime came, the trader who had extended credit usually bought the entire crop cheaply at the very beginning of the traite; the African farmer had paid his debt, but needed more credit to survive through another year. Many French administrators (as well as the president of the Saint-Louis Chamber of Commerce) criticized this system for its frequent abuses,[6] but the lack of banks and credit facilities in Africa made an alternative unlikely in an age when government finance planning was rare. The Bordeaux merchants supplied much of this local credit, but always through their own retail outlets. Except for the small operations of a few originaires, the rest of the credit was supplied by the petits colons and Creoles (both of whom usually got their training and capital by first serving as Bordeaux agents); in later years, the Lebanese joined this group. Whoever did the trading, oral contracts and a man's word of honor were essential parts of the Senegalese credit system.

Once the peanuts were sold at the provincial market, the Bordeaux group took over. Consequently, the only commercial activity open to small businessmen beyond the first stage of peanut trading was retail merchandising—selling the imported cloth, rice, sugar, tobacco, and hardware that the Africans were now accustomed to buying. But these goods had to be purchased wholesale from the Bordeaux importers; and the importers naturally reserved the best merchandise for their own retail chain stores, which were set up everywhere in the colony under various names. Africans did manage to dominate local markets in fresh foodstuffs, fresh and smoked fish, and kola nuts—that is, products both produced and consumed almost entirely by Africans. The French administration established a cattle fair at Louga in 1910 and a meat-packing plant near Kaolack in 1914, so that a small commercial market was developed for the African cattle producer. In addition, there were many wandering African peddlers, itinerants who bought wholesale or retail in the cities and sold at high prices in remote districts. Some were Wolof, but most were Dioulas from the French Soudan or Guinea; the Dioulas were a constant annoyance to the colonial administration because they entered Senegal from inland and thus avoided paying the licensing fees that applied to all merchants.

Bordeaux could not dominate retail business as completely as it monopolized the wholesale trade; the market had to be shared with Africans, petits colons, Creoles, Moors, Moroccans, and Lebanese. Ironically, these small entrepreneurs rather than the Bordeaux giants were the principal object of African xenophobic frustration. The

Africans grudgingly admitted that the large companies had to exist in order to manage trade with Europe, but they failed to see why so many foreign merchants should have a share in Senegal's local retail trade.

When chambers of commerce were created in the Four Communes after 1869, membership was reserved for French citizens. This meant that control was in the hands of the French and Creoles; urban Africans could hold only lower-level memberships, and all other Africans and foreigners were excluded. Bordeaux interests dominated the chambers of commerce and thus exercised a great deal of influence on the local business policies of the administration.[7] Technically the African members of the chambers were always in a majority. However, the categories of membership were based on personal assets and volume of trade, in which few Africans could match the French or Creoles,[8] and the chambers' statutes specified that members of the governing boards were to be drawn from the upper categories: it was a kind of pseudoeconomic assimilation that opened the doors for urban Africans but never really let them in.[9] Whereas the Creole elite struggled to control the General Council, there was never any doubt that Senegal's chambers of commerce belonged exclusively to the Bordeaux merchants and their allies.

Bordeaux controlled almost all the wholesale trade and shipping of the colony, although Marseille and Paris interests had a small share. Some of the most important members of the Bordeaux chamber of commerce were in the Senegal trade, and many of Bordeaux's oldest commercial houses had started as shippers and wholesalers to Senegal. In 1900, an official volume to illustrate life in Senegal was prepared for the Universal Exposition in Paris. It listed as the major trading houses in Senegal six Bordeaux companies and only one operating from Marseille.* (Shortly thereafter Vézia of Bordeaux began operations in Senegal, followed by the SCOA, a Swiss-French consortium based in Paris.) In time, the Bordeaux houses formed the Syndicate for the Defense of Senegalese interests, and their managing directors met in Bordeaux to determine common policy and lobbying needs. Bordeaux had the experience, capital, personnel, and ambition to direct the Senegalese trade into its own harbors, and that is precisely what it did.

---

* The Bordeaux firms were Delmas et Clastres, Peyrissac et Cie., Buhan et Teisseire, Maurel Frères, Devès et Chaumet, and Maurel et Prom; all were influential in the colony's politics. The Compagnie Française de l'Afrique Occidentale was the first important Marseille firm to operate in Senegal.

Bordeaux had had a head start over other French ports in trading with Senegal. It was active in the African trade as early as the seventeenth century. And in the nineteenth century certain families from Bordeaux took the lead in expanding trade with Senegal (the families of Maurel, Prom, Devès, and Delmas, among others, had their operations well under way before Faidherbe's day). The commercial histories of the Maurel and Delmas families, two of the most notable, may illustrate the dynastic approach that was such an integral part of French trade in Senegal.

The Maurels founded two of the largest shipping and wholesaling companies: Maurel et Prom and Maurel Frères. The founder of the family's Senegalese operations was Hilaire Maurel, the fifth son of Jean Maurel and Anne Prom (see p. 100). Hilaire and his cousin Hubert Prom, who had both traded in Senegal since the 1820's, began the firm of Maurel et Prom in 1852. The company's shipping line, vast warehouses, and chain of retail stores soon became the very symbol of Bordeaux commerce for many Africans. Hilaire's older brother Pierre had five sons who set up their own company, Maurel Frères, in 1869. Meanwhile (1857), the family had established the Huilerie de Bordeaux, a large plant for extracting peanut oil. Thus two of the largest Senegalese companies, as well as the processing plant in France, were controlled by one Bordeaux family in 1900.[10]

The beginning of the powerful Delmas family's association with Africa occurred in the tiny French hamlet of Beaucaire, where two families, the Delmases and the Lafargues, were united by several marriages after 1800. Philippe Lafargue went to Senegal in 1834, where he was introduced to colonial commerce by Hilaire Maurel. In 1855, Philippe was joined by his nephew Jean Anselme Delmas, and within ten years the two had formed Lafargue et Delmas, which soon became one of the foremost companies in Senegal. Lafargue, after making a small fortune, discreetly retired to Bordeaux and left the company in his nephew's hands, where it became successively Delmas et Laporte, Delmas et Clastres, and J. A. Delmas et Cie. Jean Delmas refused to open up shops in Dakar, holding to the view that Rufisque should be the economic capital of Senegal; but his son Philippe eventually established Delmas offices in Dakar in 1903.

The company prospered under the leadership of Philippe Delmas, and on the eve of World War II it maintained head offices in Saint-Louis, with fourteen retail outlets; in addition, there were an office and four retail outlets in Rufisque, an office and five retail outlets in Dakar, and rural establishments in eight other towns. Philippe also

# THE MAUREL FAMILY OF BORDEAUX

This genealogical table was compiled from a manuscript in the possession of Robert Delmas of Dakar; in many cases exact names and dates were not available. The following dates are of interest: 1823, arrival of Hubert Prom in Gorée; 1852, founding of Maurel et Prom by Hilaire Maurel, Jean-Louis Maurel, and Hubert Prom; 1869, founding of Maurel Frères by the five sons of Pierre Maurel.

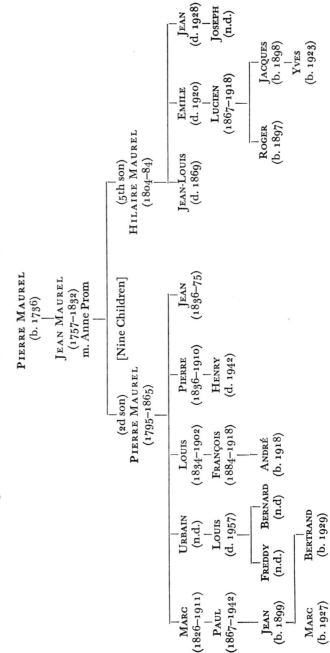

set up several new businesses: an electric company, a wholesale wine distributorship, a canned foods concern, and Manutention Africaine, a large distributorship to handle Dakar's shipping and transportation needs. Finally, Philippe's son Pierre took over the Bordeaux operations, and a nephew, Robert, was put in charge of the Senegal establishments. Delmas et Cie. was hard hit by the depression but weathered it by 1936, joining in that year with the Paquet, Delmas-Vieljeux, Fraissinet, and Cyprien-Fabre shipping lines to form USIMA, a gigantic industrial and shipping combine that dominated the port of Dakar.

Similar histories can be traced for other families. August Teisseire of Bordeaux went to Saint-Louis in 1829; in 1870, his firm was merged with an old Senegal company, J. E. Buhan et Fils, to form Buhan et Teisseire. The Bordeaux company of Charles Peyrissac began its Senegalese operations in 1872.[11] Bruno Devès, of Devès and Chaumet, was active as early as 1822, supplying millet for the French colonial army.[12] And the Gradis family, established in Bordeaux since 1688, made a fortune in sugar and slaves and eventually formed a holding company with diverse African enterprises.[13] Many of these companies were intimately linked with the great banking syndicates in France, and most of them expanded steadily. For example, Maurel et Prom, by the early 1940's, had the following assets in West Africa alone: 111 shops and buildings in Senegal; 18 bakeries in Senegal and Gambia; the largest cold storage plant in Dakar; distributorship for Socony-Vacuum Oil; and a fleet of two large steamers and 37 smaller vessels.[14]

Although the French Chamber and the Ministry of Colonies decided general economic policy for Africa and local officials often had a real voice in matters, France did little in the way of state planning or economic development in Senegal until after World War II. Economic matters were left to private enterprise; and in Senegal private enterprise meant Bordeaux.

### Political Power of the French Elite

Political power within the French community in Senegal was largely held by Bordeaux merchants and their agents. Civil servants and administrators were forbidden to run for office unless they took a leave of absence, which they did from time to time.* However, professional men or small merchants entered local politics. And the ar-

---

* Before every election, a circular pleading for neutrality was sent out by the Minister of Colonies or the Governor-General. For example, see Minister of Colonies to Governor-General, March 25, 1910. ARS, 20-G-19.

rival of more Frenchmen after the founding of the Third Republic challenged the Creoles, who soon met with keen competition for seats on the local councils. Dakar and Rufisque were dominated by the Bordeaux houses from the start, since there had been no tradition of Creole municipal rule in these cities. In Saint-Louis and Gorée the struggle was bitter.

The Bordeaux merchants were at their most cynical during campaigns. African voters were looked upon as objects to be bought—or, more precisely, to be rented for elections. French agents distributed sacks of flour, rice, sugar, and tea to neighborhood chiefs as electoral insurance; in time, this practice developed into open bribery. Lavish campaign promises and flattery were also commonplace. Some firms even transported their African workers from one Commune to another for voting under assumed names. There is no doubt that the electoral scandals uncovered by Verrier in 1905 were not entirely African in origin.

Political parties with permanent secretariats or committees were unknown in Senegal, and it was customary to organize lists of candidates about a month before elections. Two or three opposing lists were presented to the voters at each municipal election. The person who put together the list expected to be named mayor by his followers if all of them won; he would then appoint his aides from among the most faithful. By 1900, electoral lists were seldom composed exclusively of French or Creoles, since most political leaders tried to include several African names in order to attract the native vote. Usually, entire lists were elected, but on occasion the voters would prefer a group of men from two opposing lists. Candidates needed a majority of the votes cast to win. Otherwise, a runoff election took place within two weeks. This provided plenty of time for negotiations, maneuvering, and the withdrawal of some candidates in favor of others.

The list system tended to discourage individual candidates for the council elections, and it created a pattern of dynastic politics long before the African elite became an important political force; it was, in fact, the only model that the Africans had. Few modern ideas about political parties and campaigning had reached Senegal because it was advantageous for Bordeaux and the Creoles to keep the African electorate in ignorance. The ruling oligarchy regarded Africans as big children who were not really capable of political decision making; clearly, the outmoded assimilation system that had given Africans the vote had to be counteracted by intelligent manipulation.[15]

The goal of the Bordeaux merchants was simply to have a number of their local agents elected to offices in each Commune, so that no local complications would interfere with business. They were able to control all four chambers of commerce, as well as the municipal governments of Rufisque and Dakar; and they were on good terms with most of the French deputies elected from 1871 to 1902. In Saint-Louis and Gorée, and in the General Council, the Bordeaux agents shared power with the Creoles. The French civil administrators were approached less directly. Most of them longed for the comforts and amenities of France, and they readily appreciated the society of the merchant community. Since Frenchmen never met socially with Africans and only occasionally befriended Creoles, the "inner" French community of administrators and merchants formed its own society. The political desires of Bordeaux seemed very reasonable to colonial officials dining at the Yacht Club in Dakar or attending a bourgeois ball in Saint-Louis.

The usual lot of the small businessmen in Senegal was a benevolent exclusion from politics, but a few of them gained some measure of power. Fernand Marsat, a pharmacist, became an influential figure in Dakar city politics and was eventually elected mayor; Jules Couchard of Saint-Louis, a lawyer, was elected both mayor and deputy; and Jules Sergent, the postwar Mayor of Dakar, owned several taverns and a newspaper. These men had little reason to complain. Life was difficult, however, for the petits colons—the clerks, civil servants, and retail agents who kept the colony running. This group was essentially a small urban proletariat threatened by the rising number of educated Africans who could be employed more cheaply. Small businessmen not affiliated with the Bordeaux or Marseille houses had no choice but to cooperate with them in politics. The petits colons were never asked.[16]

Typical of the Frenchmen who drifted about the empire hoping to make a fortune or find adventure was Jean Daramy. Like so many colonials, Daramy was born in southern France (at Bayonne in 1876). He attended a commercial school but was expelled for failing his examinations. Despondent, he left Bordeaux and headed overseas. He worked his way through Madagascar, the Egyptian Sudan, and the East African coast before sailing for Argentina to become a cattle breeder. This venture failed for lack of capital, and Daramy was forced into bankruptcy. He fled South America for France, but had only enough money to reach West Africa. For a while he held a job on the new railway in French Guinea, but was soon fired because his pursuing creditors embarrassed his superiors.[17]

In 1912, Daramy became an assistant to the editor of *Le Petit Séné-*

*galais*, one of Dakar's weekly newspapers. When the editor, E. Post, vacationed in France shortly thereafter Daramy had his moment of glory. The paper, once a timid and conservative sheet, now spoke out on many topics usually considered taboo by the Senegalese press: administrative scandals, the private lives of the Governor and other administrators, and the business manipulations of the Bordeaux bourgeoisie. Above all, it broke tradition by printing news about Africans. E. Post returned in 1913 to find *Le Petit Sénégalais* practically the reverse of what he had left it. Daramy was sent packing, but this time he seemed to have found his element. During his fling as editor, he had taken the surname d'Oxoby as a kind of anglophilic nom de plume; it now gave him a touch of respectability in the midst of his notoriety, and he retained it for the rest of his career. He soon persuaded tavern owner Jules Sergent, a French businessman, to back him in founding a weekly newspaper that would reflect the views of small businessmen and petits colons.

With Sergent's backing, d'Oxoby published on November 5, 1913, the first issue of *La Démocratie du Sénégal*, the most important newspaper in early Senegalese politics. *La Démocratie* came on the scene like a fresh breeze amid the staid publications that modeled themselves on the *Journal Officiel du Sénégal* of Saint-Louis. Aside from the attempts of J. J. Crespin and Louis Huchard before the turn of the century, this was the first newspaper in French-speaking Africa to print satire, adopt an independent editorial policy, and criticize those in power. In his first issue d'Oxoby announced: "Without the press there is no liberty; without opposition there is no progress." He told of his being fired from *Le Petit Sénégalais* for speaking his mind, declaring that this could not happen again. *La Démocratie* would be "the tribune of the people . . . a journal of ideas, principles, and facts; a journal of republican political action for the colonies and not an ephemeral sheet in the pay of particular interests who fear opposition will bring forth the truth."[18] The first issue contained an analysis of the current sessions of the General Council, a parody of a recent speech by the Governor of Senegal, and an article decrying the brutal physical treatment of Africans by Bordeaux agents in the Protectorate.

Besides backing *La Démocratie*, Jules Sergent also organized a campaign in early 1914 to elect at least a few small businessmen to the Dakar Chamber of Commerce. With a list including small French businessmen and three respected African merchants, he planned to capture some French and all the African votes. But the all-French

Bordeaux list headed by Emile Masson had greater financial resources, and Sergent's audacious move failed. It won him the enmity
of the Bordeaux community for trying to shake the foundations of
French domination.[19]

The French political elite was anything but homogeneous. As Bordeaux's wealth grew, the interests of the large trading companies
diverged from those of the petits colons and small businessmen. Chief
agents of the companies often adopted a superior attitude toward
the small entrepreneur and linked themselves socially with the administrators; company employees at the middle and lower levels associated with the petits colons and the lower-level administrative clerks.
The conflict between bourgeois and working-class attitudes, so typical
of the metropole, was now carried to Senegal. Hostility between
northern and southern Frenchmen flared up occasionally, as did anti-
Semitism; and there was some prejudice against Corsicans, who were
well represented in the administration and in business.

Despite these economic, social, and geographical differences, which
affected political issues and the choice of candidates, the French elite
was unified on certain fundamental points. Most Frenchmen believed
in France's imperial mission and rarely questioned her right to be
in Africa.* They pictured themselves as the vanguard of a cultured
and wealthy nation that had accepted the challenge of making its
African colonies economically and politically viable. Moreover, local
questions and subtleties aside, the French electorate in the Four Communes was seen by the Africans as a single body of foreigners (*les
toubabs*) growing larger and stronger every year, gaining greater control of business, and dominating the colony's political and economic
councils. This dynamic and aggressive group was encouraged by the
French administration and backed by 35,000,000 Frenchmen. It was
therefore a formidable threat to both Creoles and Africans.

* Even d'Oxoby, who was linked with the African radicals for over a decade,
never advocated the kind of semi-autonomy that Africans really wanted at the
local level.

## CHAPTER 6

# The Creole Attempt to Dominate
# Local Politics

LIKE THE French, the Creoles were a minority in Senegal. Most of them were descended from unions between African signares and French administrators or merchants in the eighteenth and early nineteenth centuries; but by 1914, many Frenchmen customarily brought their wives to the colony, and local mistresses or marriages were no longer common.[1] Moreover, relatively few children were born to the existing Creole families. The Creole community was small and slightly aristocratic in outlook; it was probably the most self-conscious and articulate interest group in Senegal. Most Creoles were well-educated, attending Catholic schools in Senegal and the great universities in France. And over the years Creole notables had taken a leading role in Senegal's commercial and political affairs. By 1900, however, the Creole elite realized that its traditional position of leadership was threatened by the growing French community on one side and the restless Africans on the other. Clearly, the balance of political power had to be tipped in the Creoles' favor. The Africans must be kept in their place, and the French must be challenged; it was a matter of political life or death.

The Creole elite was like other groups in Senegal in having a number of internal divisions. By far the most divisive influence was family rivalry. After 1900, two opposing dynasties dominated the contest for Creole leadership. The Carpot family of Saint-Louis was descended from Durand Valantin, Senegal's first deputy; and at this time it was led by François Carpot, deputy from 1902 to 1914. The Devès family was the ostracized Creole branch of the wealthy Bordeaux family; it was led by Justin Devès, mayor of Saint-Louis and president of the General Council. Both of these major lineages were allied with other powerful Creole families by marriage and business ties. The Creoles were compelled to ally themselves with African and French voters in order to win at the polls. In addition, they spent enormous amounts of time and energy seeking alliances and support within their own families and "clans." This undoubtedly gave them a highly developed sense of political savoir faire, but it involved them in internecine battles they could scarcely afford. There were jealousies between the Creoles of Saint-Louis and those of the Second Arrondissement (Gorée, Dakar, and Rufisque). And the Creoles in private business were suspicious of those employed by the French administration. The Creole community was by no means a unified minority with a single outlook.[2]

The Creoles had diverse political interests. Some were aligned with Bordeaux commerce (a good many, in fact, took complete charge of local operations when their superiors left for France during hivernage). Some were administrators or clerks in the colonial service, and others were officers in the French Army. Many Creoles were small businessmen in the Four Communes or independent traders in the bush; others were in the liberal professions; and some, such as the lawyer and journalist Louis Huchard, were closely linked with African interests. Creole influence was present throughout the electorate and the general population; and inevitably, the Creoles had large political debts to repay in all quarters.

The Creoles of Senegal were essentially a conservative community. They had benefited from the establishment of local political institutions and had profited from the declarations of free trade in 1792 and 1864. Most important, they had achieved political and economic dominance in the colony. To them, the status quo was the proper state of things. The Creoles of Saint-Louis who were the strongest Creole community in the colony) felt that Senegal had developed to its full potential by the 1890's. They believed that Saint-Louis's predominance in Senegalese economic and political life could be maintained, and that Senegal would continue to dominate the new federation of French West Africa.[3] This dream was already outmoded. The Government-General had moved from Saint-Louis to Dakar in 1904, and economically Saint-Louis slowly lost out to the peanut port of Rufisque and the international port and naval base at Dakar. Nevertheless, between 1900 and 1915 most Creoles were still living in the world of 1890 and disregarding the real social forces at work in Senegal.

The Creole elite took pride in many of the same things that motivated members of the African elite: centuries of association with the French; a long tradition of local political institutions; a high standard of education; an early conversion to French Catholicism; and a prominent place in Senegal's history. The Creole Charles Cornier had been mayor of Saint-Louis during the Revolution. Durand Valantin was the first elected deputy of Senegal. The tenacity of Paul

Holle, Faidherbe's commander at Fort Médine, had helped turn back the conquering armies of Al Hajj Umar. General Amadé Dodds had led French army expeditions in Senegal and Dahomey. Gaspard Devès had built the most powerful Creole commercial house in Senegal. Louis Descemet was president of the General Council for fourteen years. And J. J. Crespin became secretary-general of Senegal's colonial administration. These and other illustrious names from the past contributed to the twentieth-century Creoles' sense of identification with a privileged group.

The Creoles' basic orientation was always to their own group, even though they had been assimilated to the French in education, culture, and religion at an early date. Young Creoles attended the first schools in Senegal in the 1820's, and became the mainstay of the convent schools. Many Creole girls married Frenchmen and became successors to the disappearing signares; conversely, a few Frenchmen found their fortune in the colony by marrying into respectable Creole merchant families. By Faidherbe's day, Creole women resembled their French counterparts—bourgeois housewives with some education—rather than the high-living, ambitious signares of the past.[4] Creole men tended to seek education in France; in fact, the General Council, which awarded a number of scholarships each year, saw to it that Creoles monopolized schooling in the metropole.[5]

But even though Creoles were assimilated to French culture, they retained ties with African tradition. For example, most of them spoke Wolof, the major native language of Senegal. This dualistic outlook on culture was important, for the Creoles were the chief intermediaries between French and Africans. Only in religion did they completely put aside their African past, embracing Catholicism with tremendous fervor. Creoles were the mainstay of the Church in a Senegal filled with anticlerical Frenchmen. From the Creole viewpoint, in fact, most Frenchmen in the administration were at the best Freemasons, and those in commerce were undoubtedly hedonists.

The Creoles' dualistic cultural outlook molded their political outlook, which was at once conservative and progressive. Creoles were proud of their success and high status and wanted to keep both; but at the same time, they were agents of modernization in Senegal, the link between the new world of urban Senegal and the traditional life of the Protectorate. Their lead was also followed by the urban class of Africans. They introduced Western ideas of freedom of employment, freedom of trade (without bribes and tributes), and advancement by personal merit to those curious Africans who were tempted to abandon the constraints of traditional society.[6] The Creoles' very actions exemplified the worth of individual achievement and the concept of private ownership—ideas foreign to the collectively oriented society of traditional Senegal, in which the group dominated an average man's life and possessions. This notion of individual liberty and worth was a legacy of the European Renaissance and the French Revolution, and the Creoles themselves had adopted it long ago.

### *François Carpot and the Deputyship*

A Creole deputy did not sit in Paris between 1871 and 1902, although J. J. Crespin tried for twelve years to win the office.* The post was finally wrested from the monopoly of the Bordeaux interests by François Carpot, a young Creole lawyer who had spent his education and early career training for just such a position. Carpot, born in Saint-Louis, had been a brilliant student at the University of Bordeaux. He took his degree in law at Paris and practiced there for several years; but in 1892 he decided to return to Saint-Louis and enter politics. He was elected to the General Council by 1898, and in 1902 he became Senegal's deputy.

Carpot was sophisticated and attached to French culture, and he considered himself the equal of any Frenchman. His older brother Théodore was also in local politics, on the General Council. Both men had been introduced to politics by J. J. Crespin; they remained allied to him, and later to Louis Descemet, who became mayor of Saint-Louis in 1895. The Carpots were reasonable, well-educated men, and had a sense of public responsibility often lacking in Creole politicians. In their own opinion, they were the men best fitted by education, family, and outlook to rule the colony's local affairs. The year after François became deputy, Théodore was elected president of the General Council; the two most important elective offices in Senegal were now held by one family.

Governor-General Ernest Roume, reporting on the 1902 elections for deputy, was impressed by Carpot's victory:

What really characterizes the election of April 27 is the complete triumph of local influences—the old mulatto families of Senegal over the metropolitan influence of the great commercial houses. These houses had barely succeeded in getting their candidate, d'Agoult, elected by a scant majority in the 1898 contest, and that was only because of their complete unity and extraordinary efforts. But this time they were divided.[7]

---

* Unless Alfred Gasconi was a Creole, as Idowu maintains. But Gasconi's politics were linked to Bordeaux, which is the main point here. In effect, the Creole party was excluded from the deputyship until 1902.

This time, the Carpots had won by unifying the Creole community—
by having support from Descemet as well as the wealthy Devès family
and its allies. Roume described Carpot as surprisingly courteous, and
even respectful to the Governor-General (apparently this was not true
of some Creoles). However, there was no doubt that Carpot would
fight for local interests and work for the dominance of Senegal in
French West Africa. In fact, said Roume, Carpot would be "hostile
and defiant" toward any expansion of the federation's powers; he
had, for instance, been completely silent on the campaign issue of
giving greater powers to the Governor-General, which the two French
candidates had favored.[8]

Roume and other observers noted two important factors in Carpot's election. One was the strong influence brought to bear by the
Catholic clergy on his behalf, which suggests the close link between
the Church and its Creole defenders. In addition, Carpot had won
a good part of the Lebou vote in Dakar and Rufisque. Roume commented: "The Ministry should be aware that the real power in an
election for deputy in Senegal is the sentiment of the black voters,
who are mostly illiterates."[9] Many young Lebous had voted for Carpot against the wishes of their chiefs and elders, who were, as usual,
bribed by generous subsidies to support the French candidates.

The 1902 campaign was one of the most colorful in Senegal's history, and also one of the most bitterly contested. Opposing Carpot
was the "parachuted" candidate Louis Dreyfus, a Parisian lawyer who
expected to gain an easy seat in the Chamber of Deputies for himself and his merchant backers. But the incumbent, Count d'Agoult,
though unpopular with many voters, insisted on standing for reelection and thereby split the French vote. Carpot had planned his campaign well in advance. Traditionally, electioneering began several
weeks before the April election date. Carpot's associates started in
January, holding a meeting in Saint-Louis for local notables and
even including African chiefs from the surrounding area. All those
attending pledged to support Carpot (the chiefs could not vote, but
they influenced many Africans who could). On the first of April
d'Agoult, back from Paris, got his campaign under way with a dinner
at the Chamber of Commerce and an official endorsement by its president, one Monsieur Lange.[10] Dreyfus arrived soon after, and the race
was on.

Louis Dreyfus had unwittingly transplanted an ugly aspect of
French metropolitan life to Senegal, as he soon discovered. On April
16, his first campaign speech was continually interrupted by a French

agent of Maurel et Prom, who yelled: "We don't want a Jew here! Down with the Jews!"[11] Anti-Semitism took root quickly in the charged atmosphere of the campaign, and Dreyfus found himself explaining frantically to crowd after crowd that he was in fact Jewish but no relation to the famous Captain Alfred Dreyfus. Léopold Angrand, a wealthy Catholic Creole merchant, warned the Muslim Lebous against voting for a Jew "whose religion is completely opposed to yours."[12] All Catholics, both Creole and African, were told the same. The French police reported that a strong wave of anti-Semitism was sweeping through the Africans, fomented by the preaching of local marabouts.[13] And when Carpot's victory was finally announced, crowds jammed the main plaza in Dakar chanting, "Down with the Jew!"[14] Despite his handicap, Dreyfus made a better showing than d'Agoult. In addition to being a lawyer, he was a wholesale businessman and a reserve lieutenant in the French Army. Moreover, he had the support of the powerful Dakar merchant Fernand Marsat, who hoped to use Dreyfus's influence in Paris to good advantage. Marsat's political machine was able to swing the older Lebou voters to Dreyfus.

Each candidate was identified with definite groups. Carpot championed local interests, especially those of the Catholics and the Creoles. Dreyfus acted for Marsat's Dakar machine and many Bordeaux agents who were tired of the ineffective incumbent deputy. And d'Agoult spoke frankly as the official candidate of big business. Louis Huchard, a Creole lawyer of Saint-Louis, charged that Marsat had arranged a payoff of the Lebou chiefs to hold the Lebou vote for Dreyfus. Carpot hurried to Dakar, where he held an open-air rally for African voters under the chairmanship of the French mayor of Gorée. Carpot's plea was direct: "I'm just a local boy, not a title-seeking foreigner. I don't have propaganda money to distribute; I have only a knowledge of this colony and its needs."[15] The crowds were filled with young Africans who were tired of taking voting instructions from their elders. The drums beat for Carpot, and there were torchlight parades to the Catholic community center, where young Muslims and Catholics cheered his praises until midnight.

Carpot's platform caught the imagination of the younger African voters, who were more accustomed to the cynical bribes of Bordeaux candidates or the patronizing flattery of other Creole politicians. He called for increased local power and freedom of action, thought that the opinions of local councils should be made known in France (an attack on the French absentee deputies), and favored creating more communes de plein exercice in direct rule areas. His economic views were just as radical. He thought that vacations and salaries should match those prevailing in France, criticized the local taxes on businessmen as excessive, and opposed applying the protectionist Méline Tariff to France's colonies. He felt that France should respect Senegal's traditional customs and institutions, but declared that the interests of the African population and those of European commerce could easily be reconciled.[16] Carpot was a new kind of political candidate—progressive and open-minded, sympathetic to certain African wishes yet not hostile to the Bordeaux interests, and a striking figure by contrast with the tired hacks the voters were used to. When the votes were counted, he polled 3,292 ballots, twice as many as the 1,640 Dreyfus had gained with his machine support in Dakar and Saint-Louis. Count d'Agoult received only 281 votes.[17]

Carpot went to Paris filled with energy and ambition. He impressed his colleagues in the newly formed Radical Party, with which he affiliated, and was soon named to the Radical executive committee. Eventually, he also became secretary of the Chamber of Deputies. Carpot was no mere provincial lawyer lost in the turbulence of Parisian parliamentary intrigue; on the contrary, he had a Parisian education and many influential friends. He was judicious, politic, and calculating in his advancement; and despite his narrow bourgeois background and Creole ties his sympathies were liberal.

In 1906, covered with glory, Carpot returned to Senegal to stand for reelection. He was confident of victory, even insinuating in a letter to an African supporter that he had the French administration's support.[18] And he was backed by Justin Devès, who brought the many Devès family supporters to his cause. This support was needed. Bordeaux had seen that absentee candidates could no longer win votes, and Carpot was opposed by two local politicians in this election: Fernand Marsat, and Mayor Edmond Teisseire of Dakar.

Marsat had been suspended as mayor of Dakar because of serious financial scandals in his administration. Nevertheless, he had decided to run for deputy rather than choosing another Dreyfus to front his political machine. Marsat followed a pattern established by former deputy Jules Couchard and sought to win by courting the masses. He drew his greatest support from Dakar's large Lebou community, which still maintained its traditional form of government despite the administration's insistence that everyone in Dakar was under French rule and institutions. Marsat played upon Lebou grievances, flattered the older chiefs, paid off the younger leaders, and posed as a strong advocate of Lebou rights.

Edmond Teisseire was a Frenchman from the Bordeaux oligarchy, and his family had been known in Senegal for almost a century. He was also connected with the colonial Church hierarchy, which now discreetly supported him rather than Carpot.[19] The administration feared that the question of separating church and state, so recently a burning issue in France, would affect the Senegalese campaign as anti-Semitism had in 1902; but the candidates preferred to discuss local issues. Teisseire told the public that the mission of Senegal's deputy in France was mainly a commercial one, and that a representative of big business like himself should therefore be elected.[20] Once again the factions were clearly defined: Teisseire represented Bordeaux, Marsat the small businessmen and the Lebous, and Carpot the Creoles, the younger Africans, and some businessmen.

Carpot again took a liberal position. Among other things, he favored establishing a secret ballot in Senegal, abolishing the death penalty, and instituting a progressive income tax. He called for a decentralized colonial administration that would allow more decision making by local councils, and wanted to convert some communes-mixtes into full communes. As the keynote of his campaign, he attacked France's existing colonial policy. "It should be recognized that the conquest is over and we are now in an era of development; we should have a policy of association based on justice and humanity. We should therefore respect the mores and customs of the natives as well as their property, and should improve their moral and material well-being by a better usage of the funds derived from the taxes they pay."[21] This was a direct appeal to restore to the General Council control over the tax budget of the Protectorate; it also revealed Carpot's approval of the new policy of association.

Carpot's reputation, skill, and policies carried the contest for him, and he was reelected overwhelmingly.[22] He now stood at the pinnacle of his career, serving as deputy from Senegal and sitting on the General Council. François and his brother Théodore had united most of the Creoles and had won over enough Frenchmen and Africans to control the deputation and the General Council. Only the municipal councils were out of their grasp, for except in Saint-Louis these bodies were still controlled by the French elite. However, a new Creole politician now emerged to challenge French supremacy in the municipal arena.

### Justin Devès and the Challenge to French Leadership

Municipal and conciliar politics in Senegal had always been complicated. Given the divisions in both the French and Creole communities and the constant maneuvering of factions to get votes from one another and from the Africans, it was usually difficult to discern any general pattern or definite alignment of forces that lasted for more than a few years. On the whole, the battle resolved itself into a struggle between the French and Creole elites, whose relative strengths shifted with each election. Both French and Creoles practiced clan politics, and each camp was built on several major political figures who put together the lists of candidates. In general, the Creoles were the more successful group; they were a permanent community and took a serious interest in local politics, whereas many Frenchmen regarded Senegalese politics as a joke, an amusing pastime to occupy an otherwise monotonous stay in the colonies. Under Louis Descemet, and after 1903 under Théodore Carpot, the leadership of the General Council was in Creole hands (although the French were often able to force decisions through); and when Descemet retired from the General Council, he became mayor of Saint-Louis and won the support of the Bordeaux merchants in that city.

In Gorée, Dakar, and Rufisque the story was different. The wealthy Frenchman Le Bègue de Germiny shared power with the Creoles in Gorée, which was rapidly diminishing in importance, trade, and population.[23] Maurice Escarpit ran an almost exclusively French administration in Rufisque. And in Dakar Fernand Marsat and his aide Emile Masson had a powerful political machine based on the Lebous, whereas Edmond Teisseire had the support of Creoles and Frenchmen. The French elite clearly dominated the municipalities.

Justin Devès, a son of Gaspard Devès, set out to change this. At first he based his efforts on the power of his brothers Hyacinthe and François (members of the General Council), the reputation of his family as the wealthiest of the Creoles, and his innate political ability; but he quickly built up his own political machine and alliances after 1907. Devès became so powerful and controversial that in 1910 he was charged with financial irregularities and was suspended from politics by the French administration. By 1911 he was back in politics; and within two more years he was able to wrest the Creole leadership from François Carpot, and even to challenge the French themselves everywhere in Senegal. Here was an energetic, shrewd political boss. He first supported the Carpots and then turned against them; he feared none of the traditional political leaders; and he openly flaunted his contempt for the administration, the Governor, and the Governor-General. The base for all this confidence was the Devès family fortune, which the Carpots could not begin to match—indeed, the family assets rivaled those of some Bordeaux firms in size.

Justin undoubtedly inherited his energy from his father Gaspard, who had built up the Senegalese branch of the Bordeaux family into the most powerful of Creole commercial houses. This branch had begun with Gaspard's father Bruno, who had married a Senegalese and had promptly been ostracized by the family.[24] Bruno left Gaspard a sizable fortune and a business whose interests ranged inland along the Senegal River, southward toward Guinea, and northward along the Mauritanian coast. In fact, the Devès of Senegal claimed ownership of Arguin Island, an abandoned Dutch stronghold 300 miles north of the Senegal; they built up a commercial entrepôt on the island and then negotiated a settlement with Paris when the government decided to construct a naval base there. The family brought rural Africans to Saint-Louis for training in business methods and then sent them out as agents. By 1900, it was estimated that the Devès had 300 retainers in Saint-Louis alone, and it was often charged that they were actually maintaining their own system of slavery and bondage. Other Creoles feared them; and many sought alliance with them. Even Faidherbe had at times relied heavily on Gaspard Devès's support.[25]

Justin attended a lycée in Bordeaux and eventually won a law degree in France. He married a French girl, Mlle. Laplène, and returned to Saint-Louis to work in the family businesses. He entered the municipal council briefly in the 1890's, allying himself with J. J. Crespin against Louis Descemet and Théodore Carpot. But Crespin lost his majority in 1892, and Devès left office. After this he retired from politics for several years, devoting his time to business. But when Gaspard died in 1901, the family business was rearranged; and within a few years Justin was able to participate more fully in the colony's political life. He entered the political scene at a time when many changes were taking place. The Carpots had become dominant in the General Council, but the influence of Louis Descemet, mayor of Saint-Louis and dean of Creole politicians, was waning.

Descemet had dominated local politics by astutely mediating between wealthy Creoles and Bordeaux businessmen. He had represented the conservative wing of the Creole party, whereas J. J. Crespin had been the spokesman for those Creoles who wanted more power in local affairs.[26] Neither had any special interest in Africans, except in a polite sort of way when election time rolled around. A few Creoles (notably Louis Huchard and Georges Patterson) were interested in African affairs, but they were in a minority. Beyond these three groupings it was difficult to sort out the various factions in municipal politics. As Governor-General William Ponty noted: "Politics as practiced in France is unknown in Senegal, where it is difficult to classify members of newly elected assemblies into groups or parties. In a general sense, it is the large commercial houses that continue to hold most of the seats."[27]

But the African element in Communal politics was finally beginning to stir. It was becoming apparent even to Saint-Louis's Creole community that urban Africans should be given some representation, if only to encourage their participation in voting; and by the turn of the century, African names started to appear on most electoral lists.

In 1900, the Africans of Saint-Louis formed a Native Committee intended to accomplish the reverse: that is, to persuade sympathetic Frenchmen and Creoles to join an African list of candidates. The attempt failed in its basic purpose, for the only person of political substance who decided to join the list was former deputy Jules Couchard, seeking a political comeback. However, a few French and Creole politicians who were out of power seized on the Native Committee as a convenient way to pick up some important African backing. The Africans lost confidence and threw their support to these men, eventually running only two "safe" candidates on the native list. The incumbent mayor, Descemet, took the hint and added four Africans to his own list, which handily won the elections.

In these same 1900 elections, Africans won at Rufisque; and five were elected in Dakar on Fernand Marsat's machine-dominated list. It appeared that new political opportunities, albeit small, had opened up for the Africans. But the 1904 elections proved otherwise. Descemet, aided by his son-in-law Louis Guillabert, triumphed in Saint-Louis; but the respectable Pierre Chimère, a Catholic, was the only African on his list. The Frenchman Le Bègue de Germiny was re-elected in Gorée, and he likewise ran with only one African, the conservative Thiécouta N'Gom. It was the same story in Rufisque, where Maurice Escarpit added Aly Guèye to his French list for the sake of form. Dakar was the only city with several African candidates in 1904. Marsat had previously brought "safe" Africans into politics there, but this time he was unseated by Edmond Teisseire, who had also collected a group of African "yes men," five of whom were elected (including three Catholics).[28] This was a general defeat for the more radically oriented Muslim Africans, who were in the vast majority.

Governor Camille Guy, a learned and skillful executive, had much to do with the outcome of the 1904 elections. Because of the Creoles' unexpected success in the General Council that year, he feared that a violent struggle for municipal seats would break out, especially in

Saint-Louis.[29] Not wishing to see unrest in the colony, he worked patiently to bring about a rapprochement, calling his efforts *la politique de conciliation*. And in his post-election report to Governor-General Roume, he triumphantly announced that the expected war had not broken out. In Saint-Louis the French and Creoles put together a compromise list of eighteen candidates, and much the same thing happened in the other Communes. Governor Guy glowed with pride at arranging this truce, but noted in an aside at the end of the report: "I should add, Mr. Governor-General, that an unexpected result of this conciliation was the almost complete disappearance of natives from the councils of Rufisque and Saint-Louis."[30] To colonial administrators like Guy only the dominant French and Creole community mattered.

Justin Devès looked on with interest. By 1907 the local political scene was conveniently partitioned between Creole and French groups. The Creoles had General Council president Théodore Carpot, the recently reelected deputy François Carpot, and Mayor Descemet of Saint-Louis. The French had mayors in the other three Communes: Maurice Escarpit in Rufisque, Le Bègue de Germiny in Gorée, and Edmond Teisseire in Dakar. Creole politics were at their most successful because the Creoles were more or less united and had compromised with the French. But was there room for new men who wanted to share the monopoly of power? How did the ambitions of Justin Devès fit into this tidy arrangement, which enjoyed the Governor's blessing?

In 1908, Devès decided to run candidates for seats in the General Council and in all four Communes. But he was soundly defeated everywhere: Saint-Louis, Rufisque, and Gorée returned their incumbent lists to office; Dakar, wooed by the incessant intrigues and overtures of Fernand Marsat, welcomed him back as mayor and elected his reorganized list; and the Carpots continued to dominate the General Council. Undaunted, Devès brought suit before the Council of State in Paris, charging a fraudulent election in Saint-Louis. He won his case, and new elections were set for 1909.*

Devès began his list with Georges Crespin, Georges d'Erneville, Charles Pellegrin, and Durand Valantin—all from illustrious Creole

---

* Saint-Louis had removed a great many Africans from its voting lists because of the 1905 Verrier report on electoral irregularities. Now, Devès alleged that over a thousand of the men whose names were struck off had never been notified of their removal. The Senegalese courts rejected his contention that this had influenced the 1908 election, but the high court in Paris reversed the decision. The case is analyzed in ARS, 20-G-17.

families, and all eager to create a party that could break the power of Descemet and Carpot. Then Devès recruited the Catholic Wolof Pierre Chimère as bait for the African vote; and he eventually put a total of eight Africans on his list instead of the customary one or two. Like the machine politician Marsat, he had realized that political strength in Senegal was derived from firmly controlling a single bloc of the African electorate. Consequently, he concentrated his campaign on the fishing suburbs of Guet N'Dar and N'Dar Toute. The hardy Wolof fishermen of these villages had steadily increased their numbers and had stayed on the voting lists; and they were now the largest bloc of votes in Saint-Louis. When the ballots were counted, Devès's strategy was borne out: he had defeated Descemet and turned out Descemet's party after it had controlled Saint-Louis for more than a decade. Descemet, shaken, could not understand what had happened; but his son-in-law Louis Guillabert easily saw that Devès had won because he had eight Africans on his list and the total backing of the Wolof fishermen.[31]

All did not go well in the Devès camp, and soon Georges Crespin complained bitterly about Devès's high-handed manner of ordering the municipal council about. Eventually, Crespin and the popular Alexis Cornu resigned their seats in protest. This mattered little to the ambitious Devès, who was busily preparing a long-range strategy to gain eventual control of the General Council. In November 1909 half the Council seats came up for reelection. Devès and his ally Pellegrin were elected, but their antagonists Crespin and Guillabert also won seats. Clearly, Devès would not dominate the Council this year.

The most surprising event of the 1909 Council election was the victory of Galandou Diouf, an independent African candidate from Rufisque. After the election, Diouf's right to run was challenged because of his nonaffiliation; but when it was shown that appearing on a list was merely customary and not required, he was allowed to keep his seat. His election was greeted as a curiosity in most circles because so far his only reputation was that of being a man who changed jobs often (he had worked as a farmer, a railway agent, a schoolteacher, and a business agent). Diouf later said that his eyes were opened to the "finer points" of politics after he had accompanied Justin Devès on a stroll through the city: Devès had greeted all the men he saw by name and had inquired about their families, whose names he also knew.[32] Diouf admired Devès greatly; and at first he invariably voted with the Devès faction and worked closely with Justin's brother, François Devès, the other Council member from Rufisque. In time, however, Diouf gained confidence and became a real spokesman for African interests.

Justin Devès, with his colorful temperament and penchant for action, soon caught the attention of the Paris press, which lionized him as the coming boss of local politics in Senegal. *La Presse Coloniale* observed at the end of 1910:

> From 1907 to 1909, two political parties took turns dominating Senegal: one was led by M. Théodore Carpot, president of the General Council, and M. Louis Descemet, then mayor of Saint-Louis; the other was under the direction of M. Justin Devès. We have previously written of our admiration for the political energy of M. Devès, who bases his power on the youth of Senegal. The General Council, the municipal council—he conquers everything. In fact, if M. Devès had decided to run for deputy in the 1910 elections, he would undoubtedly have taken the post away from the honorable François Carpot.[33]

## The Carpot-Devès Struggle

On the advice of friends, Justin decided not to run for deputy in 1910, since Senegal would presumably be difficult to control from Paris. This was fortunate for François Carpot, who returned to Senegal for the 1910 campaign totally absorbed in parliamentary politics and out of touch with local issues. However, the wily Marsat now challenged Carpot for the deputyship. Also in the 1910 race were Jules Couchard, still unreconciled to losing the deputyship in 1898, and Paul Sabourault, a liberal Dakar lawyer. All three were Frenchmen, which gave Carpot a great advantage in campaigning for the Creole and African vote.

The 1910 campaign involved several important issues. A recent decree had provided that French citizens would be eligible to vote regardless of where they lived or worked in Senegal; but the local interpretation of the decree distinguished originaires from full citizens and gave them voting rights only within the physical limits of the Communes.[34] Carpot himself raised a number of issues. Alarmed by Germany's growing population, he accepted the French military's idea of bringing France's colonial empire into closer association with the metropole, so that France would have greater manpower reserves. He proposed creating eight more full communes in Senegal in order to "win the hearts" of the colonial peoples. He also wanted to hire more native clerks for the colonial bureaucracy—a policy warmly applauded by younger members of the African elite.[35] Carpot introduced two new campaign techniques in 1910. First, he managed to have his candidacy endorsed by political luminaries in metropolitan

France—Henri Brisson (president of the Chamber of Deputies), Senator Léon Bourgeois, and others. Second, he set up a newspaper in conjunction with the campaign; this journal, *Le Radical Sénégalais*, was managed by the Creole Alexandre Angrand and addressed its arguments to educated Africans.

Carpot tried to present himself as a liberal lawgiver, respected in Paris and sincerely interested in his people's problems. He emphasized his accomplishments in the Chamber, where he had presided over the petitions committee and sat on the naval colonial, and parliamentary initiative committees; he had even submitted a plan for reorganizing the autocratic Ministry of Colonies to give colonial administrators more local initiative. But all these laurels seemed to fade in the hot sun of Senegal, where two political bosses were after Carpot's post and the electorate was usually wooed with gifts, bribes, and promises.

The first ballot of the 1910 election was remarkably even: Couchard 1,417, Marsat 1,185, Carpot 1,052, and Sabourault 1,003.[36] A breakdown of figures by Commune shows the candidates' areas of strength.*

|  | Saint-Louis | Dakar | Rufisque | Gorée |
|---|---|---|---|---|
| Couchard | 796 | 47 | 459 | 7 |
| Marsat | 42 | 733 | 312 | 30 |
| Carpot | 392 | 293 | 294 | 35 |
| Sabourault | 137 | 405 | 401 | 33 |

Couchard and Marsat understandably swept their home cities; Carpot picked up respectable support in all the Communes but won only in Gorée. A runoff election was set for two weeks later. It was now apparent to Carpot that he had lost touch with the voters and could win only by persuading another candidate to withdraw in his favor. He found his man in Sabourault, who was jealous of his Dakar rival Marsat and quite willing to support Carpot in order to keep Marsat out of the Chamber.

With Sabourault's votes, Carpot managed to win the runoff election: the final tally showed Carpot 1,790, Marsat 1,587, and Couchard 1,370.[37] It was a hollow victory, and Carpot was now convinced that he should devote more time to local matters. No one was more impressed with the results than Justin Devès, who had stood by giving tacit support to Couchard and sizing up the political situation. He

* This includes only the Communes proper; hence the total number of votes for each candidate differs from the figure given above, which includes votes from direct rule areas outside the Communes. Election report in ARS, 20-G-19.

concluded that the Carpot machine was extremely vulnerable, that Marsat's strength was more vaunted than real, and that Couchard was actually a political liability. Bordeaux had not bothered to put up a candidate, preferring to back the local politicians. It seemed clear to Devès that the political future belonged to him.

Within two months this dream was shattered. Devès was suspended as mayor of Saint-Louis in July 1910 for "financial irregularities"; in September he was recalled from office, and an investigation of his affairs began in both Paris and Saint-Louis. Over forty witnesses gave sworn depositions that they had been induced to pay cash retainers to Devès to "protect them from the French,"[38] and the financial records at Saint-Louis showed large discrepancies between receipts and expenditures. From the conflicting reports, it was difficult to tell whether Devès was actually running a profitable political machine and extortion racket or whether the administration, alarmed by his growing influence and urged on by Carpot, was trying to nip him in the bud. But it was shown that his direct influence on political activities extended deep into Senegal—along the railway line to Louga, Tivouane, and Thiès, and along the river to Dagana and Podor. From the Governor's point of view, Devès was building a personal patronage system within the framework of the colony and could eventually become dangerous. Despite the protests of his supporters, he was dismissed and publicly humiliated. Governor Guy cheerfully noted: "These events have given M. Devès a blow from which he will never recover."[39]

In 1911 a new decision by the Council of State in Paris voided the 1909 special elections, which had brought Devès and his party to power in Saint-Louis. Louis Descemet, the object of the suit that had brought about the 1909 elections, had successfully counterattacked Devès in Paris. According to the evidence, Devès had illegally promised the Wolofs of Guet N'Dar suburb that he would eliminate their house taxes. Moreover, he had led Africans to the polls, given them printed ballots for his list, and then accompanied them into the polling precincts. Special elections were authorized for Saint-Louis in 1911. But Descemet's comeback failed: not only did he lose his second straight election, but he made it possible for Devès to re-enter politics after having been discredited a few months earlier. With the Wolof vote assured, Devès and his list were victorious to a man.

Undaunted, Descemet tried again in 1912, entering the regular municipal elections. And once again he was defeated by the seem-

ingly invincible Devès. The administration was alarmed, and Guy
observed: "We must keep a careful watch on Devès and his system-
atic opposition to the local administration."[40] The Devès list signifi-
cantly included nine Africans; the Saint-Louis council was now half-
filled with natives, and most of the remaining members were Creoles.
Clearly, Devès intended to create an unassailable political base of
African voters, who would be led by the Creole elite; Frenchmen
would have only a token role. However, the Bordeaux community
was not visibly alarmed, since its candidates had won in the other
three Communes.[41]

The municipal elections of 1912 determined Senegal's city government until 1919, for all such elections were canceled during World
War I. To be sure, the war would bring some changes as Frenchmen
left Senegal for France. But the basic pattern was maintained: a compromise between Frenchmen and Creoles in the colony as a whole,
with a façade of African participation in Saint-Louis and Dakar.
And Justin Devès was once again in politics, in spite of the Governor's fear that his quest for political power would upset the delicate
French-Creole balance. Devès became president of the General Council in 1913, and the deputyship was the only remaining barrier to his
total domination of Senegalese politics. He dedicated himself to gaining this ultimate prize in the 1914 elections. But in so doing, he risked
widening a split that the Creole community could ill afford—not because of competition from the French elite, which was also divided,
but because of rising expectations in the African electorate, which
no French or Creole politician took seriously.

## CHAPTER 7

# The African Political Awakening, I

FOR OVER a dozen years before World War I, a general mood of unrest and frustration existed among the urban and rural Africans of Senegal. Even before the turn of the century there were signs that the French presence in Senegal was not a settled matter, despite the complacent reports of French administrators and governors. Open rebellion seemed remote and many French officials assumed that occasional outbreaks of violence during this period were simply an indication of African stubbornness. But in retrospect, the many instances of rioting, murder, and insubordination were a sure sign that African resistance to French domination had not ceased with the passing of Lat-Dior and other traditional leaders.[1] A new generation of Africans created its own kind of resistance to the European attack on African values, institutions, and freedoms.

The general mood of frustration was not translated into effective political action until after 1900, although the members of the African political elite had occupied a privileged position in the Four Communes since 1848. Why this political reaction was delayed is a difficult question to answer, especially since there is comparatively little data on urban African political activity before the turn of the century. However, there are several factors that may have contributed to the slow politicization of African voters. For one thing, there was a dearth of political leadership in the African camp. To be sure, from the 1870's on occasional Africans sat in the municipal councils and General Council, but none commanded the respect of the French and Creoles until Galandou Diouf entered politics in 1909. The late emergence of leaders is related to two other factors. It took several decades for the African mass of voters to become politicized; political questions were raised only at election time, and the personalistic emphasis on the candidate often obscured more important issues. Moreover, the level of Western education in the Communes rose only slowly until the twentieth century, so that few Africans received the training needed to compete in the French-inspired institutions of local politics. Until 1912, there was apparently no group of Africans familiar enough with political tactics to organize a lasting political action group.

In addition, the consolidation of French colonial rule at all levels became increasingly more oppressive for Africans (whether rural or urban) after 1900 as more Frenchmen came to the colony and impeded the advance of young Africans in business and administration. Administrators took full control of the Protectorate, and direct rule was tightened up in the urban areas. The various French attempts to eliminate urban Africans from the electoral rolls created a climate of oppression that inspired greater African interest in local politics, but this did not occur until after 1900. Economic conditions, increasingly favorable to urban Africans as the Communes grew, contributed a new spirit of independence to African traders; but the growth of peanut culture also brought larger French trading companies, which threatened many African middlemen. It was the combined threat to African voting privileges and to African opportunities for economic participation that helped change the African attitude toward local politics. Hence the conditions necessary for an African political awakening emerged only after 1900.

There were also several specific reasons for African unrest: the dynamic expansion of Islam in both rural and urban areas; the growing number of Africans receiving a French education; the growing realization of Africans in the Protectorate that they were not as well off as their fellows in the Communes; the old grievances of the Lebou community on Cape Verde; and lastly, the emergence of an aggressive African youth movement with capable leaders. These phenomena were either unnoticed or largely ignored by most French and Creoles, who believed, like most European colonials in Black Africa, that European rule would be a necessity for countless decades to come.[2]

Africans in Senegal definitely sought assimilation to French political institutions; but at the same time, they staunchly maintained their traditional and Islamic values in personal matters. This paradoxical dualism grew from the hopes and fears of the African elite, which wanted the political power made possible by French republicanism but opposed complete cultural assimilation. To be sure, some Africans willingly became totally assimilated, whereas others vehemently rejected assimilation in favor of traditional values; but most pursued a dualistic goal. The French considered this contradictory, for in colonial logic there was no such thing as partial assimilation. As a result, a decree promulgated in 1912 set forth definite requirements for natives who wanted French citizenship.[3]

In reality, the originaires were giving substance to an attitude best defined by Léopold Senghor forty years later: "to assimilate, not to be assimilated." That is, to adapt European ideas to an African base (much as Islam had been adapted) and to resist being swallowed up by Western culture. The end result was confusion: Africans were never certain how much assimilation they wanted, and Frenchmen were equally uncertain of how much assimilation to give or expect. The issues were especially clouded at election time.

## The Growing Dynamism of Islam

One of the most important causes of the African awakening was the advance of Islam in Senegal. As the French altered the indigenous society by deposing traditional rulers in the countryside and building towns for the emerging class of urban Africans, several traditional power roles disappeared. In the bush, Africans were accustomed to having strong, legitimate chiefs in authority. When these were removed, the French-appointed chiefs, who often had no claim to legitimacy, were seldom able to guide their charges through the difficult period of adjustment to French rule. In the towns, new immigrants were often released from the duties and sanctions of traditional society, cast adrift without moorings.

It was the Islamic marabout who filled this power vacuum during the period 1860–1920. He offered the solace of Islam as a cure for the afflictions of French rule in the countryside; and even urban Africans responded to the call, for this was a militant Islam that seemed to provide an effective defense for the African way of life. In short, Islam, which many Senegalese had long regarded as an alien influence in their midst, now became a major focal point for resistance to French authority. However, converts were rarely attracted by specific doctrines or ideas.[4] For many Africans, Islam was incarnate in their own marabout, and his word was more important than any from the Koran, which the ordinary *talibé* (faithful adept) could not read. This situation produced many sincere marabouts who realized the importance of their influence in helping their followers adjust to a changing society; but it also produced charlatans and tyrants motivated by hopes of personal gain.[5]

Although there were hundreds of marabouts actively proselytizing throughout Senegal, the two most important leaders during this period were almost recluses—pious men in the monastic tradition rather than great evangelizers of the jihad. By their example of devotion to learning and prayers, and their reputed possession of supernatural attributes, they were able to exercise both moral and spiritual authority. In the bush and the rural villages, Amadou Bamba M'Backé created a new Islamic brotherhood for Senegal, the Mourides, and extended his personal spiritual domain far and wide. Al Hajj Malick Sy of the Tijaniyya sect wielded great influence among the inhabitants of the direct rule territories and the Communes. The two men were rivals in many ways, since most of their converts came from the same population. Their respective "ministries" provided the basic orientation of Islam in modern Senegal, and their activities and respective spheres of influence explain much about the importance of Islam in Senegalese politics.

*Amadou Bamba and rural Islam.* Bamba was descended from an aristocratic Toucouleur family of marabouts that had been Wolofized by several generations of marriage with Wolof women. His father, Momar Antasali, had been a marabout in Sine-Saloum, where he had taught the young children of the revolutionary marabout Ma Bâ. Momar was also on intimate terms with the Wolof king Lat-Dior and eventually married the king's niece Thioro Diop.[6] In 1871, after Lat-Dior was recognized as Damel of Cayor by the French, Momar and his family moved to Cayor, where Bamba took his place as a marabout in Lat-Dior's entourage after Momar's death in 1880.

When Lat-Dior fell in battle in 1886, Bamba left Cayor and returned to M'Backé, a town in Baol that his ancestors had founded four generations earlier. Originally trained in the Qadiriyya brotherhood, he now became preoccupied with making his religion more acceptable to the African peasant. His new tariqa, the Mouridiyya, emphasized the values of hard work and complete obedience to one's marabout. In addition, Bamba encouraged the belief that his supernatural power was more effective than that of the animist cults. His reputation as a powerful marabout grew rapidly; and soon he rarely traveled, preferring to receive his talibés at Touba, a village that he had founded near M'Backé as the headquarters of his new sect.[7]

From 1888 on, the French administration was increasingly suspicious of this powerful new marabout. Bamba's sect was rapidly becoming the dominant force in Baol's traditional society, and hundreds of new talibés arrived weekly to seek his blessing and offer him presents. At the same time, African parents complained that Bamba did not educate their children, as a marabout was expected to, but kept them in bondage as laborers and servants; moreover, he was denounced by certain local chiefs in Baol, who were jealous of his growing influence. In 1891 he was persuaded to visit Saint-Louis as a gesture of loyalty to the new French order, and a short period of calm ensued. But many tiédos, displaced nobles, and former followers of traditional resistance leaders like Lat-Dior continued to gather around the young marabout. Consequently, it was rumored that he sought the legitimate rulership in both Djolof and Baol. Bamba's followers were supposedly stockpiling arms and ammunition, and some Frenchmen believed that he intended to set up a new theocratic state in the strategic heart of Senegal.

In the summer of 1895 the French deported Bamba to Gabon for seven years of exile.[8] (There he met the future deputy of Senegal, Blaise Diagne, who was then a young career officer in the French customs service. The fruits of this friendship were to become important for Diagne and Senegalese politics during World War I and the 1920's.[9]) When he was allowed to return home in 1902, thousands of pilgrims clogged the roads to visit him, and enormous offerings of money and valuables were brought to Touba. But unrest was evident throughout the countryside; and the French soon put Bamba under house arrest and sent him to Mauritania for the next several years. Bamba told the French, "I am a captive of God and know no other authority"—words that his followers repeated in defiance of the French.

It is difficult to say whether Bamba was actually planning a jihad in 1895; in spite of the conflicting evidence and claims, it seems that he probably was not. After his return from Gabon, he was understandably hostile to the French, but he never preached directly against them.[10] The same was true in 1907, when the French allowed him to return to Senegal after "good behavior" in Mauritania. Nevertheless, he was distrusted and received harsher treatment from the French than most suspect Africans—which helped his movement grow and increased his personal fame as a living martyr.

The French native affairs officer Paul Marty, writing on the eve of World War I, observed that Bamba had four legal wives and a harem of about 70 concubines "kept for reasons of social prestige"; that there were about 100 students in his koranic school and about 1,000 persons connected with his household; and that although numerous conversions took place every day, there were as yet few of Bamba's talibés in the Four Communes.[11] By this time, the French had realized that Bamba could not be suppressed, for deportation had brought him even greater fame and respect. A judicious manipulation of Senegalese Islam seemed the best solution, and France now started to exploit rivalries between Bamba's lieutenants. Governor Henri Cor encouraged this policy, but cautioned his administrators to watch Bamba's disciples closely, since these men were gaining much influence over village and regional traditional chiefs, and even over French-appointed chiefs.[12] Cheikh Anta M'Backé, Balla M'Backé, Ibra Fall, and other possible successors to Bamba's leadership were put under especially close surveillance.[13] Bamba himself was carefully watched until his death in 1927, even though he and the administration had worked out a modus vivendi in 1912.

The expansion of Islam in rural Senegal transferred much local authority to marabouts. The French were in command at the regional level, where their administrators were aided by some traditional chiefs. But at the lower levels, the years 1900–1920 saw a number of chiefs appointed for local affairs. Most appointed chiefs held their power from the French, had no traditional legitimacy, and were generally weak men. Moreover, many of them were converted to Islam, and therefore came under the very influences that French policy sought to diminish. The rural growth of Islam, then, was a real threat to French colonialism, and in the case of the Mourides a veritable state within the Protectorate.

Rural Islam helped negate the apathy bred by African defeats during the conquest. Its ultimate significance emerged after World War II, when it became evident that many marabouts dominated the newly enfranchised rural voters and should be courted by politicians. In the meantime, the Mourides and other marabouts were anxious to influence French colonial policy. It was generally known that if an African political party wanted success in local politics the rural marabouts could often provide important financial and moral backing.[14]

*Malick Sy and urban Islam.* The other major figure of Senegalese Islam during these years was Malick Sy, whose spiritual domain extended to Senegal's rural heartland, especially in Cayor, but whose greatest influence was his leadership among the faithful of the towns. Sy was an intellectual who produced dozens of short scholarly works and commentaries on the Koran; and his reputation grew from this intellectual achievement, whereas Bamba's power depended on a mystical, supernatural orientation. Sy was trained in the Tijaniyya brotherhood, the largest in Senegal, and he kept in touch with its headquarters in Morocco. His orientation, unlike Bamba's, was essentially orthodox and traditional. Sy and Bamba were great rivals for conversions to Islam, especially in the animistic areas of Senegal (e.g. among the southern Wolofs and Sereres); and apparently their personal relationship was cool. At one point, Sy warned his faithful against "certain parties" who imposed a heavy burden on believers by requiring holy gifts to one's marabout.[15]

Many Senegalese marabouts of the Tijaniyya sect claimed descent from Al Hajj Umar, the first Khalife of the brotherhood in West Africa. But Malick Sy's reputation was built on his own attainments. Like Bamba and so many other marabouts, he came from a Toucouleur family that had been actively proselytizing in Wolof country for several generations. Born in 1855, he was educated locally and made his pilgrimage to Mecca in 1889, returning with a knowledge of literary Arabic unsurpassed in Senegal at the time. Sy studied Islamic theology, law, and custom, wrote on the life of Mohammed, and composed poetry in Arabic. His work was praised by the director of the Medersa (koranic Academy) in Saint-Louis; and he quickly won the respect of the French administration, which considered him the most intelligent and important marabout in Senegal.[16]

Sy's influence spread over the western part of Senegal, especially in the direct rule areas. In fact, all of Senegal's Muslims acknowledged his leadership in one sense, since he annually fixed the date for Senegal's greatest feast day, Ramadan. His prayers became famous, and thousands of the faithful visited his headquarters in the mosque of Tivouane to hear him conduct the Friday services. Most of his talibés came from the Four Communes, and Paul Marty characterized them as members of the urban elite:

Many of the old Wolof families of Saint-Louis and Dakar, the old Lebou families of Dakar and Rufisque, and the merchants from these families in the towns along the railway line and the Senegal River boast of having Malick Sy as their marabout. And since these families, because of birth and residence, include many of the Communes' voters, Al Hajj Malick Sy exercises a very real influence on an important part of the electorate.[17]

Sy was discreet in using his influence: that is, he never overtly opposed French rule. Consequently, the French honored him and helped him build the mosque at Tivouane. In 1912 he specifically recommended French rule to his spiritual charges. The French, he said, had been chosen by Allah "to protect us and our property." Before the French conquest, "we lived in a world of captivity, murder, and pillage—a point on which Muslims and infidels will agree."[18] In other words, Sy accepted the basic rationale of the French themselves: that traditional Senegalese society had been submerged in warfare and chaos, and that only *la paix française* could provide order and stability. From his point of view, this was a valid assumption, since he had seen Islam grow and prosper in the new urban areas after the French conquest and consolidation. (But the idea was anathema to Amadou Bamba, who felt that the same events had disrupted traditional society and threatened Islam as a result.) Sy also told his followers that it was a good thing to pay French taxes in order to maintain the colonial administration.

When World War I started, Sy denied reports that the French were in danger of collapsing. He urged his faithful to serve in the French army if they were called, and regularly said prayers for the French forces in his mosque. It is not surprising that he was given the Légion d'Honneur for these actions. To the French, Sy was "the devoted servant of our administration."[19] To the urban radicals and some Mourides, by contrast, he was a traitor to the African cause. But from a third point of view, Sy was a perspicacious leader who recognized the needs of the growing urban masses, realized that French rule and Western institutions were firmly implanted, and knew that his followers were now free of the arbitrary cruelty imposed by the tiédos and the traditional Senegalese rulers. This "progressive" brand of Islam dominated the Communes and greatly influenced the education of the growing African political elite.

Perhaps the greatest measure of Sy's power was the number of koranic schools that he directly influenced. A 1912 survey found the majority of schools taught by Tijani marabouts. Marty, who conducted the survey in his capacity as Officer for Islamic Affairs, found 1,385 marabouts who claimed to give instructions in the Koran, and he estimated the total number of students at 11,451.[20] Marty acknowledged that many marabouts (especially in the rural areas) refused to admit they maintained schools, and that others claimed them when in fact they had only one or two pupils. But the survey clearly indicated that in the urban areas the Tijaniyya had displaced the Qadiriyya as the most important brotherhood, and the Tijani who followed Sy were by far the most numerous.

Islam in twentieth-century Senegal was both conservative and progressive: in the rural areas it reinforced traditional values, which had suffered greatly from the French conquest; in the cities, it helped to unify and acculturate Africans who had been cut off from traditional society and family life. The unorthodox rural Islam of Amadou Bamba and the more sophisticated urban Islam of Malick Sy brought about a bloodless Islamic revolution that the swords of Al Hajj Umar and Ma Bâ had failed to carry through. This success, superficially improbable because of the differences between Mouride and Tijani, was an indication of the adaptability and flexibility of Islam in the African milieu. Islam provided a foundation for political activity in both rural and urban areas, though only the urban participation would be obvious until after World War II. Because of their faith, urban Africans avoided total assimilation to the French system and retained Islamic forms of marriage, family life, and inheritance. And Islam became the driving force behind the concerted bid of many young Africans for advancement and recognition.*

### Revival of African Protest in the Protectorate

The spirit of opposition to the French regime had never died in the Protectorate, although the means of resistance had collapsed with the demise of the traditional states and their armed power. For some, the will to resist lived on in the memory of Lat-Dior's valiant stand against the French; for others it was centered in the anti-French teachings of Amadou Bamba. But memories and prayers were not able to halt the French disruption of traditional life and the multitude of petty tyrannies that sprang up under French rule.

Many Africans naturally looked to their chiefs for aid, but found little support. Independent-minded chiefs who had actively resisted the French had been killed, imprisoned, or bought off. And many of the younger legitimate chiefs had attended French schools and become partly assimilated. Finally, Senegal had an increasing number of chiefs appointed by the French. Governor-General Ponty had spoken against this (as did Governor-General Van Vollenhoven, who also recommended choosing chiefs who had a traditional link with their subjects).[21] Appointed chiefs were often from lower castes or unrelated ethnic groups and sometimes did not speak the same language as the villagers under them; indeed, appointed chiefs were usually chosen because they knew some French. The typical chief was an African interpreter, clerk, or typist, appointed because the French could communicate with him and trust him.

In these circumstances, to whom could a rural African turn if he felt persecuted by the French? The French announced that any aggrieved person should see his chief or local administrator; but since these local officials were often the cause of the grievance in question, the African had to turn elsewhere. In the 1890's, when this problem first arose, urban Africans and Creoles were beginning to move into

---

* It can be argued that Islam in the Four Communes provided the same motivation and leadership for Africans that voluntary associations and clubs provided in the British colonies of West Africa. The Communes themselves developed more voluntary associations after World War I, and some of these were affiliated with the tariqas or with individual marabouts.

the Protectorate as commercial agents and small merchants. These urban exiles brought with them political ideas that gave new hope to discouraged rural Africans, who soon realized that the battle-ground of resistance had shifted from the countryside to the cities, and that the urban elite had replaced the vanquished traditional chiefs as leaders. The power vacuum created by the French (which Amadou Bamba had exploited so successfully) now provided a chance for these urban Africans, who were determined to maintain their own political rights and work for the political betterment of their rural cousins.

Even before urban Africans invaded the Protectorate in any num-bers, it had become apparent to rural Senegalese that the only pos-sible redress for French injustice had to come through the mecha-nism of local government in the direct rule areas. For example, in the early 1890's Jules Couchard offered his political influence as deputy for a price, and upriver chiefs arranged payoffs, hoping he would protect their interests in Saint-Louis and Paris. This incident introduced the idea that Senegal's deputy acted for the entire colony and not just for the areas from which he was elected.* The growing influence of urban politics in the countryside had also preoccupied the General Council's Creole members—so much so that the budget of the Protectorate had been separated from that of the direct rule areas in 1890. But both Council and deputy were concerned more with what they could get out of the Protectorate than with what they could do for its inhabitants. It was the new wave of urban emigrants who acquainted Africans in the Protectorate with the realities of local government in the Communes. They set up businesses and talked about free enterprise; they became teachers or monitors in the new schools and spoke of African political liberties; in short, they began to politicize the countryside.

By 1903, the Secretary-General of French West Africa was suffi-ciently impressed with the situation in Podor on the Senegal River to report to Paris:

In the district of Podor the disposition of the population is less than satis-factory. One can sense hostility that is only restrained by the fear of reprisal; and certainly there is no sympathy for us. This state of feeling can be attrib-uted in good part to the presence in the town of numerous Wolof merchants

---

* This idea was consolidated under Carpot, and it was "expanded" to include all of French West and Equatorial Africa under Blaise Diagne. It was strictly political fancy, however, since only the originaires of the Communes participated in the voting.

who have connections in Saint-Louis; some of them, who are voters in that city, often arrogantly refer to their status and to the influence that they supposedly have with certain political personalities in the capital or with business agents, who are increasingly getting mixed up in native affairs.[22]

The report also cited an incident in nearby Dagana, where the populace had refused to accept Racine Kane, a French-appointed chief; this attitude was supposedly encouraged by bribery, which was again attributed to Africans from Saint-Louis. The case of Dagana, in fact, was considered typical of the disruption caused by the intervention of the urban political elite.

Another example occurred in 1912 at the peanut center of Kaolack in Serere country. A group of Saint-Louisians were accused of trying to establish an independent community at Kaolack, to be presided over by one Saër Guèye. An anonymous bureaucrat commented: "Saër Guèye declares he is in charge of the community of Saint-Louis originaires in Kaolack and absolutely refuses to submit to the local authorities." Investigating what was at first believed to be a Muslim plot, the French found that Guèye and company had actually created a mutual-aid society of the type common in many new urban centers in French and British West Africa. Called into court, Guèye testified: "I am the president of an organization founded to aid, in case of need, all natives of Saint-Louis, Dakar, Gorée, and Rufisque who live in or pass through Kaolack."[23] The alarmed *commandant du cercle* still thought the group dangerous, and prosecuted the society's leaders for "misappropriating" funds that the 83 members had paid in.

### The Radicalism of Mody M'Baye

There were other indications that Western political ideas and institutions were being introduced in the Protectorate. The most striking was the sudden appearance of the public letter writer (*écrivain public*), who was usually an urban African with some schooling and much political savoir faire. The letter writer was a kind of rural notary, an embryonic lawyer, and a public tribune. Essentially, he translated the grievances and petitions of thousands of rural folk into French so that they could reach the local French administrator or appointed chief. And his open letters to the French regime on behalf of rural clients took the place of formal protests in the Protectorate, where there was no recourse to the French codes that prevailed in the Communes. The letter writers exposed administrative injustices, the tyrannies of appointed chiefs, and the bribery or payoff of officials, thereby incurring the wrath of French officialdom.

The most famous and influential écrivain public was Mody M'Baye, a Wolof born in Saint-Louis in 1871. Through a series of harsh personal experiences M'Baye became an embittered critic of French rule; and more than any other man he helped to create a new climate of unrest in the Protectorate during the period 1900–1914. Because of his birth in the Commune of Saint-Louis, he considered himself a citizen even though he spent most of his life working in the Protectorate. He began his career as a schoolteacher; but in 1902 he was suspended from his job at Toul (near Thiès), charged with establishing himself on the side as an écrivain public. It was alleged that he traveled through Baol claiming he would defend the local people, who "naïvely thought M'Baye was listened to in high circles."[24] He soon lost his job permanently for these political reasons, although he had evidently been a popular teacher.

Setting out on a full-time career as an écrivain public, M'Baye created his own intelligence network among the Africans. For example, one Khaly Boye, the local telegrapher in Toul, secretly copied all important wires that arrived for French officials and sent the copies to M'Baye's archives. With such information at his disposal, M'Baye soon became a thorn in the administration's side. In 1907 Governor Cor proposed to have him deported to another colony as "politically undesirable"; but Governor-General Ponty quashed this idea, observing that such a sentence should only be passed on natives who actually bore arms against France.* Ponty himself preferred to put M'Baye under house arrest.[25] Ponty obviously sympathized with the African cause, and other liberal administrators felt the same. But M'Baye, by his accusations of injustice and corruption, had made a good many enemies.

In 1904 M'Baye had been instrumental in locating the suspected murderers of a French administrator, Monsieur Chautemps. He then wrote to Martial Merlin, the acting Governor-General, and hinted that the administration should reward him by naming him chief for western Baol province. "My nomination, Mr. Governor-General, would teach the traditional princes that the Republic gives its favors to the son of a peasant who is well-trained and patriotic rather than to the son of a noble who has no virtue but his birth."[26] M'Baye believed in the ideal of assimilation and wanted to help the French put into practice the ideals of republicanism that he had learned

---

* Of course, Amadou Bamba had not borne arms and had nevertheless been exiled on two occasions. Clearly, Ponty did not regard M'Baye's actions as a significant threat to French rule.

from young administrators in the field. But his intractable foes blocked his appointment. By December of 1904, seeing that his chiefship would not materialize, M'Baye asked to be reinstated as a teacher in return for his help in capturing the assassins. Even though there was an acute shortage of teachers, his request was denied. From that moment on, M'Baye became an unmerciful critic of the colonial regime.

In 1907 M'Baye again ran afoul of the administration because of his own private investigation into the affairs of one Monsieur Manetche, an administrator in the Protectorate. M'Baye had posted his agents to gather information for an intended exposé; but whether Manetche was guilty of any irregularity never came to light, since the administration promptly accused M'Baye of running his own police network. A transcript of the resulting inquiry revealed the following exchange:

*Inspector Aubry Lecomte:* A recent statement by Governor Guy warned the population against public writers like you, who profit from the naïveté of the natives by boasting of authority that you don't have and promising them aid and protection while actually exploiting them . . . .
*M'Baye:* Let me say just one thing. When one has seen the truth, doesn't one have the right to tell the proper authorities?
*Lecomte:* The Governor has his own informants. Natives who want to complain about something can go to their natural defenders, the agents of the administration.
*M'Baye:* But if someone confides his grievances to me and entrusts me to present them to the Governor in a letter, don't I have the right to send that letter?
*Lecomte:* Yes, but the Governor won't pay any attention to it. If the natives want to complain, all they have to do is speak to the agents of the administration.[27]

M'Baye remained free after this investigation partly because of his ties with the Ligue des Droits de l'Homme, which took an active interest in complaints received from French citizens and subjects in the colonies. The League had important connections in Parliament and had previously brought about investigations in other colonies; hence Ponty acted carefully toward M'Baye, who claimed membership.

In 1909 Ponty decided that M'Baye's services could actually be of some use to the administration, and he informally proposed giving M'Baye a small government post or reinstating him as a teacher. But Governor Cor, still hostile toward M'Baye and annoyed that Ponty was interfering in a strictly Senegalese problem, could not agree. He answered Ponty diplomatically, but argued: "The past of this teacher leads us to believe that, as is the case with most gifted natives, his moral character is not commensurate with his intelligence; it is probable that he would make poor use of any authority given him."[28] Hardened by this rebuff, M'Baye continued his career as a letter writer, managing to keep out of trouble with a colonial regime he now hated.

M'Baye was abetted in his quest for African rights by two professional lawyers: the Creole Louis Huchard and the liberal Frenchman Paul Sabourault. Huchard came from an aristocratic famly in Gorée but spent most of his active career in Saint-Louis and Dakar. After his death in 1922, *L'Eveil Colonial* hailed him as a champion of native rights and as the founder of Senegal's independent press.[29] An official gazette, *Le Moniteur*, had existed in Senegal since the days of Faidherbe; but Huchard founded what might be called the first modern independent newspaper in Senegal. This was *L'Afrique Occidentale*, which flourished in the 1890's and publicized the plight of many oppressed Africans. Huchard also printed articles by such outspoken liberals as Senator Alexandre Isaac of Guadeloupe, a personal friend who lauded Huchard's unselfish efforts in collecting complaints from Africans and making them known to the authorities.[30] Paul Sabourault was an attorney and politician in Dakar who also did much to help rural Africans. Both Huchard and Sabourault were derisively referred to by the authorities as écrivains publics.

In 1912, M'Baye was embroiled in a dispute that became an important test case in Senegal's political history. He had written a letter of intervention for an African in Sine-Saloum who was about to be judged by the local administrator, Paul Brocard. None of the French or Muslim legal safeguards available to residents of the urban areas applied in the Protectorate. Consequently, rural Africans were literally at the mercy of their local administrator—and Brocard was known as a driving, tough-minded official who ran Sine-Saloum efficiently but despotically. Annoyed by M'Baye's initial intervention, Brocard was enraged when further letters appeared in the Dakar journal *Le Petit Sénégalais*. Ordinarily this would not have occurred; but at that precise moment the soldier of fortune Jean Daramy d'Oxoby had temporarily taken over the paper, and he was happy to give M'Baye a platform.[31]

In April 1913, M'Baye made the mistake of setting foot in Sine-Saloum, where he was immediately arrested. After he admitted authorship of the articles criticizing Brocard, the vengeful administrator sentenced him to fifteen days in prison without appeal. Brocard's decision was specifically based on a 1907 arrêté that gave administrators the power to do this to any French subject in the Protectorate. M'Baye replied that he was an originaire of the Four Communes and a voter, and hence was not liable to summary administrative justice. Producing his voting card as proof, he demanded a court trial but was refused. Through friends, he immediately appealed the sentence to the Paris office of the Ligue des Droits de l'Homme and to Governor-General Ponty.[32]

All of this happened on April 10. General Council member Galandou Diouf came to the rescue within the day, wiring Ponty that M'Baye simply could not be treated this way: he was a citizen of the Four Communes and had stood for election three times. As in 1907, Ponty overruled Governor Cor, who had backed Brocard; and on April 11 M'Baye was released pending a fuller investigation into the circumstances. Meanwhile, the Paris director of the Ligue des Droits de l'Homme, François de Pressensé, demanded an explanation from the Ministry of Colonies, which in turn cabled Ponty for full details.[33]

On April 19, 1913 Brocard defended his action in a carefully written letter to his superior and friend, Governor Cor. He described the activities of M'Baye, Diouf, Huchard, and Sabourault as dangerous agitation that should be suppressed before it led to general rebellion. Moreover, he was humiliated because d'Oxoby's newspaper had published the fact that Ponty had arbitrarily ordered M'Baye's release. And he even hinted that such leniency toward African unrest had been responsible for the recent assassination of Police Chief Bourdennec in Rufisque. But Brocard had to swallow his pride, for Ponty ordered the entire affair closed.

In June 1913, Ponty wrote Cor about the incident and explained his position. First, he personally felt that no administrator was justified in giving such a harsh sentence for a mere newspaper article. Second, he chided Cor, saying that a Governor-General had to keep in mind overall considerations not always apparent to the Governor of Senegal or a mere regional administrator: proposals were then pending in Parliament for the suspension of administrative disciplinary powers in Algeria, and Ponty did not want the M'Baye affair blown up for the benefit of anticolonial deputies. Third, Ponty reminded Cor that it was, after all, perfectly legal for a native to appeal to a higher authority in the administration, given the absence of any legal rules on the subject.[34]

M'Baye's case captured the attention of urban Senegal, for the principle of African citizenship rights was at stake. Were the originaires exempt from administrative justice when traveling outside the Communes? The Decree of August 16, 1912, stated that only Africans complying with its detailed requirements were considered citizens; otherwise, originaires had limited rights. M'Baye's detention dramatized the possible implications of this decree for the political elite, who were now alerted to the need for preserving their historic rights. (At the same time, the incident greatly discredited deputy François Carpot, who was thought to have arranged the promulgation of the decree.)

Mody M'Baye and the many other écrivains publics were the vanguard of urban influence on rural life. But at the same time they kept the urban elite informed about attitudes and problems in the interior. It was apparent by 1914 that Africans throughout Senegal had become conscious of their place in the political scheme of things, and even more apparent that they were about to demand changes.

CHAPTER 8

# The African Political Awakening, II

*The French Education of the Senegalese*

BY THE turn of the century, a good many Africans were able to attend schools financed and managed by the French. At first, these schools had been under the jurisdiction of various Catholic religious orders; but even before the separation of Church and state in France (1905) state education had become increasingly important, although the schools were mostly confined to the Communes and the areas of direct administration. The French schools became centers for implementing the ideals of assimilation at a practical level. Africans learned about the French Revolution, the Third Republic, and France's civilizing mission in her colonies; and as France extended her schools with the intention of training new clerks, messengers, and schoolteachers, she spread these potent ideas.

The advent of Western education in Senegal can be traced to the earliest Catholic missionaries in the 1630's; but no serious effort to create permanent schools for Africans occurred until after the Napoleonic Wars, when French priests tried to establish a parochial school in Saint-Louis. A courageous Catholic nun, Mother Javouhey of the Sisters of Saint Joseph of Cluny, organized girls' schools at Saint-Louis and Gorée in 1826. She was the first to envisage educating Africans in Senegal and sending the brightest ones to France for training as schoolteachers. The idea was opposed by Governor Roger, who favored training Africans only in manual skills. But since Mother Javouhey had excellent connections in Paris, her scheme prevailed. In a sense, she was the founder of modern education in Senegal.[1]

An important step was taken by the French government in 1841, when the Frères de Ploërmel, a Catholic teaching order from Brittany, were asked to found several schools in Senegal. Small schools were set up in Saint-Louis and Gorée, and for a time classes were given in the river posts of Bakel, Dagana, Podor, and Sédhiou. Also during the 1840's, the Abbé Boilat, a Creole priest (and the author of an important work on nineteenth-century Senegal), founded a private secondary school in Saint-Louis.[2] He even managed to send some scholarship students to France, but they were all from the Creole Christian community.[3] Boilat was forced to close the school in 1849 because of a lack of funds and the turmoil caused by the Revolution of 1848. Louis Faidherbe's contributions to Senegal's education system have already been mentioned—e.g., his creation of the School for the Sons of Chiefs and his invitation to the urban Africans and Creoles to gain an education and enter the ranks of the new elite. He also encouraged the Frères de Ploërmel to expand their schools at the same time.

Religious education was most successful in the new towns where the state did not have funds or personnel to expand. In 1847 Father Libermann and the Frères du Saint-Esprit founded a mission and school on the site of modern Dakar. Other Catholic orders established schools on Cape Verde during the next several decades, and also moved down the petite côte, which was more receptive to Christian proselytizing and Western education than the Muslim lands of the Senegal River. The Serere and Casamance regions ultimately became the most fruitful areas for Christian missions in Senegal. Joal, one of the original Portuguese enclaves, proved to be an especially strong Catholic center; and nearby N'Gazobil also became important for Catholic education.

After 1900, the increasing anticlerical sentiment in France spread to the colonies, where many officials regarded the Church as a rival to the state. In 1904, Governor Camille Guy made his position quite clear: "In a recent circular I have reminded the functionaries of their duties to the Republic by warning them not to place their children with the religious orders and not to further the nefarious attempts of these orders to regain their influence on the youth of the colony."[4] The battle lines were drawn quite clearly before the official separation of Church and state in the metropole in 1905; in fact, a quasi-monopoly of education in Senegal had been settled on the state by 1901. But official action did not halt the Catholics' efforts in Senegal; although their influence and prestige diminished, a few religious schools continued to educate young Senegalese.

For many years Africans had refused to send their children to Catholic schools for fear they would be converted to Christianity. Many African children stayed in the koranic schools until twelve years of age in order to finish their religious instruction, and those who went on usually entered the state-supported schools.* Moreover, the Africans knew that the Church and the powerful Creole community were closely linked, and they reasoned that Catholic education would only produce more supporters for the Creole oligarchy. Men like Governor Guy—trained in French universities and cosmopolitan in outlook—indirectly reinforced these attitudes, for they were confident that Republican France and not the Church offered the best model for new African recruits to the elite. An official report in 1903 observed: "It has been necessary to replace certain books [of the Frères de Ploërmel] because of their religious nature, which is clearly hostile to democratic principles; they have been replaced by books truly secular and republican in outlook."[5]

A department of education was instituted in Senegal in 1903, an inspector of education arrived from the metropole to organize education along secular lines, and the first public girls' school was started. This was a boon for African girls, who had been barred from most religious schools unless they conformed to Western dress and behavior. In the past, the religious orders had considered themselves autonomous in running schools and appointing teachers. But Governor Guy was determined that only the state should decide which teachers were fit to work in the colony, and he imposed this restriction on the religious schools that continued to operate.

Since Faidherbe's day, the religious schools had performed valuable service by operating evening schools for adults. Courses in arithmetic, French grammar, and conversational French were available to urban Africans who wanted to qualify for new jobs in administration and commerce. By 1903 more than 700 students were enrolled in night classes; and by 1910 this had grown to 1,357, out of a total of 5,854 students in French schools.[6] Much of this expansion occurred because the state schools picked up the idea of evening school from the Church schools and made it an important part of government schooling for Africans.

The new public school system was composed of primary schools and middle schools. The primary schools, in turn, were subdivided into rural, regional, and urban schools. Urban schools had good facilities and French teachers, whereas regional and rural schools usually had poor facilities and African teachers. This was natural, since the

---

* In later years, it became difficult for African students who finished the koranic schools to enter French lower-grade schools. The French balked at mixing twelve-year-olds with younger primary children and consequently refused admittance to many Africans, who naturally felt the French were prejudiced against them.

urban schools also served the Creole and French communities; in fact, more and more places were reserved for French students as time went on. However, the overall increase in public schools did make it easier for Muslim Africans to become monitors or grade-school teachers, and there was a great expansion in the African teaching force after 1900. African teachers were in particular demand for remote inland schools where few Frenchmen cared to work. (Time and again official reports told of a new school functioning without a French teacher, or of a school opened by a Frenchman who soon quit his post and left an African assistant in charge.)

What happened to African students after they left these schools? A 1910 survey of 515 boys who had recently graduated from primary school showed that most had become useful members of the urban community (see Table 3).[7] Most of the educated young Senegalese were absorbed into trades, artisan jobs, and the world of business. Relatively few became domestic servants or farmers. Not many were employed in the administration, since there were not many positions open for educated Africans. Africans were usually employed by the French as drivers, guards, runners, and the like—positions that required little Western education. Very few students went on to school in France, and most of these were Creoles who had access to scholarship funds voted by the General Council. The normal school, where African teachers and monitors were trained, had only begun to operate. Few Africans were sent to advanced trade school because the French intended that most of the colony's master tradesmen would be French petit colons.

Another 1910 survey measured the total number of students and teachers in Senegal's French schools (see Table 4). Most of the effort was concentrated on primary schooling, with the adult evening

TABLE 3

*Later Occupations of African Primary Students*

| Occupation | Number of students | Occupation | Number of students |
|---|---|---|---|
| Trades and crafts | 104 | Normal school | 17 |
| Commerce | 137 | Secondary school | 15 |
| Agriculture | 27 | Advanced trade school | 5 |
| Civil service | 15 | Koranic academy (Medersa) | 10 |
| Domestics | 25 | No occupation known | 46 |
| Miscellaneous | 30 | Unemployed | 60 |
| At school in Europe | 24 | | |

TABLE 4

*Teachers and Students in French Schools, 1910*

| School | Students enrolled | Teachers | Number employed |
|---|---|---|---|
| Adult courses | 1,357 | French teachers: | |
| Secondary school | 21 | Secondary school | 4 |
| Koranic academy (Medersa) | 65 | Primary school | 45 |
| Mechanics school | 65 | African teachers and | |
| Trade school | 26 | monitors (almost all | |
| Primary schools | 4,497 | in primary schools) | 54 |
| Total | 6,053 | Total | 103 |

courses taking second priority. Education for young Africans beyond primary school was practically nonexistent. More than half the teaching force in Senegal was composed of African teachers and monitors, but this was primarily because French instructors were hard to come by. Only in 1904 had it been decided to train and use these African auxiliaries in a methodical way.[8]

This involvement with Western education inevitably made Africans aware of France's discriminatory practices in several spheres: the urban schools tended to exist more for French students than for Africans; newly arrived Frenchmen replaced Africans or stood in the way of young Africans in the administration; and Africans qualified to teach were given the least desirable assignments and paid on a much lower scale. By this time the Western ideals of individual opportunity and advancement according to merit had been impressed on most urban Africans and had begun to spread to the rural areas. And the policy of assimilation, so unjust in practice, had changed in African minds from a vague hope to a practical reality. The situation resembled our modern "revolution of rising expectations."

The lack of opportunities beyond middle school meant that the great majority of the educated African elite did not have a secondary education; and not until the 1920's did even a small segment of this elite begin to acquire degrees from French lycées. Nevertheless, young Africans in the Communes were usually able to comprehend the complicated political issues of the day and penetrate the smoke screen of French colonial propaganda, and they behaved in far more sophisticated ways than their level of schooling might indicate. Moreover, about the time that urban youths began to value the advantages of a French education, pressure was put on the urban schools to accept all French and Creole students, leaving Africans to the regional and rural schools. This added greatly to the growing discontent in the colony: urban school programs were almost identical with those in France, but students outside the Communes received a watered-down curriculum that gave little preparation in arithmetic and practically none in French grammar.[9]

In summary, the emphasis on state schools after 1901 shifted the debate in the African community from arguments over attending religious schools to discussions of how to get the best education possible.[10] Urban schools reserved fewer places for Africans, regional schools offered an inferior program, and both denied admission to Africans who had finished koranic school. Even so, a vociferous educated minority developed after the turn of the century; and by 1914 this group took the lead in the African struggle for political participation.

### The Lebou Community and Galandou Diouf

Another major cause of unrest among Africans during this period was the continued disaffection of the Lebou communities on Cape Verde. With the arrival of French merchants in Rufisque and international shipping in Dakar, thousands of Africans from elsewhere in Senegal sought jobs that the conservative Lebous refused to accept. Intractable in the face of urban advance, both old and young Lebous were still obsessed with regaining their expropriated lands or getting what they considered adequate compensation. The French had actually paid extra compensation on several occasions; but the Lebous had quickly spent the money and then resumed their complaints. The younger Lebous, in fact, had never seen evidence of any compensation and hence believed that it had never been given in the first place.[11]

Only a few younger Lebous were permitted to attend the new lay schools in Dakar and Rufisque; most were illiterate and subject to the iron rule of the diambours, or traditional elders. Hence the Lebou community remained a closed, taciturn group fighting a losing battle to retain their lands and privacy. The Lebous of Dakar and Rufisque were considered originaires and had exercised voting privileges ever since the two cities became full communes. But they took little interest in the Western political institutions that surrounded them, and aside from voting for city councilmen, General Councillors, and the deputy they remained apolitical.

French politicians in the two Communes had long recognized that Lebou support was necessary to win any election; consequently, the traditional leaders of the Lebous were always deferred to by French merchants at election time. For their part, the Lebou chiefs seemed to feel that supporting whichever party promised to take up their grievances with the colonial administration was the best way to seek redress. Before an election they decided which list of candidates the entire Lebou community would support, and it then became a matter of collective honor for the various families and clans to vote for the chosen list. The average Lebou, to keep faith with his kinfolk, had to vote for the endorsed candidates; otherwise he would lose face.[12]

In return for supporting an electoral list, the Lebou community was given bags of rice, tea, and sugar, as well as a collection of lavish promises that usually proved worthless after the election. Fernand Marsat, the Dakar pharmacist who organized Senegal's first real political machine, won several elections with Lebou votes, which he gained simply by distributing more favors and bigger promises than his rivals. He was able to muster the Lebous for Louis Dreyfus in the 1902 race for deputy even though other candidates made anti-Semitism the basis of their campaigns. After this campaign, Louis Huchard attacked Marsat for paying off the Lebou chiefs; but his charges were ignored, since most candidates had done the same with other groups of voters. Marsat enjoyed the continuing support of the Lebous despite the fact that he had been suspended as mayor of Dakar for financial irregularities. He flattered the older chiefs and came to terms with the younger Lebous. He also put several Africans on his lists for the municipal elections to please the Lebous (all of these, of course, were "safe" Africans who knew their place).

When Marsat was defeated by Edmond Teisseire in Dakar's 1904 mayoral campaign, he managed to gain additional Lebou support in the face of defeat; for Teisseire added some Catholic Africans to his municipal council list, which outraged the intolerant Lebous. In 1908, Marsat reconquered his "fief," as it was now popularly called, but was obliged to install his lieutenant Emile Masson as mayor. Masson, however, was just as skillful at flattering the Lebous, and he was reelected in 1912. It seemed that this sort of thing could continue for years. But there were many Lebous, especially the younger men, who were thoroughly dissatisfied with the cynical politics of Marsat and his machine. They wanted a change, and as time went on their demands became more urgent.

The Lebous of Rufisque also desired a change. They had been dominated from the beginning of municipal politics in Rufisque by the French merchants, who occasionally put an African yes man on the lists to curry public favor. The Lebous had been courted, bribed, promised remuneration, and then forgotten after every election.* Maurice Escarpit, long-time mayor of Rufisque, kept the situation in hand with funds from the Bordeaux merchants. Then, in 1909, a new personality appeared on the political horizon: Galandou Diouf, a Wolof originally from Saint-Louis, was elected by the Lebou community as their representative on the General Council.[13] A new era dawned for African politics in Rufisque and all Senegal, for here was a man who thought for himself and was not afraid to criticize the French and Creoles. Besides his Lebou support, Diouf had the backing of several important Bordeaux houses, since he had been associated with Senegalese commerce. And, as we have seen, he was well regarded by François Carpot.

Diouf was born in Saint-Louis in 1875, of Wolof parents (and possibly had Creole ancestors, since his father was named John Legros Diouf).[14] He was reared as a Muslim and always considered himself part of the Islamic community in Senegal; however, his family sent him to the boys' school kept by the Frères de Ploërmel, and he later studied at the short-lived Catholic secondary school in Saint-Louis. Since teachers were in demand when he finished school, his first job was at the Dagana primary school upriver from Saint-Louis.

Diouf quickly tired of his passive life as a teacher; and in quick succession he became postmaster of Dagana, conductor on the Dakar–Saint-Louis railway, and chief of the Dakar railway station. He found that all these posts paid African employees only a fraction of French salaries, and decided in 1900 to enter Senegal's commercial world as an accountant for Abdou Salam Boughreb, the largest Moroccan merchant in Dakar. He found this career more to his liking, and in 1902 the large Bordeaux firm of Buhan and Teisseire named him chief accountant for its Rufisque office. This put Diouf in a position to meet many important personages in Rufisque, both French and African.

In 1909 Diouf became a candidate for the General Council—undoubtedly because his job seemed to mark him as a "safe" African. He received some Bordeaux backing, but his campaign appealed primarily to the Lebous, who were disgruntled and ready to try any new face. (Even Louis Huchard, a veteran campaigner for African rights, was defeated in the election.) Diouf did not pose as a radical during the campaign, but instead supported the moderate political

---

* The Lebous' policy of not sending their children to French schools now worked against them, for they had no trained leaders who could aspire to political office in the Communes.

program of François Carpot. He campaigned for "increased local industry" to please the French and "increased local justice" to please the Lebous.[15] In November he won his seat on the Council; and although his election was at first challenged because he had run as an independent, he went on to carve out one of the most remarkable careers in Senegalese politics.

Diouf soon heard from the man who was shortly to follow him into politics and become Senegal's first African deputy: Blaise Diagne, then Senegalese customs inspector in French Guiana, sent a congratulatory letter to Diouf upon his victory. This and other signs convinced Diouf that the significance of his election was interpreted very broadly by Africans in both the towns and the Protectorate. Before long, he considered himself a spokesman for the African community at large and not just for his Lebou constituents. He soon parted company with Carpot and joined the camp of Justin Devès, whose political savoir faire and organizational ability he had long admired. Both Carpot and Devès were political models for the young African aspirant; but Diouf was basically an independent, and after he got his bearings he became a radical independent.

In 1910, for example, when the inhabitants of Dagana attempted to have the French-appointed chief Guibril Gaye removed from office, Diouf joined forces with the French "écrivain public" Paul Sabourault to fight their cause. An official French inquiry had simply stated, "There is nothing discreditable to be found about this chief."[16] But this missed the point that Diouf and Sabourault pressed. A later report admitted:

[Guibril Gaye] was not promoted to his post by an act of superior authority but by the simple decision of an associate native affairs administrator; consequently, Gaye has not had the authority to resist attacks on his position by his adversaries. The best course now is to have Gaye resign and put in his place someone who has the confidence of the local elders.[17]

And in 1912, the rumor of abuses in Sine-Saloum during the tenure of Administrator Paul Brocard (who had tried to put Mody M'Baye in prison) caused Diouf, in his role as a Council member, to demand an inquiry into the true state of affairs—much to the consternation of Brocard and other rural administrators, who bitterly resented any interference from the Communes, let alone interference by an African.

The Brocard affair led Diouf to address the General Council on the alarming fact that Senegal's local government had functioned for so long without responsible criticism from the Senegalese press: "Our (local) institutions are in an enviable position compared to those of the great French nation, whose acts are held in check by the great tradition of the press in France. . . . It's too bad that each newspaper in this colony kowtows to the government and winds up showering it with compliments." Moreover, he complained, "Words don't seem to be worth anything when we expendable Negroes write them."[18] Already Diouf was acutely aware of the attack on the originaires' voting rights, the lack of political expression and participation available to Africans, and the effective denial of the rewards that assimilation had promised.

During all this, Diouf did not forget the specific interests of his Lebou constituents in Rufisque. He was influential in having *La Démocratie* attack the administration's policy on the Lebou land question. Certainly, there were numerous incidents to report. In November 1913, *La Démocratie* alleged that the French army had evicted numerous Lebous from their fields near Ouakam on Cape Verde in order to hold cold-season maneuvers. No compensation had been paid. And later, when the French needed a new cemetery between Dakar and Rufisque, they bought a plot from Maurel et Prom instead of the Lebous, although the large Bordeaux firm owned one small parcel in an area of many Lebou owners who would have been happy to sell.

When he was criticized for collaborating with *La Démocratie*, d'Oxoby's new liberal journal, Diouf replied that he considered it in the tradition of Clemenceau's *L'Homme Libre*, Jaurès's *L'Humanité*, and Hervé's *La Guerre Sociale*—newspapers that he read regularly and considered good examples of a vigorous opposition press. He went on to proclaim the need for a new order in Senegalese politics. Since neither the existing French-Creole entente nor a hypothetical Creole-African entente would work, the future should belong to the Africans:

Forgetting the past of their ancestors and themselves, certain undesirable Frenchmen from the metropole would like to try keeping us under the yoke of slavery, despite all the liberties generously granted us by the great French Revolution. The French Republic, gentlemen, has freed *us*, the same as *you*; if we are the slaves of the last hour, you were among those of the first hour.[19]

Despite his courage, independence, and zeal at crusading in the General Council, Galandou Diouf did nothing to unify the various forces of discontent at work in Senegal. Like Mody M'Baye, he was a leader without a political organization. He never forgot that he was elected at the pleasure of the Lebous; but he could not control them as Justin Devès could control the Wolof fishermen at Saint-Louis or Fernand Marsat the older Lebou chiefs in Dakar. Diouf, in a very real sense, did not transcend his own bailiwick of Rufisque. He was a symbol rather than an effective leader for the many restless young Africans in Senegal.

## The Young Senegalese

Senegal's first African political group, the Jeunes Sénégalais, was founded in Saint-Louis in about 1912—probably the first political action group in French-speaking Africa. It developed from the Aurora, an urban voluntary association for young men that had been started in 1910. The young Senegalese were mostly educated Africans such as clerks, schoolteachers, and interpreters; they met regularly to discuss ideas, put on plays, engage in French sports, socialize, and cement the bonds of African friendship in an urban setting.[20]

Lamine Guèye (later deputy from Senegal) helped in organizing the Aurora during his student days in Saint-Louis. His memoirs recount the good times he and his friends enjoyed fishing, boxing, and hunting. A number of musically inclined members formed a group called La Lyre de Saint-Louis, which gave occasional vocal concerts on Faidherbe Square. Curiously, their favorite number was the national anthem of the Transvaal—which they regarded as a demand by the black Africans to be freed from British rule. Guèye also recalled the Aurora meetings at his house or at Papa Mar Diop's place, where the young members talked of news from France, tried out English, Arabic, and Latin phrases on each other, and discussed politics in the colony.

Booker T. Washington was one of the Aurora's idols: "For us he stood as an example of determination, a sign that one day we, too, would succeed in our own country."[21] But there were other heroes nearer home. The young Papa Mar Diop was the natural leader of the group, but it also idolized older Senegalese like Mody M'Baye and Galandou Diouf. Guèye recalled: "When he [Diouf] gave his maiden talk in the Senegalese [General] Council, the young men of Saint-Louis could hardly contain their wild enthusiasm."[22] The young men were also impressed with Masylla Diop, a local notable who wrote satirical verse in *La Démocratie*, and with Rémy Naintousha, a West Indian who worked as a French veterinary inspector. Naintousha , in particular, impressed his youthful admirers with stories of Negroes participating in local politics in Guadeloupe, Martinique, and French Guiana.

In response to a mounting interest in political problems, the Aurora soon formed a section for political discussion called the Young Senegalese, and in 1912 this section became an independent political club. Among the active participants were Papa Mar Diop, Lamine Guèye, Aby Kane Diallo, Amadou Assane N'Doye, Amadou Duguay-Clédor, and others who eventually became leaders in local politics. But rather than choosing one of their own number as chief, the Young Senegalese picked the elderly Thiécouta Diop, an articulate Wolof notable who had strong opinions about local politics and French policy. Diop was an unassimilated African who did not know French and spoke to white men through an interpreter; in spite of this, he followed political developments closely and maintained an independent frame of mind that appealed greatly to his young admirers.

Diop presided over weekly meetings at which the young Africans aired their grievances. Among other things, they wanted better chances for administrative jobs, better salaries, cost-of-living benefits (then reserved for French only), better educational facilities, and scholarships to French schools (in theory, these were already available, but they were monopolized by the Creoles). A new, militant spirit pervaded the meetings, and it was succinctly expressed in various open letters published by *La Démocratie* for the benefit of the administration and the French-Creole entente:

Watch out! You now find yourselves face to face with twenty generations [of Africans] who are waking up, evolving with such rapidity that you don't realize it because your points of contact with the natives are so sorely lacking.

Senegal has suffered too much from these internecine battles between families.... The youths of Senegal are now awake, conscious of their political rights and duties, of the implications of universal suffrage under a democratic government.[23]

In November 1912 Galandou Diouf brought some of the African grievances into the open during a session of the General Council. He pointed out the discrepancy between appointments for clerks and administrative cadres hired in France and others hired in Senegal. It had previously been possible for Africans to aspire to the *cadre-général* (highest rank in the civil service), but this had become virtually impossible in the last decade. Subsidies to cover the increasing cost of living had recently been raised from 33 francs to 50 francs for Frenchmen but had been discontinued for all African personnel of equivalent rank. Diouf also demanded to know why postal clerks from France were excused from taking an entrance examination that was mandatory for Africans, and why qualified African employees were paid less for working overtime than their French counterparts. Even Justin Devès joined Diouf in demanding an investigation of this last injustice.[24]

The Young Senegalese thought of themselves as similar to the famous Young Turks they had read of in the newspapers, and they were constantly seeking ways to make their views known. Coincidentally, Jean Daramy d'Oxoby was looking for support to found *La Démocratie*; and he hinted that his columns would be open to the Young Senegalese if he were guaranteed their financial and moral support. After much debate, the group decided to use part of its treasury to subsidize the new weekly. *La Démocratie*'s principal backer, the liberal tavern owner Jules Sergent, was pleased that his young African friends were joining in the enterprise. Other backers were less enthusiastic (notably Jean Théveniaut, the resident administrator of the wealthy province of Baol).

The first issue of *La Démocratie* contained a torrent of invective from the irascible d'Oxoby, mostly directed at E. Post, who had fired him from *Le Petit Sénégalais*. But several columns were reserved for d'Oxoby's African colleagues; Mody M'Baye, for instance, was a regular contributor. For the first time, sessions of the General Council were analyzed and criticized. The Governor, the Governor-General, and other officials were satirized in a piquant style reminiscent of the Parisian press. A special report exposed alleged French brutality toward Africans in the Protectorate; and d'Oxoby took up M'Baye's vendetta with Administrator Paul Brocard of Sine-Saloum, calling him "Boubacar I, King of Sine-Saloum . . . who has depopulated the country of human beings and replaced them with cattle."[25] D'Oxoby announced his motto as: "Without the press there is no liberty; without opposition there can be no progress."

D'Oxoby's satires, lampoons, and personal attacks appeared each week, together with M'Baye's allegations of corruption in government. Governor Henri Cor was ridiculed, and was criticized for having his son privately tutored rather than sending him to a public school.* Governor-General Ponty was dubbed "Seigneur Guillaume I of French West Africa," and was also referred to as "Rome's ambassador in Africa, Guglielmo Ponty Africano." Cor and Brocard were enraged by the new sheet, and many others in the French adminstration and merchant community shared their feelings.

---

* "Cor-ricide" was recommended for those suffering from "mal-de-cor"—a jibe that infuriated the Governor.

How could this journal flourish at a time when the French Empire was highly autocratic and kept various deviant groups, such as the Mourides, under constant surveillance? The answer may well lie in Governor-General Ponty's attitude toward the Africans and the French liberals. Though not openly sympathetic to these groups, he respected their views and aspirations, for he was a confirmed Republican who considered it his personal mission to bring France's ideals to the Africans. Ponty intervened to help M'Baye and Diouf on several occasions, and was a personal friend of Louis Huchard. It seems probable that his personal influence made possible a free press in Senegal during these crucial years—something the colony did not enjoy after World War I, when a reactionary Governor-General heavily censored all newspapers. La Démocratie, recognizing its debt, paid homage to Ponty after his death in 1915: "William Ponty knew the African mind well; no aspect of the black soul was foreign to him."[26]

All during 1913 attention was focused on the forthcoming elections for the deputy. When the Young Senegalese contributed to La Démocratie, they had also agreed to back d'Oxoby's friend Jean Théveniaut as a candidate, since they were disillusioned with the Bordeaux-Creole entente and thought a liberal Frenchman, even an administrator, might be favorable to their cause if elected. They ridiculed the incumbent deputy, François Carpot, and blamed him for the decree of 1912 (which had actually helped to stimulate political consciousness among members of the African urban elite, who saw their political rights jeopardized). But in late 1913 Théveniaut, who was a neophyte in politics, quarreled with d'Oxoby, withdrew his cash investment in La Démocratie, and announced that he would seek political support elsewhere.[27] D'Oxoby, the petits colons of Jules Sergent, and the Young Senegalese were left without a candidate.

This occurred a few weeks before a former resident of Gorée, François Pouye, arrived in Senegal to test the reaction to a possible new candidate. Pouye talked to many Africans, Creoles, and Frenchmen, and concluded that the general mood of dissatisfaction might work to the advantage of a newcomer. But only Galandou Diouf expressed interest in Pouye's suggestion that Blaise Diagne might seek the colony's highest elective office. Diagne had been absent from Senegal for over twenty years and was an unknown quantity. Besides, commented many Africans, who had ever heard of an African running for deputy? Not even Diouf, the bright young man of African politics, had aspired to that honor.

Pouye returned to France and told Diagne about the general disaffection in Senegal. The originaires were tired of the political bossism of Marsat, Masson, and Devès, and they disliked Carpot's absenteeism. As a group, they feared that their historic liberties and political privileges were in peril. Lebous, Young Senegalese, petits colons, and Africans in the Protectorate all longed for someone to plead their cause. But save for Diouf, all were indifferent to the idea of backing an unknown outside candidate.

CHAPTER 9

# The First African Political Victory

THE FIRST hint that an African might run for Senegal's deputyship came in 1912 in a badly distorted account printed by *L'A.O.F.* (one of the earliest French newspapers to serve all West Africa, at that time from Conakry and later from Dakar). "A Senegalese originaire is reported to be entertaining the possibility of seeking Senegal's seat in the legislative elections, which will take place in about sixteen months at the expiration of Deputy Carpot's term of office. This candidate is [supposedly] M. Blaize N'Diaye, director of customs in Martinique, who will be backed by the Devès brothers."[1] The article further stated that "important money" was thought to be available for "N'Diaye's" campaign.

Blaise Diagne, at the time, was in fact a customs collector in French Guiana. However, he had spent much leave time in France studying the metropolitan political questions of the day, especially those pertaining to the French colonies. From the appearance of this 1912 article until February 1914, when his steamer docked in Dakar, rumors of Diagne circulated among the Africans. But few knew who he actually was and what he had done during his 22-year absence from the colony.

Diagne was born in 1872 at Gorée. He was the son of Niokhar Diagne, a Serere cook, and Gnagna Preira, a housemaid whose maternal line was Lebou but whose paternal ancestors had come from Portuguese Guinea. It is possible that some remote ancestor was Portuguese or had adopted a Portuguese name; but the family never thought of themselves as métis.[2] Diagne always presented himself as purely African, and this came to be the major factor in his appeal to Senegalese voters.

It was traditional among Creole families to take in African boys as servants, houseboys, or companions for their children; and Diagne's parents made no objection when Adolphe Crespin, a wealthy Catholic Creole, offered to adopt their son and send him to the local Catholic school. Young Diagne's intelligence impressed

Crespin, who soon came to be a real father to the ambitious young man. Years later, Diagne recalled what a privilege his education had been.

Almost fifty years ago, when I was a young boy in school on my rocky island home of Gorée, some French infantry and artillery soldiers were brought to us. They were Bretons who didn't know how to read or write, and it was to us, little fellows of eight to ten years, that these soldiers were marched, two by two. And to the best of our ability, making use of what we had learned, we wrote out short letters that the soldiers wanted sent to their families.[3]

Diagne was sent to Aix-en-Provence to finish his secondary studies; but he suffered apparent homesickness, failed his examination, and had to return to Senegal. He redeemed himself by graduating at the head of his class in 1890 at Saint-Louis's short-lived secondary school. For the graduation, the students presented a version of Molière's *Le malade imaginaire* in the chambers of the General Council, and were afterwards honored at a reception.[4]

Cheered by his scholastic success, Diagne decided to compete for a post in France's colonial customs service. At the time, few Africans were being educated in Western schools, hence few tried to enter the French civil service. However, there were no official bars if one could pass the qualifying examination. (Only after the turn of the century, when more Africans began to apply, did administrative action seriously limit the access of educated Africans to these jobs.) Diagne failed the first time, but succeeded a year later. In November 1892 he entered the customs service as a second-class clerk and was sent to Dahomey.

Diagne's career was turbulent and colorful. On successive assignments he made a virtual tour of the colonies—Dahomey, French Congo, Gabon, Réunion, Madagascar, and finally French Guiana. On leaving each assignment, he received the same notation on his personal dossier: "Never to be sent to this colony again." Diagne was not afraid to jeopardize his job by defending persecuted Africans or egalitarian ideas. He was suspended from the service for two months in 1898 because of insubordination and then had to take a six-month furlough when his attitude did not change. An inspector described him as well-dressed and enthusiastic but very pretentious, and noted that he pushed his superiors to the limit of their endurance. The secretary-general of the French Congo considered him "an undisciplined fellow, with a talent for intrigue, who will never make a good agent."[5]

What had Diagne done to merit such criticism? His immediate superior, when questioned, replied:

Monsieur Diagne, the Senegalese originaire, has tried to play the role of emancipator of the African race here in the Congo. All of his remarks exhibit a burning hostility toward the white race. At election time certain of his compatriots in Saint-Louis yell, "Senegal for the Senegalese!" In the same way, he seeks to implant in this colony the doctrine of "Africa for the Africans."

Diagne soon became hypersensitive to the slightest criticism or negative opinion regarding Africans, West Indians, and Negroes in general. He was teased, taunted, and bullied; but he did not give in to his detractors, although his outraged reactions more than once blocked his promotion or earned him a temporary suspension. For example, when a fellow African named Sangué was charged with insubordination Diagne acted as lawyer at the hearing.[6] To the discomfort of his superiors, he took this opportunity to accuse the customs service and the French administration in general of blatant discrimination and racist policies.

It is hard to say why Diagne was never dismissed, especially since his dossier was filled with complaints and criticism from his superiors. In fact, recommendations for dismissal or nonpromotion did occur frequently, for Diagne's volatile temper, aggressiveness in official matters, and total candor toward his superiors had long ago established him as anything but a dependable, steady civil servant. Nevertheless, although he was transferred again and again, he remained in the customs service, always managing to make his promotion at the eleventh hour. One possible explanation for this durability was that Diagne became a Freemason early in his career, probably during his stay in Madagascar; as a result he enjoyed a certain measure of fraternity with many important French administrators.

Diagne needed whatever help he could get. Despite his precarious position, he was not afraid to antagonize such august persons as Governor-General Joseph Gallieni of Madagascar, or Gallieni's successor, Victor Augagneur. Augagneur at one point determined to have Diagne sacked, but was prevented from doing so by pressure from fellow Freemasons (both Diagne and Augagneur were members of the same lodge). In 1908, after several incidents in Madagascar during a period when Diagne was serving as a temporary municipal judge, he was ordered away from the island by Augagneur.

In the midst of this controversy, Diagne had fallen ill and undergone an appendectomy. He charged that his case had been diagnosed improperly, and his superiors were happy to let him stay in France for the next fifteen months on sick leave. Thus he was able to observe at first hand the working of French politics and colonial lobbies while he waited for a new assignment. In 1909 he married a French girl, Mlle. Odette Villain of Orléans, whom he had previously met in Paris. And in 1910 he was finally ordered to French Guiana.

Diagne's extraordinary energy was not always used to antagonize his opponents. During his Paris stay he managed to befriend a number of important political personalities, including Senator Alexandre Isaac of Guadeloupe and Gratien Candace, the deputy from Martinique. Diagne had met Isaac a decade earlier and had since corresponded with him about political ideas and philosophies; in fact, Isaac may have been instrumental in having Diagne transferred from Gabon to the French Congo in 1897 after Diagne complained of racial discrimination among the local officials.

In April 1910 Diagne and his French bride arrived in Cayenne, one of the most remote posts of the French empire. Diagne plunged into his new job enthusiastically, and nothing but praise resulted from his first year's efforts. In December 1910 Governor Fernand Levecque recommended Diagne for the Cross of the Order of Agricultural Merit in recognition of his aid in developing public gardens and carrying out a general beautification scheme in Saint-Laurent du Maroni, a penitentiary city. But Diagne's interest in politics and his crusading zeal for African rights eventually reemerged in Guiana, and again he became embroiled in bitter conflict with his superiors. On one occasion, for example, he was insulted by three drunken French sailors; he demanded, and ultimately got, severe punishment for them, but he antagonized his own colleagues by his obstinacy and insistence on his rights.

Diagne applied the letter of the law in his customs work, much to the chagrin of local merchants who were used to agents they could bribe or influence. Complaints were rained on Governor Levecque; among other charges, it was alleged that Diagne, by serving as an adviser to the Saint-Laurent municipal commission, had violated the rule that civil servants should display neutrality in politics. Diagne's immediate superiors demanded his expulsion from Guiana; but Governor Levecque, not convinced that Diagne was entirely to blame for all the trouble, granted him a respite and shipped him to France on leave in 1912. Levecque noted:

Monsieur Diagne is difficult to employ. Wherever he serves he causes his chiefs trouble and often draws violent protests from merchants. Some of his superiors, on the other hand, consider him one of their most intelligent agents. Personally, I know that Monsieur Diagne does possess an excellent memory. But he is an ambitious fellow who believes he is constantly being persecuted; he [likes] to play politics. Perhaps I can summarize my appraisal as follows: *Souffre d'une indigestion d'assimilation.*[7]

Diagne nursed his pride in Paris and reflected on his deteriorating career. His quest for equal status had actually become more difficult since he had taken a French wife. Increasingly, he found himself and his fellow Africans barred from the assimilationist ideal of colonial theory. He put his ideas into writing for *L'Action* and *Les Annales Coloniales*, and undertook a program of lectures about France's colonial problems. Diagne soon caught the public interest: he was tall, striking in appearance, and conveyed a sense of earnestness that set him apart from the ordinary speaker. He audaciously challenged his old foe Governor Augagneur to a public debate, and also crossed swords with Pierre Mille, an influential writer on colonial affairs.[8] Diagne's appetite for public life was whetted by this activity, and the prospect of returning to Guiana as a mute civil servant galled him. He first broached the idea of running for office in his native Senegal during this leave in France—hence the origin of the distorted *L'A.O.F.* article on "Blaize N'Diaye, customs officer of Martinique."

In 1912, Diagne returned to Guiana, where he began to study for an impending examination for the rank of inspector, the highest customs post open to a career civil servant. In September 1913 he was granted six months' leave in France, presumably to compete for this advancement. During his absence, there was increasing speculation about his intention to run for deputy. In April 1913 (fully one year before the elections for deputy), *L'A.O.F.* ran a feature story on possible new candidates to oppose Carpot's bid for reelection. Diagne was listed—this time correctly—as an outside possibility, mainly because his public activities in France had built up his reputation. He was referred to as "an independent socialist who is often mentioned in the French press."[9]

In late 1913, as we have seen, Diagne dispatched his friend François Pouye to survey the Senegalese political scene. When Pouye reported that there was much dissatisfaction in Senegal but no general support for Diagne's candidacy, Diagne had to make a momentous decision. He could stay in France, compete for the inspectorship, and try to achieve preeminence in his field; or he could seek the deputyship and pass up his chance for future promotions, which would ruin his career if he lost the election. Diagne weighed the alternatives. Pouye had reported that only Gorée, the smallest of the Communes, could be counted on; that the various African voters would be difficult to unite; that liberal French and Creole candidates were already active; and that the incumbent Carpot was generally conceded another term. The chances seemed slim. But Diagne was confident of his ideas and his ability, and was further encouraged by his friend Gratien Candace.[10] On January 30, 1914, he sailed from Marseille for Dakar.

## The Candidates in 1914

The forthcoming election of 1914 had been discussed in Senegal since the 1912 decree went into effect, for most Africans were convinced that François Carpot was determined to eliminate them from the local political scene.[11] Senegal's rising political entrepreneur, Justin Devès, also questioned the desirability of Carpot's staying in office. In fact, Devès, after capturing the presidency of the General Council from Théodore Carpot in 1913, was once more thinking of seeking the deputyship himself, especially since the Paris newspapers constantly referred to him as Senegal's outstanding politician and predicted that he would undoubtedly win the deputyship whenever he chose to run. But serving as mayor of Saint-Louis, leading the Council, and directing the vast Devès commercial interests were more than enough for one man. Devès and his brothers therefore asked Henri Heimburger, their Alsatian lawyer in Paris, to come to Senegal and enter the race, assuring him of easy victory in their political fief. Heimburger's election would have been a great aid to the Devès business activities in France. Heimburger himself was agreeable to the idea; he knew nothing of politics in Senegal, which he thought of as a political backwater, and thought that his election would be automatic.

This action by the Devès clan was in effect a drastic break with the rest of the Creole elite, and two other Creoles soon decided to enter the contest. One was Georges Crespin, a young lawyer from Saint-Louis who was already serving on the General Council. He was the son of J. J. Crespin, the articulate Creole who had unsuccessfully contested the deputyship with Alfred Gasconi and had later become mayor of Saint-Louis. Georges had his father's flair for politics; and his statements during Council debates revealed his great sympathy for the plight of Africans in Senegal. The other new candidate was the merchant Louis Pellegrin, also the bearer of a venerable Creole name. His ancestors had been engaged in trade in Senegal for over a century, and he had some experience in the local politics of Louga, a trade center on the railway near Saint-Louis. Neither Crespin nor

Pellegrin was well known outside his home city. But they were both Creoles, and they intended to run against Carpot and the Creole-sponsored Heimburger; this meant that the Creole community's vote would be split four ways.

Most upper-class Frenchmen in Senegal were perfectly satisfied with the regime of François Carpot in Paris, since his actions there were far less radical than his campaign statements in Saint-Louis.* But there were many who could see the advantage of electing a man like Heimburger, despite the fact that he was obviously the tool of the Devès interests. To support Carpot would maintain the French-Creole alliance; but Heimburger was French, and he could probably be dissociated from any radical moves that Justin Devès might attempt. There were, however, Frenchmen who thought that either course was an abdication of French initiative and therefore opposed Creole power. They did not favor keeping Carpot in what had previously been a Frenchman's seat, and they did not trust Heimburger, because he was a foreigner to Senegal.

For these reasons, among others, three Frenchmen came forward to enter the campaign. The first was Fernand Marsat, who was the power behind the political machine that Mayor Emile Masson had inherited in Dakar. The ambitious Marsat loathed Africans and Creoles but pandered to them for votes. He had friends from Bordeaux, but was considered an independent candidate.[12] In reality, he was too small a power to be officially backed by Bordeaux but too big to gain the confidence of the petits colons. Marsat counted heavily on receiving a decisive Lebou vote in the first round and then winning a runoff election.

But two other Frenchmen had little sympathy for Marsat's political style: Colonel Henri Patey and Administrator Jean Théveniaut. Both were technically government employees and were required to take leave of absence to participate in the election. Patey was popular in some quarters because he had taken an interest in African problems during his tour as an artillery officer in Senegal. The same could be said of Théveniaut, whose liberal record as chief administrator of Baol had impressed the Young Senegalese and many petits colons. Each man felt that his experience in the colony would enable him

---

* For example, Governors Camille Guy and Henri Cor were favorably disposed toward Carpot. William Ponty also worked with Carpot on a number of projects. This led Carpot to imply in the 1906 campaign for deputy that he was "approved" by the government. See an extract from Carpot's letter of January 19, 1906 (ARS, 20-G-15).

to usher in a new era of closer relations between the metropole and Senegal; and each hoped to succeed as a compromise candidate if there were a deadlock on the first ballot. The foremost of the seven contenders was unquestionably the incumbent deputy, Carpot. Carpot had received a setback when Justin Devès took over the General Council, but he was still confident that Senegal's voters would stand by him for a fourth term. Governor Cor agreed, and wrote to Paris that Carpot would probably win, Thèveniaut and Marsat would run strong, and Heimburger would make a weak showing. As for the rumored candidacy of Blaise Diagne, Cor observed: "Diagne n'aura aucun chance de succès."[13] Cor's predictions convinced Paris that all was normal in Senegal. As a result, the Ministry of Colonies was simply not prepared for the tumultuous election of 1914, the most important in the history of the Four Communes. Nor was it prepared for the appearance in French politics of Africa's first black deputy, Blaise Diagne.

## Diagne's Return to Senegal

As soon as his steamer docked in Dakar, Diagne went straight to the leaders of Dakar's Lebou community to pay his respects. He spoke at great length with the grand marabout Assane N'Doye, who was convinced that the time had come for the Lebous to abandon the Marsat-Masson machine and assert their independence by supporting an African candidate. N'Doye soon gained the support of the younger Lebous for Diagne. But many older Lebous were not impressed by this new arrival—a man more European than African in his bearing, dress, and speech. Some asked about his family: Was it not true that his father was Serere? N'Doye and his supporters overlooked this and claimed Diagne as a true Lebou, "one of our own sons."[14] This initial support from the Lebous of Dakar (and eventually from those of Rufisque) proved to be Diagne's greatest political asset. But not all the Lebou diambours followed Assane N'Doye, nor did they think that Diagne could win. The majority decided to remain loyal to Marsat, at least until the campaign officially opened in April.

Diagne next met with Galandou Diouf, who had been trying with limited success to stimulate interest in the new candidacy. Mody M'Baye soon joined them, and the three discussed the most immediate problem of Diagne's campaign: how to build strong bases of support in Dakar and Saint-Louis. M'Baye convinced Diagne that the only way to capture any votes in Saint-Louis, where Devès and Carpot were strongest, was to ally with the rebellious Young Senegalese. But even though Diouf and M'Baye were greatly admired by the Young Senegalese, the cautious Thiécouta Diop managed to prevent his followers from hastily endorsing Diagne.

For over a month after Diagne's arrival in the colony the Young Senegalese argued over the choice of a candidate to back for deputy. At a meeting on March 18 Thiécouta Diop accused M'Baye of misappropriating from the Young Senegalese treasury certain funds that had been set aside as a contribution to *La Démocratie* to help support Jean Théveniaut's candidacy. Théveniaut had broken with d'Oxoby and his paper, and M'Baye had evidently taken the money and promised to found a new paper for the Young Senegalese, which he had not done. At a meeting of the club on March 20, Diop ridiculed M'Baye, called him a bandit, and censured him for spreading word that the Young Senegalese supported Diagne, whereas they had not yet chosen a candidate. Diop and the enraged M'Baye came to blows, and the meeting was adjourned.[15]

Two nights later, the Young Senegalese met again, and M'Baye was given the floor. He reviewed Diagne's career in the customs service and spoke glowingly of his great potential as a candidate. Here at last was a man who could deal with the French on their own terms because of his background, education, and excellent spoken French; moreover, Diagne could also speak to Africans on their own terms, since he could still muster passable Wolof. Finally, M'Baye charged that the French and Creoles had banded together to eliminate the Africans from politics, which made it necessary "to fight for our rights as French citizens."[16]

Diagne then faced the crowd, which had swollen to more than 800 Africans and about 30 Frenchmen. He reminded them that if a Negro had attempted to address such a crowd even ten years earlier, he would have been laughed down. "But today, reason and progress have changed that. One of your own people does not fear, despite the opposition, to ask you to help him become your representative so that he can help you with your grievances."[17] Diagne criticized the "infamous decree" of 1912, which directly attacked the political rights of the originaires. He then accused both François and Théodore Carpot, as well as Joost Van Vollenhoven, and Gabriel Angoulvant (both French administrators who would later become Governors-General of French West Africa) of implementing the decree and urging Paris to promulgate it.

And who opposed this, who protested it, who warned you of its implications? It was Mody M'Baye, was it not? Friends, they want to diminish our claim to French citizenship so that in another fifteen years there will be no more voters among us. From Cape Blanco to the remotest limit of our African colonies your fathers, your brothers, and yourselves have stood beside the French to conquer this vast domain. What kind of recompense is this for all the devotion we have shown toward France? . . . I ask myself, do we really belong to a democracy? We're no longer slaves. We're French citizens with the same rights as anybody else![18]

Diagne admitted that the job before him would be difficult; but he promised, if elected, to work for the abolition of all oppressive decrees and taxes aimed against the Africans of Senegal. The crowd was enthusiastic.

Diop stalled for time and still refused to commit the Young Senegalese to formally endorsing Diagne's campaign. But during the next few days, speaking at similar rallies, Diagne won the hearts of the young elite. They were convinced that this tall, handsome leader, who impressed even urban Frenchmen who came to hear him, should be their candidate. Diagne could inspire confidence in the young because he was an African who had achieved equality and success within the assimilationist system; he was a leader who could command respect as a Galandou Diouf could not.

Having established firm ties with the Young Senegalese, with M'Baye and his network of écrivains publics, and with d'Oxoby and Sergent, Diagne set about creating a committee to run his campaign. He appointed Diouf chief lieutenant and campaign manager; M'Baye was second in command and was in charge of soliciting votes outside the Communes. D'Oxoby, much impressed by Diagne's liberal views, offered the columns of his journal to the campaign. And eventually the flamboyant Frenchman made Diagne "political director" of *La Démocratie*; this title was printed in large letters on the masthead of each issue. Through all this Diop remained intractable, gave Diagne only tacit support, and jealously retained his titular leadership of the Young Senegalese. For this reason it was impossible for Diagne to transform the club into a true political party along French lines; Diop remained in control of the young members and Diagne was simply a candidate they endorsed. The young elite may have called itself *le parti jeune sénégalais* in the columns of *La Démocratie*, but Diagne's campaign was basically in the hands of his trusted advisers.

Diagne also had support from a few old acquaintances in Gorée, but this was of minimal importance owing to the island's decline in population. More important was Diagne's new friendship with Jules Sergent, who rallied many petits colons and small businessmen to Diagne's side and helped fill his campaign coffers. In Rufisque,

Diagne relied on Diouf's influence and a certain good will springing from the fact that Diagne's mother had lived in that city. Aside from this support, however, Diagne remained an unknown candidate for most Senegalese. To many, he resembled the "parachuted" Louis Dreyfus, whom Carpot had defeated in 1902; and he was linked in the popular mind with Henri Heimburger, also a new arrival from Paris.

Diagne and his lieutenants set out to change this. Numerous rallies were organized wherever voters might be located in an effort to spread Diagne's name throughout the colony. He traveled up and down the Dakar–Saint-Louis railway, visiting towns, villages, and whistle-stops. Evening *palabres* and house-to-house visits were organized to introduce Diagne to all Africans, voters or not. He sought both moral and financial support, asking Lebou and Wolof, Mouride and Tijani to make common cause on his behalf. For his part, M'Baye seized on the issue of the French-Creole effort to keep Africans out of politics. "Until today," he thundered, "only the whites and métis have campaigned for deputy. Today it is a black man like you or me that I give you!"[19] Diagne, however, who had suffered at least as much from the color bar and who was equally color-conscious, astutely underplayed this potent grievance. Unwilling to risk open hostility from white voters, he pursued a moderate line, emphasizing a reasonable outlook: "I am black, my wife is white, and my children are mixed. What better guarantee of my interest in representing all our population?"[20]

In his campaign statement of purpose (*profession de foi*) Diagne appealed to French voters by pointing to his years of faithful service in the customs corps, and claimed his ideas were based on "rational evolution, not brutal revolution."[21] On the other hand, he told the Africans that they deserved full equality, that the opposition feared them because they were finally awakening to political realities, and that his opponents were openly prejudiced against blacks. Diagne was able to project his anger and outrage at these injustices without seeming like a cheap demagogue.

## The Campaign and Elections of 1914

After several months of informal politicizing in the Communes and and the Protectorate, the official electoral campaign for the post of deputy got under way in April 1914. Nine candidates filed their petitions with Governor Cor in Saint-Louis. Diagne was first and Carpot second. The other major candidates—Administrator Jean Théveniaut, Fernand Marsat, Colonel Henri Patey, Louis Pellegrin, Georges

1. The fort and village of Saint-Louis in the early nineteenth century.

2. A waterfront in the port of Dakar, shortly after 1900.

3. Blaise Diagne, Senegal's first African deputy. The photo most likely dates from his first election as deputy in 1914.

4. The liberal journalist Jean Daramy d'Oxoby, one of Diagne's earliest supporters.

5. A marabout from eastern Senegal. From a late nineteenth-century print.

6. Joost Van Vollenhoven, Governor-General of French West Africa 1917–18.

7. William Ponty, Governor-General 1908–15.

8. The Governor-General's Palace in Dakar during the early 1900's (now the Presidential Palace).

9. After Diagne's electoral victory in the 1914 elections for deputy, Diagne and his lieutenants speak to a crowd of supporters.

10. François Carpot, deputy of Senegal from 1902 to 1914 and Diagne's chief opponent in two elections.

11. Louis Guillabert, Diagne's chief Creole lieutenant.

# SÉNÉGALAIS

Demain! Vous affirmerez à nouveau votre volonté inébranlable de rester « Libres ».

Demain! Vous irez tous aux urnes; toute défaillance serait un crime envers votre « Pays ».

Demain! Vous remettrez de nouveau à **Blaise DIAGNE**, le mandat qu'en 1914 vous lui aviez confié.

Demain! Verra la Victoire décisive du Prolétariat Africain sur les forces de réaction.

Sénégalais! Veillez à ce que demain — nos adversaires y songent — toutes leurs manœuvres soient impitoyablement réprimées.

Pour un Sénégal libre à tous.

**Le COMITE.**

12. A campaign poster for the 1919 election.

13. Lamine Guèye, one of Diagne's early
supporters (later deputy from Senegal).

14. Tirailleurs sénégalais and their officers, in Paris for the Bastille Day parade, 1913.

15. Senegalese troops from the 43d Battalion of Tirailleurs displaying their battle honors, 1918.

16. Galandou Diouf congratulating a sergeant of African troops in the early 1930's.

17. Diagne as deputy, in the early 1930's shortly before his death.

Crespin, and Henri Heimburger—filed within a few days. Finally an obscure civil servant, one Monsieur André of the public works department, also declared his candidacy.[22]

Never had there been so much interest in a Senegalese election. Usually, campaigning did not even begin until after the petitions were filed. But the break in Creole unity as Devès challenged Carpot, the African unrest in town and countryside, the tension built up by the decree of 1912, the emergence of groups like the Young Senegalese and the petits colons of Sergent, the appearance of an independent newspaper, *La Démocratie*—all of these combined to produce a climate of expectation that Senegal had never experienced. Moreover, the idea of an African running for deputy was greeted with suspicion and hostility in many quarters. None of the other candidates took Diagne seriously, and none would agree to meet him in public debate.

Carpot returned to Senegal several months in advance of the election to plan his campaign. He was publicly confident but secretly worried, for he had stirred up a hornets' nest with the Decree of August 16, 1912. Ironically, both Carpot and Governor-General Ponty, unknown to the general public, had long tried to have African rights increased. In February 1909, Ponty had drawn up a proposal to extend voting rights to Frenchmen and originaires living outside the Communes, and had recommended that certain qualified Africans in the Protectorate be given the vote as well.[23] But all that the conservative Ministry of Colonies would agree to was a decree applying to Frenchmen living outside the Communes, which was ordered in time for the 1910 election. Carpot had gone on record as approving Ponty's project. But this only seemed to associate him with the Ministry's exclusion of Africans, which was made explicit in the Decree of 1912.

After the 1912 decree came under attack by African radicals, Carpot realized that he would have to do something to counter the impression that he had authored it. He labored behind the scenes, trying to revive the 1909 Ponty project as a spectacular coup to regain the confidence of his originaire constituents. But in this attempt, which was reviewed by the Minister of Justice in Paris on January 10, 1914, Carpot admitted that he did not consider originaires to be French citizens; he thought they possessed only limited local voting rights, which he felt should be extended elsewhere in Senegal. In essence, he was trying to have Senegal's deputy legally recognized as representing all Senegal and not just the voters of the Four Communes.[24]

Carpot felt that he was bending over backward to help the Africans of the colony, but the local press took a cynical view of his actions. *L'A.O.F.*, the voice of the French community, complained that he was too liberal toward Africans, and that his plans to improve the treatment of Africans in the civil service would provide them with higher wages than workers in France.[25] *La Démocratie* complained that Carpot had come back to Senegal thinking he could give a few reassuring speeches and be elected. "But Monsieur Carpot did not realize that a great awakening had taken place among the young people during the past four years. He could not see this progress because he had not deigned to pay us a visit during that time."[26]

Carpot was even at odds with his own Creole community: Justin Devès had imported Heimburger to seek office, and Crespin and Pellegrin were also in the race. None of these four could see the handwriting on the wall, or realize that the Creoles' minority position might become untenable if the Africans seriously entered politics. Carpot could think only of reelection, for his twelve years in Paris had made a Parisian of him. Devès, after tasting power as mayor of Saint-Louis and president of the General Council, was determined that his candidate Heimburger win so that the Devès family could completely dominate local politics. Crespin, one of the few liberal voices in the General Council, wanted to bring new life to the Creole community; and Pellegrin, a solid merchant, intended to unseat Carpot and provide a powerful representative for Senegal's small businessmen. The Creole political leaders approached the impending election with little sense of reality, too preoccupied with factional rivalries to realize the hazards of disunity. Others were not so blind. As early as December 1913 *La Démocratie* had called for a change, and remarked: "Senegal has suffered far too much from these fratricidal battles between families."[27]

Justin Devès was more confident than Carpot, since he had managed to enlist some Bordeaux supporters for Heimburger, who rarely appeared in public. And the Devès machine in Saint-Louis was prepared to deliver a large Wolof vote, especially from the rotten borough of Guet N'Dar, where its control was unquestioned. The fisherfolk liked Devès, appreciated his gifts, and obeyed his orders. Their political outlook can best be summarized by the Wolof proverb *gane yomba na mougnal* ("the caprices of one's host are easy to tolerate"). They had previously voted for Carpot on orders from Devès; but now Heimburger, who shrank from meeting them in public, was announced as their candidate.

But even though some Senegalese voters could be bought for a sack of rice, elections in the Four Communes were not contests where voters ignored issues. Many African voters were illiterate, but they nevertheless discussed the merits and weaknesses of candidates by word of mouth. (As a result, police inspectors who visited rallies were forced to learn Wolof or have interpreters at their sides.) The Africans' rallies were not simple meetings where a candidate or his seconds spoke. All public meetings were organized according to French law, in which a presiding body (bureau) took charge, kept order, and introduced the speakers. The Senegalese took this French pattern and fused it with their traditional *palabres*, which meant that ten or twenty speakers might hold the floor at one meeting, with anyone from the floor having the right to challenge the speaker of the moment. Freedom of speech and assembly was largely unimpaired; only when tempers flared, rocks flew, or drums beat too loudly did police move in and break up a rally. In smaller assemblies at the village level, local family politics, neighborhood quarrels, and clan rivalries became part of the debate. But the larger rallies discussed the major issues, candidates, and alternatives, although the participants might talk around the subject endlessly in an African manner that perplexed police inspectors.[28]

The Wolof language was vital to Senegalese politics. It had resisted encroachments by Arabic and French for centuries, even though it was never written down; in a way, it was synonymous with the traditional Africa it helped to preserve. It was easy for casual observers of elections in Senegal, knowing no Wolof, to blandly assume that Africans, because they could neither read nor write French and could barely speak it, must be incapable of understanding politics. Nothing was further from the truth; and yet reports from inspectors, *chefs de cabinets*, specialists on native affairs and Governors reiterated this fallacy decade after decade.* Moreover, the fact that about 10 per cent of the Four Communes' inhabitants could read and write in 1914 was overlooked. Ideas, facts, and opinions spread swiftly in the urban areas and almost as swiftly through the rural suburbs, where some relative was always visiting.

The three Dakar newspapers, *L'A.O.F., Le Petit Sénégalais*, and *La Démocratie*, had a much wider influence than their combined press run of about 3,000 would suggest. All three were weeklies and en-

---

* Many of these critics were inspectors who visited the colony briefly and returned to France as "African experts" (like M. Verrier in the registration inspection of 1907). They forgot that France herself had some rural districts where illiterate Frenchmen made reasonably intelligent choices at the polls.

joyed considerable freedom during the Ponty administration. *Le Petit Sénégalais*, despite its conservative French editor, employed several African writers (such as Amadou Duguay-Clédor, later to become Diagne's chief lieutenant); and *La Démocratie* regularly published columns by M'Baye, Diagne, and Diouf. Even Eugène Ternaux, the pro-administration editor of *L'A.O.F.*, wrote that the campaign of 1914 was to the Africans' credit, for it showed they read newspapers, understood posters, knew the importance of political rallies, and could no longer be considered "automatic votes at five francs a head."[29]

The major issue at stake for Diagne was the preservation of voting and citizenship rights for Africans in the Four Communes. Whereas other candidates paid ambiguous lip service to this ideal or opposed it, Diagne made it the central point in his campaign: "They say you and I aren't French. I tell you that we are, that we have the same rights!"[30] Heimburger, prodded by Justin Devès, demanded to know if Africans really wanted full citizenship. Were they prepared to give up traditional law, follow the French civil code, and make themselves liable for military service? (Enormous Heimburger posters asked if the African voters were ready to join the French army.)[31] Moreover, he charged that Diagne had never voted in a Four Communes election and hence could not be a local citizen. Diagne replied that he had been baptized a Catholic, had married a French woman, and had been a loyal civil servant for almost 22 years; in short, he was "a citizen of the empire."* Moreover, he argued that his compatriots in the Communes were also full citizens, and that their customs, traditional or Muslim, should be respected. The French candidates laughed at this notion: how could an African with four wives, as koranic law allowed, possibly be considered a French citizen?

Other issues came up, and again Diagne was specific in the reforms he called for. He declared that the Lebous should be recompensed for their lost lands. He wanted to stop Senegal's contribution to French West Africa's budget—a tax that paid the lion's share of Dakar's administrative costs and drained Senegal's treasury—and instead create a Colonial Council empowered to vote a budget and raise funds for the entire federation.[32] He demanded that the head tax be abolished in all the Communes, pointing out that France's West

---

* Diagne then appraised Heimburger's patron: "M. Devès est noir aussi, mais il n'a pas une carrière comme la mienne, et il n'est pas marié avec une Française."

Indian colonies had no such burden. His wide experience abroad reinforced his argument. He pressed for the establishment of a medical school at Dakar, patterned after those France had established in Madagascar and Indochina, and for a full-fledged French lycée in Saint-Louis. He favored extensive social legislation that would provide such benefits as payments for expectant mothers, pensions for older workers, weekly sabbatical rest laws, and recognition of the Africans' right to organize labor unions. Drawing from his personal experience, Diagne argued that customs rates should be altered to favor the small businessman. He charged that the Bordeaux firms were favored by the current arrangement, but declared: "Those sharks and their agents are bewildered to think that natives will now freely use their votes and will be joined by many French workers."[33]

François Carpot's response to Diagne's energetic campaign was ineffectual. He issued striking purple posters that reiterated his old campaign slogans from 1906 and 1910, but did little else and rarely appeared in public. His only fresh effort for the new campaign was the publicizing of his successful effort to have the Decree of 1912 modified. The reform had come on March 9, 1914, altering the decree to provide that originaires would always be tried by French courts regardless of where they were in Senegal. This change was directly opposed to the views of Governor Cor and his ally Administrator Brocard of Sine-Saloum, who both felt that Africans should remain liable to summary administrative justice if they were tried in the Protectorate. In fact, the change did show Carpot's concern for African welfare; but it seemed insignificant to an African electorate that wanted major changes. Diagne spoke to the heart of the issue: "We are convinced that you will go to the polls with one purpose in mind: your complete [political] emancipation. To demand justice for yourselves is not to eliminate it for others."[34]

Diagne's electoral campaign gathered momentum all through April. But his principal opponents remained unperturbed, each certain of his own victory. *L'A.O.F.*, which supported Heimburger and considered Diagne a racist, was forced to admit: "Blaise Diagne is the only candidate who is really campaigning with such energy that he is attracting attention on all sides. If elected, he will have neglected nothing. He alone is conducting a campaign as it would be conducted in France."[35] Nevertheless, the French and Creole communities refused to take Diagne seriously, and election day on April 26 produced a real shock for them.[36] The vote went as follows:

| Blaise Diagne | 1,910 | Henri Patey | 365 |
| François Carpot | 671 | Louis Pellegrin | 252 |
| Henri Heimburger | 668 | Georges Crespin | 71 |
| Fernand Marsat | 516 | Miscellaneous | 2 |
| Jean Théveniaut | 408 | | |

The implications were clear: too many French and Creole candidates had divided the vote, and Diagne had profited. His victory was not a majority of registered voters, however, and a runoff election was proclaimed for May 10. The specter of an African deputy in Paris alarmed the lethargic French business community; the possibility of an African winning Senegal's leading political post rudely awoke the Creoles. It was apparent that if four or five other candidates pooled their resources, Diagne could be defeated. Both Frenchmen and Creoles determined to act before it was too late.

On April 30, the Hotel Agard in Rufisque was the scene of a hastily convened meeting of all candidates but Diagne; a number of important agents and merchants were also present. Frenchmen and Creoles argued over what course to follow, and how to bridge the gulf that separated them. Carpot asked to be named the coalition candidate, since he had come in second to Diagne. The Devès were intractable and would not agree to this; in fact, Justin Devès clung to his plan for a puppet deputy and finally convinced the caucus after much argument that the man who divided them least was Heimburger. The Parisian lawyer won a vote of confidence (30–3); Bordeaux and Saint-Louis petits colons and administrators were now allied against the Africans and Diagne.[37] When it became apparent that the real issue was one of color, however, the three Creole candidates walked out of the meeting. Carpot, refusing to believe his constituents would abandon him, thought victory was imminent and stayed in the race. But Crespin and Pellegrin were shocked by the emergence of a color bar and gave their support to Diagne.[38] The Creole community as a whole committed political suicide by dividing its support between Heimburger, Carpot, and Diagne.

The ensuing campaign was a vicious one. Diagne was painted as a hypocrite and a demagogue, a bigoted rascal who sought to introduce racial strife into the colony. Muslims were told that he was a nonpracticing Catholic, had sold his soul to the Freemasons, and had applied to the grand marabout of Saint-Louis for circumcision in order to win their votes and sleep with their women. French merchants refused to give further credit to African customers who would not agree to support Heimburger. Mayor Masson of Dakar threatened to cut off the water and electricity of the Africans unless they ceased campaigning for Diagne. Rumors had it that all appointed chiefs and African civil servants would be dismissed if Diagne won.[39]

Loyal Africans were brought forward to speak in favor of the official candidate. For example, Jean Thiam, a respected jeweller and merchant of Gorée, said that he, like Diagne, had traveled far and wide in Europe and Africa; this experience had convinced him that Africans should keep in their place and show gratitude by electing the French candidate.[40] And once again the question of whether Diagne was a citizen was raised in speeches and in the French press. Editor Ternaux acidly observed in *L'A.O.F.*: "It's absurd to imagine that a native deputy could have the slightest bit of influence in parliament. Furthermore, he couldn't sit there because he's not a citizen."[41]

Diagne countered this onslaught with front-page editorials in *La Démocratie*. His opponents' attacks, he said, were being made "not on behalf of certain ideas or issues but in the name of that abomination racial prejudice."[42] To counteract certain heated remarks that he and M'Baye had let slip earlier in the campaign, Diagne wrote: "We have also said that this country belongs to the three races who live here, and equally. We want justice and legal rights for everybody. To seek these for the natives, however, does not mean that we intend to suppress them for others."[43] When Mayor Masson threatened to turn off water and lights in Dakar, and when Bordeaux cut off credit to Africans, Diagne persuaded African food merchants not to open their stalls in the markets; and he threatened to call for a general strike of all African labor unless the French desisted. Even Governor-General Ponty did not escape Diagne's charges of bias and illegal attempts to influence the election.[44] Diagne's followers issued posters portraying him as a true socialist and a friend of the people; Heimburger was depicted as a capitalist reactionary. Thus the vocabulary of metropolitan politics entered the struggle.

*Le Petit Sénégalais*, in trying to understand what had happened, attributed Diagne's success to his dynamic personality:

After the thunderous electoral rally of April 19, the cause of Blaise Diagne was already won. The Lebous could believe that their community would be totally revived by this man, who seemed more powerful than all others . . . . The mayors of Gorée, Dakar, and Rufisque were swiftly abandoned with great enthusiasm. Even the great benefactor of the Lebous, Monsieur Marsat, was betrayed.[45]

*L'A.O.F.* agreed that Diagne had made a spectacular impression during his campaign tours. A Diagne rally was the first time many Africans had heard one of their own people openly speak back to the French. "The thrilled blacks see in him a superior man, predestined for the greatest of public careers."[46]

Even in such a race-oriented campaign, the battle lines were not drawn exclusively on color. The Devès brothers managed to retain their large bloc of bought votes among the Wolofs of Guet N'Dar. Marsat still had the support of many of the older Lebou diambours. And Carpot, though greatly weakened, had scattered Wolof and Creole followers whose votes he refused to release. Crespin and Pellegrin swung some Creole support to Diagne. D'Oxoby and Sergent worked tirelessly to enlist petits colons of all types—petty clerks, small businessmen, independent agents, and others who were willing to give Diagne a chance because he was a government employee like themselves. Besides, he promised tariff relief, an issue that the other candidates ignored.

Carpot's stubbornness proved to be the deciding factor on the second ballot. The vote was close: Diagne, 2,424; Heimburger, 2,249; and Carpot, 472.[47] Diagne held on to his first ballot supporters and picked up more Africans and a few Creoles. The French-Creole consortium could possibly have triumphed if Carpot had cooperated and thrown his support to Heimburger. But whatever the reasons for their defeat, the French and Creoles now had to face the question they had ignored for so long: how to come to terms with the African majority in the Communes.

## The Aftermath

Diagne's victory seemed to take everyone by surprise. From Paris, a dazed Ministry of Colonies demanded an explanation; and complaints from the Bordeaux merchants poured into Governor-General Ponty's office. The older Saint-Louisian Wolofs charged the younger Wolofs, active in the Young Senegalese, with selling out to the Lebous and Diagne. Congratulatory letters for Diagne arrived from Senegalese expatriate groups in Dahomey, Guinea, and Ivory Coast. The Young Senegalese were jubilant; Diagne's election was a personal victory for each one of them against all griefs, real or imaginary, inflicted by the French. The Lebous were ecstatic, supposing that Diagne would immediately find a way to reimburse them for their lost lands. The Lebanese and Moroccans, now important business minorities in Dakar, hastened to pledge future financial support to Diagne, since they could not vote.[48]

The most profound reactions were in the Protectorate. The

Mourides—specifically, Amadou Bamba and his brother Cheikh Anta M'Backé—had donated funds that made possible much of Diagne's campaign.[49] Consequently, many Mourides thought that Diagne's triumph would protect them from further persecution by the French administration. Elsewhere, Serere peasants supposedly believed that Diagne would restore lands taken away from them centuries earlier by Wolof invaders; and administrators reported rumors that Diagne would lower the head tax, reduce the prices of millet and rice, and eventually replace the Governor-General himself.[50] These and other stories soon created a mystique that surrounded Diagne in every part of Senegal.

Diagne had fully earned his victory. He was the first candidate in over a half-century of Senegalese elections to break away from the cynicism of rotten-borough politics by appealing to the intelligence of the voters. He doubtlessly profited from his role as an underdog pitted against the Bordeaux interests and the colonial administration. He also benefited from the secret ballot, first used in Senegal in this election. Many Africans paraded into the booths displaying marked ballots given them by their patrons but once in private substituted ballots of their own choice.[51] This was probably the most honest election ever held in the Four Communes, despite the stakes involved. There were few cases of stuffed ballot boxes, voters casting two or three ballots, and altered registration lists composed of names from graveyards—all standard practice in most Senegalese contests.

Diagne was aided immeasurably by *La Démocratie* and its editor, who gave him the means to make his case known and to answer opponents who refused public debate. D'Oxoby and Sergent also did much to persuade the petits colons to help finance Diagne's campaign. Diagne had left Marseille in January for Senegal with meager resources.[52] Apparently Assane N'Doye raised some funds from the Lebous in Dakar, and Diouf from the Lebous in Rufisque; it is doubtful if any Young Senegalese funds went to Diagne, since Thiécouta Diop's support of his candidacy was minimal. The greatest single financial support for Diagne came from the Mourides; Diagne's friendship with Amadou Bamba during Bamba's exile in Gabon was undoubtedly a major reason for this.

Diagne's victory perplexed Governor-General Ponty, who blamed the situation on Senegal's bizarre electoral traditions. Acting Governor Raphael Antonetti wrote Ponty from Saint-Louis that perhaps Diagne could be bought off by a lucrative civil-service post in France; but as a good republican Antonetti felt this would be "grossly immoral." Ponty, also a fervent republican and still liberal toward Africans, agreed, and omitted this suggestion in his report to Paris.[53] Ponty's feelings about the whole affair were ambivalent: he made no attempt to have the election invalidated, which he certainly could have arranged; on the other hand, he was annoyed with Diagne for complaining to the Ministry that he had tried to pressure African civil servants to vote for Heimburger.

Governor Antonetti's letter pointed out that from the beginning Diagne had told the Africans they were a majority of the electorate and therefore held the balance of power. This had made an especially great impression on the Lebous, whose marabouts had whipped their followers to a pitch of fanatical excitement. It also rallied together the Young Senegalese, of whom Antonetti said: "All of these young men, some of whom are quite commendable, suffer from having very modest resources and limited opportunities."[54] More perceptive than his immediate superior, Governor Cor, who had gone on leave, Antonetti also commented:

The coming of Blaise Diagne profoundly affected [the masses]. He personified the realization of their wildest dreams—a black man who wasn't afraid to attack the whites, who often spoke to them with disdain, who declared (quite truthfully) that he was superior to most of them. Diagne had his newspaper, he campaigned mightily . . . he spoke in public on a platform. He exalted the most secret African desires: "Today him, tomorrow me." He opened a door through which all hoped to pass. They dreamed of the public offices they would have. The General Council, the municipal councils—all of it would fall into their hands.[55]

Antonetti claimed that Marsat or Patey, who were known to many local people, might possibly have won the election if Justin Devès had not insisted on running Heimburger. This contrasted with the situation in the African camp, where many Saint-Louisian Wolofs had united with the southern Lebous, whom they ordinarily held in low esteem, to elect Diagne.

Antonetti saw several future consequences of the election. Although Diagne was highly intelligent, politically astute, and responsible, his victory had engendered a new, irrational political climate that could become dangerous. Diagne's election was a victory for the younger Senegalese over the more conservative older generation. The two generations had frequently misunderstood each other in the past, and few older men had taken the younger educated men seriously. But Diagne's campaign awakened some older Africans to new ideas, so that their camp was split, some supporting Diagne and the young men and others remaining faithful to the old order.* Antonetti expected the election to have even more serious effects on the Protectorate. He quoted an important chief:

> I suspect . . . that Blaise Diagne and company will try to make our charges believe that they hold [ultimate] authority and can run the colony. At that point it is they who will be listened to and we chiefs who will be disobeyed. I have good reason to believe the new party will make common cause with the marabouts, since both have obscure backgrounds and will never accept the fact that we should hold authority by traditional right.[56]

This was a direct confirmation of Islam's tremendous influence on the Senegalese political scene—and of the fact that Islam was hated by French and Creoles in the Communes and many traditional chiefs in the interior. Despite Diagne's Catholic background and present Freemasonry, he was adopted wholeheartedly by the Muslim communities, whether Tijaniyya and Qadiriyya in the Communes or Mouridiyya in the bush. Other chiefs also complained that the example of Diagne and the Young Senegalese encouraged similar young radicals in the rural provinces and paved the way for marabout influence. Senegal's proud traditional chiefs, once opposed to French advance, were now anxious to cooperate with the French against the Muslims, who seemed to threaten what was left of traditional life.

At the end of his report, Antonetti discussed the general attitude of the French merchants in Dakar and Rufisque. Most of these men, he said, favored abolishing local municipal institutions if the followers of Diagne seemed likely to take over local government. "They can accept the rise of Blaise Diagne, who is educated and cultivated, but they abhor the thought that his ignorant followers might come to power."[57] Antonetti closed by remarking that unless the electoral laws were changed Senegal had difficult years ahead. Even the liberal Ponty was taken aback by the implications of African political power. His next report to Paris stated: "The present electoral system . . . represents a dangerous situation for the future of white men in Africa."[58]

Like Antonetti, Ponty rejected the notion of buying off Diagne. But he did write the Ministry that he thought Diagne was not a registered voter in the Communes and was therefore ineligible for office —a questionable argument, considering that Heimburger was also unregistered in Senegal.[59] In the event, the French officials in Sene-

---

* Antonetti mentioned one older notable who reasoned: "Our young men have as much education as the whites; maybe they are just as smart." But others argued: "We owe everything to the whites; no question of race should be raised in this election." Antonetti to Ponty, June 10, 1914. ARS, 20-G-21.

gal did nothing to prevent Diagne from taking his seat; and the Ministry of Colonies also took no action, except to forward protests and arguments to the Chamber of Deputies. The African's unexpected victory was a turn of events that the Ministry was simply not prepared to face.

The opposition candidates did not capitulate so easily, however. Justin Devès soon appeared before the Electoral Commission in Saint-Louis, which had the responsibility of validating election results, and demanded that Diagne's victory be annulled. Heimburger drew up a complaint for Devès, which was also endorsed by Théveniaut and Marsat, and was eventually attached to the Electoral Commission's report; it demanded that the election be invalidated because Diagne was not a French citizen and was not eligible to sit in the Chamber.[60] This protest was supported by the Bordeaux merchants and other French colonial interests, who feared that once Diagne took office the floodgates would be opened for any African to aspire to high elective office. After all, they argued, republican institutions had been given to Senegal on the supposition that Frenchmen, or at least highly assimilated Creoles, would be elected.

Carpot was humiliated at his defeat by an unknown upstart and filed a separate complaint with the Chamber of Deputies, hoping to gain a hearing from his former colleagues. His views were summarized in the final report presented by G. Leredu of the Credential Committee to the Chamber on July 7, 1914.

(It is alleged that) Monsieur Diagne preached . . . racial strife during the entire campaign making the native voters (who comprise eight-tenths of the electorate) believe that the French and Creoles of Senegal considered them mere slaves and capitalizing on this to call for their awakening and emancipation. [He] was aided in this campaign by the marabouts, who induced a great many voters to swear on the Koran to vote for Diagne . . . . The marabouts proclaimed that anyone failing to vote for Diagne would not be considered among the faithful and could not be married or buried according to Islamic law.[61]

But the complaints of disgruntled candidates and the arguments of William Ponty seemed to fall on deaf ears in the Chamber. Leredu's report was sympathetic to the historic voting rights of the originaires and declared that Diagne's victory was legitimate within the special context of Senegalese politics. The committee members did not attempt to pronounce on whether Diagne was a citizen; but they were obviously impressed with Diagne's arguments that he had served as a French civil servant for over two decades, had voted in numerous colonial elections, had been married in France to a Frenchwoman, had exercised the functions of criminal judge in Madagascar, and had served as a member of the Saint-Laurent municipal commission in Guiana. To Heimburger's argument that Diagne had not fulfilled his military service obligation, Leredu answered that because Africans were barred from the regular French Army, this was not possible, and thus Diagne was not liable for service.[62] After considering each complaint, Ponty's report, and the statement of the Electoral Commission of Senegal, the Credentials Committee had voted to seat Diagne as a deputy without any further questions.

Justin Devès still thought he could control the deputyship, and arranged for Heimburger to be appointed as "special consultant" to the Ministry of Colonies. This appointment was supported by the Devès-controlled General Council, which voted an annual salary for Heimburger. But when the Parisian lawyer called on the Ministry of Colonies, he was politely informed by the Chef de Cabinet that the Minister would not receive "this kind of deputy, elected outside of constitutional law."[63] The Devès scheme collapsed, and Heimburger faded from the political scene.

In 1914 Diagne was on the threshold of a great career, flushed with the thrill of victory. The election was his personal triumph; he had united the forces of discontent in Senegal and had given the colony its first serious electoral campaign. To a vigorous people who had finally found their champion, he penned these lines after the first ballot:

Springing from the heart of our native society, we had as much right as anyone to seek this high office and honor, and did so without resorting to cheap demagoguery. We kept ourselves on a high moral plane without falling prey to numerous traps put in our way. Now we are rewarded by the historic spectacle of Senegalese democracy breaking the chains of darkness and aspiring to certain liberty by means of the ballot.[64]

◇◇◇◇◇◇◇◇◇◇◇◇◇◇◇◇◇◇◇◇◇◇◇◇◇◇◇◇◇◇◇◇◇◇◇◇◇◇◇◇◇◇◇◇◇◇◇◇◇◇◇

## CHAPTER 10

# The Quest for Political Assimilation

THE VICTORY of Blaise Diagne in 1914 caused an immediate realignment of Senegal's political structure. The deputyship, in Creole hands since 1902, now became the preserve of the new African group. The General Council and the municipal government of Saint-Louis remained in the hands of Justin Devès; Dakar, Gorée, and Rufisque were controlled by French mayors. The three institutions of local government were thus almost evenly divided between French, Creoles, and Africans. How long this arrangement would last was a matter for speculation. Diagne was well aware of this fact, and took steps to consolidate his position before leaving for Paris at the end of May 1914. Galandou Diouf was appointed his chief lieutenant for political affairs in Senegal, with Jean Daramy d'Oxoby second in command. Diouf was specifically responsible for Rufisque, and d'Oxoby and Jules Sergent were in charge of Dakar. Thiécouta Diop, now reluctantly reconciled to Diagne's ascendancy, was made responsible for Saint-Louis, Mody M'Baye for Diourbel and the important railway areas, and Ambroise Mendy for Dakar and Gorée.[1]

The African elite, encouraged by Diagne's victory, now voiced its long-standing frustrations in the local press. Maurice Delafosse, a colonial administrator and a professor of African languages, was attacked by the young Africans for suggesting that the time had come to end assimilation in Senegal because it was hypocritical for France to allow two classes of Africans in one colony when justice demanded only one, that of sujet français.[2] Mody M'Baye, in a series of polemical articles in La Démocratie, declared that there were also two kinds of Frenchman: one served France loyally and believed in the principles of 1789; the other thought of himself as a free agent in the colonies, seeking to make a huge profit in Africa and then return to France. M'Baye said that Africans were now able to distinguish between these two types, and to show the first respect and the second defiance.[3]

Several questions were left unanswered by the election. Most important was the status of the originaires: were they French citizens, with full rights and duties, or were they something else? During the campaign, Diagne had claimed to be a French citizen and had repeatedly told the urban Africans, "You are citizens." The Credentials Committee had refused to rule on whether he was a citizen but had seated him nevertheless. Those who believed that originaires were citizens because they voted and lived under French law in the full communes of Senegal could now argue that Diagne's presence in the Chamber was proof of their contention. Their opponents pointed out that the originaires' rights had developed as an historic accident, that most of them were governed by Muslim law in personal and family matters, and that Diagne was either a special case or was in office illegally.

The Chamber's refusal to clarify Diagne's status implied that the question would be left to the courts—an ominous implication for the originaires, since court decisions after 1900 had consistently gone against them. True, the 1912 decree had been modified in 1914 to assure that originaires would not be liable to summary administrative justice in the Protectorate; but it was cynically observed that this had been done as an election expediency by Carpot and would soon be changed. Diagne had made the clarification of his constituents' political rights his primary campaign promise. He now addressed the herculean task of trying to do something about it.

A second question, directly related to the question of political rights, had also been raised during the election. If the originaires aspired to citizenship, argued hostile French observers, they should be liable for service in the French army. The same argument was made by Africans who sought to confirm their citizenship; in fact, many Africans had tried to enlist in the French army but had been barred by discriminatory regulations (Africans could not even join the Foreign Legion). This issue inflamed many originaires as much as the citizenship question; in fact, it proved to be the first major issue confronting Diagne after his arrival in Paris.

## The Senegalese and the French Army

The Wolofs of the Senegalese coast were among the first Africans to be associated with a European military force. Since the founding of Fort Saint-Louis in 1659, Africans had been employed on a random basis as guards, interpreters, and messengers by the chartered companies that operated in Senegal. And after the establishment of crown rule at Gorée in 1765, Governor de Mesnager created for the first time a regular corps of *laptots*, or African marines. The troops were divided into two sections, freemen and former slaves. The freemen were required to dress French-style, and those attaining the rank of sergeant were given long waistcoats and hats trimmed with silver. The former slaves were dressed rather like Turks, with white turbans, short jackets, and full trousers.[4]

The laptots of Gorée disappeared after the French lost the island to the British. African troops were next used on a regular basis in 1789, when Governor Blanchot raised two companies of volunteer African infantrymen at Saint-Louis. This corps of Senegalese served in the town and vessels trading along the river and the nearby coast; they proved extremely valuable during the years the colony was cut off from France, since few replacements arrived for the French forces in Senegal. These troops were disbanded in 1809, when the British captured Saint-Louis.[5] During the 1820's a shortage of French troops prompted the Governor of Senegal to reform the African auxiliary units for use as needed. Some troops were recruited for service in Madagascar on an enlistment of fourteen years;[6] and a few years later others were enlisted for service in French Guiana.[7]

The principal problem in Senegalese units was friction between slaves and freemen, which continued until France emancipated slaves throughout her empire in 1848. Military service then became less desirable to some Africans, who had previously found it more attractive than slavery. By 1854, when Faidherbe took over the governorship of Senegal, the African forces were depleted and of little value. But more native soldiers were needed if France were to move inland, and the new Governor recruited many African units for his campaigns against the Moors and Al Hajj Umar. In 1857 Louis Napoléon belatedly sanctioned Faidherbe's plan by officially creating an infantry battalion of Senegalese. These were called the *tirailleurs sénégalais* and were the first permanent African unit in the French army. Men were recruited for two-year enlistments and drew exactly the same pay as their French counterparts. This battalion was the first to wear the familiar uniform of fez, red sash, and Turkish trousers.[8]

Senegalese were recruited for service everywhere in the French Empire. They fought during the Crimean War, went with the French to Mexico under Maximilian, and battled with Frenchmen in vain to repulse the Germans in 1870–71. Heroes emerged to become a part of French Senegal's oral history. N'Gam Seck became Faidherbe's flag bearer, Lieutenant Alioune Macodé Sal defeated the chief of the Trarza Moors at Lake Cayor. Bouel Mogdad explored Mauritania for the French. Meissa Ley rescued Governor Pinet-Laprade from enemy hands during the campaigns in Rip. Men like these were as famous among urban Africans as heroes of resistance to the French were in the Protectorate.[9] Raymond Auriac, the French editor of *L'Union Africaine* (one of Senegal's first independent newspapers), also praised the African soldiers: "With the help of these natives of Senegal we have been able to succeed in many difficult undertakings. . . . With the aid of the Senegalese race we have been able to introduce civilization and the French spirit into our other colonies in West Africa."[10]

The question of military service and its relationship to the status of originaires arose soon after the General Council was reinstituted. As early as 1882 African Muslims asked for the right to serve in the regular French army (rather than in separate African units). This problem was discussed often during the next two decades. In 1902, the Governor of Senegal wrote to Paris on the subject:

[This is a country where] all of the towns have been endowed for many years with European organization, inhabited by people subject to our laws and, up to a certain point, our customs; and they consider themselves so thoroughly French that their principal goal at present is to obtain the right, sanctioned by Paris, to accomplish their military service without restriction.[11]

In 1904 provision was made for conscripting West Africans for service in the French colonial army, in case enlistments sagged. And in 1905 France reduced the service obligations of Frenchmen to two years in an effort to build up reserves more rapidly. The Comité de l'Afrique Française, one of the most important colonial lobbies, argued that the time had come to enlist more African troops. But again, these troops were to serve in the colonial army. No mention was made of Senegalese soldiers serving in France.

In February 1910 the Chamber of Deputies authorized using Senegalese troops to help with the occupation of Algeria, since so many French troops were needed on the Rhine. Jean Jaurès led the opposition to this measure, and he was vigorously supported by François Carpot.[12] Finally, a commission headed by General Charles Mangin was sent to Africa to assess the situation. For five months Mangin and his staff toured the Communes and the countryside, talking with chiefs, administrators, and other regional officials; his report concluded that it would be possible to recruit up to 40,000 Africans annually for service in the French colonial army.[13]

By 1912, with European tensions mounting, the Chamber decided to follow Mangin's recommendations and create a much larger African corps. The Decree of February 7, 1912, provided that French West Africans between the ages of 20 and 28 could be conscripted for four years. However, this process was to be carried out through traditional political structures—that is, local chiefs would be empowered to raise the necessary men. Carpot, annoyed that his constituents would now be liable to the draft, attacked the government for promulgating the decree without adequate discussion and authorization by parliament; and in December he moved a resolution calling upon the government to totally renounce the idea of conscripting Africans.[14] The motion failed, but the Minister of Colonies agreed that conscription would be moderate, so that native feelings would not be injured. This meant that before 1914 roughly 10,000 Africans per year were conscripted.[15]

For all this time, the originaires had been demanding the right to serve in the regular French army rather than the colonial troops, since anybody in West Africa who was considered a French citizen automatically performed his service with the metropolitan troops on duty there. Buell notes: "The government originally decided to conscript them into the metropolitan army upon the same basis as Europeans. After they had served four months, the government discharged the originaires without giving any reason."[16] Because originaires were not allowed to join the French army, they were also exempted from service in the colonial troops. In 1911 the members of the General Council had again called on Paris to allow Senegalese citizens, regardless of color, to perform their military obligations; and in 1912 Carpot had asked if Senegalese might volunteer for the Foreign Legion. The first request was ignored and the second refused.

Meanwhile, Mangin's plan for recruiting soldiers from the Protectorate got under way. The recruiters had fair success until August 1913, when enlistments fell off. To stimulate interest, the colors of the First Regiment of Tirailleurs were paraded by smartly attired soldiers through the streets of Saint-Louis and Dakar; and over 300 chiefs from all parts of Senegal were brought in to participate in the ceremonies. This effort was a resounding success, and enlistments returned to normal.[17] By 1914, however, many areas of Senegal that had cheerfully furnished men in the past had become reluctant to cooperate with the authorities. Young Lebous living south of Cape Verde simply moved to Dakar or Rufisque to avoid conscription. The same happened in Baol, where growing resentment was reported. Special parties of French soldiers were assigned to prevent the young men of Thiès from fleeing to Rufisque. The usually cooperative

Serere peasants now complained that their sons should not be taken if the Lebous were going to escape military service.[18]

Acting Governor Antonetti blamed the originaires for much of this unrest. "The opposition that one encounters among the natives of the Four Communes has, since the election of a deputy from their race, created a clear danger because of the deplorable example they set for neighboring tribes."[19] The originaires were in a difficult position. They desired incorporation in the regular French army and were refused. In order to press their claims for this right they refused to serve in the colonial troops; and they could not be forced to serve because they were not sujets françaises. By 1914 the originaires' freedom from conscription was envied by young men throughout the Protectorate.

### The Diagne Laws of 1915 and 1916

France's entry into World War I created innumerable problems overnight. Not the least of these was manpower, and Mangin's thesis that West Africa could furnish substantial numbers of men was now tested. Recruiting rose from under 10,000 per year to more than 30,-000 during the first year of the war.[20] African troops were quickly brought to France and sent into the trenches. France's "reservoir" of black manpower now became a real asset.

At the outbreak of hostilities, Blaise Diagne had served in the Chamber for only six weeks. He had identified with his intellectual heroes, the Socialists, and had taken his seat on the left of the Chamber. It was never apparent why Diagne had been seated in spite of the many objections to his election. But the Chamber of 1914 was liberal in composition and progressive in outlook. The elections of that year had returned 102 Socialists, as against 72 in the previous Chamber; the Radicals lost six seats but remained the strongest party in the Chamber with 136 delegates; and the Republican Socialists and Independent Socialists together picked up 30 seats. The Left now had close to an absolute majority in the Chamber, with a total of 268 seats. Moreover, a new Ministry of Colonies was formed on June 14, at the precise moment Diagne's credentials were being examined.[21] The combination of a liberal Chamber and a new, untested Ministry had worked to Diagne's advantage.

The declaration of war captured the imagination of the new deputy, who could easily see that France was soon going to need every man available, regardless of race. On August 3 he telegraphed Galandou Diouf in Senegal:

In the light of yesterday's events, I appeal to you to ask the administration that we be allowed to defend our own territory by enlisting for the duration of the war in the French corps stationed in Senegal. . . . [They should] recognize that all our people are worthy of the rights and duties of citizens, especially after my election. Notify the Governor-General and our compatriots of this [plan] while I tell the Ministry.[22]

Diouf cabled back the next day: "Will demand extraordinary session of the General Council in order to make patriotic appeal and ask for the enlistment of all ages twenty to forty. Bravo!"[23] Diouf then visited Ponty and told him that the originaires definitely expected to serve in the metropolitan French troops stationed in Senegal and not in the tirailleurs sénégalais. Ponty was impressed by the sincerity of the offer and promised he would discuss the matter with the local French commander. Diouf also spread the news to Diagne's lieutenants and supporters throughout the colony. The young Africans were enthusiastic,* especially since the intent of Diagne's plan was perfectly clear: the war had precipitated consideration of military service and citizenship for originaires, an issue that would otherwise have bogged down in the courts.

But hope was short-lived. On August 16 Ponty wrote Diouf that the law on recruiting forbade voluntary enlistments for the duration of the conflict, at least for those who were not otherwise liable to serve.

Nevertheless, in view of your many ardent manifestations of patriotic sentiment since the start of mobilization, and because of the numerous requests for enlistment, I have asked the Minister of Colonies to obtain from the Government a special authorization to accept enlistments from native volunteers of this colony.[24]

Diagne, however, wanted to hold firm. He cabled Diouf to go slowly, to win acceptance among local originaires of the idea that they should not fight unless given full rights and privileges:

We must show that we are no longer inferior to our brothers in the Antilles, Guiana, and Réunion in the sense of responsibility that we bring to our patriotism. . . . This is a chance to prove to the many Negrophobe functionaries in French West Africa that we are truly worthy of our status as voters and French citizens.[25]

---

* At the very outbreak of the war, Mody M'Baye had written a call to arms that showed the depth of assimilation in the Communes: "Faithful to the ancestral tradition of our Communes, we demand the privilege of marching side by side with the French and mulattoes to fight our hereditary enemy. . . . We believe we will accomplish a sacred task by combating the German enemy; hate for him is as profoundly rooted in us as in those who were subject to his cruelties in 1870." *La Démocratie*, Aug. 14, 1914.

Diagne added that Senegal's originaires must pay for the honor of being represented in Paris; and that if they were to serve in the French forces, Diagne's position in Paris would be strengthened and he could present their grievances on other subjects. He noted that he had the support of the director of African Affairs and the director of the Military Section of the Colonial Ministry.[26]

Diagne wrote to Senegal frequently during the first two months of war. In some of these communiqués he gave his own interpretation of why the war had started. "In effect it is ourselves, the French of overseas territories, that the Germans had in mind in attacking France, land of law and justice. It is our homeland that the savages of Central Europe would like to annex by iron and fire."[27] To set an example of patriotism, Diagne joined the army, announcing to his friends in Senegal that he was now a private in the Fourth Regiment of the Line.[28] During the war, however, mobilized deputies were allowed to stay in the Chamber as long as it was in session. After parliament returned to Paris from Bordeaux on December 22, 1914, it met continuously until the end of the war; hence Diagne saw little active service.

Throughout the long winter of 1914–15, Diagne continued to lobby for incorporating the originaires in the regular army. In Senegal, Diouf held the line by persuading urban Africans not to join up until their status had been clarified.[29] But recruiting continued in the interior. Even Bouna N'Diaye, claimant to the title Bourba of Djolof, notified the Governor in September that he wanted to go to France and fight for the French cause.[30] During the first four months of 1915, Amadou Bamba produced 551 men for enlistments; the French found his followers good soldiers "because they have already been trained by Mouride discipline."[31] The French changed their recruiting tactics, relying more on persuasion (Antonetti admitted that in the past many administrators had used *la chasse à l'homme* to fill quotas).[32] Nevertheless, many young men still avoided their homes, fearing the recruiting teams. Since intensive recruiting had begun in 1912, few Africans had returned on furlough; and speculation grew that those who joined the army would never return.

Early in 1915 Diagne visited Senegal to urge his originaire constituents not to be cajoled into joining the colonial troops. Antonetti was furious at this interference, and at Diagne's charge that Africans were being used to fill up the garrisons so that Frenchmen could leave the army and return to business. He reported that Diagne's cause had been lost because of its insistence on equal rights; in fact, **Diagne** was now "a dangerous obstructionist."[33] The Acting Governor reiterated Governor Cor's statement that the originaires should be treated like all other natives in West Africa. Under the present arrangement, Africans from the Protectorate were infuriated because they had no political rights but were required to serve, whereas the originaires had privileges but no duty.

Diagne returned to Paris convinced that he must act. On April 1, as the Chamber was discussing routine business pertaining to conscription of men in the 1917 contingent, he arose and asked that an amendment be added giving the originaires in the 1899–1916 groups the chance to join French troops serving in Equatorial and West Africa. The Minister of War, Alexandre Millerand, interrupted and suggested that Diagne's amendment should be taken up separately at a later date. Diagne replied that since August 1914 he had tried unsuccessfully to get a decision from the War Ministry on his request, which was also supported by Minister of Colonies Gaston Doumergue and Governor-General William Ponty. "If we can come here to legislate, we are French citizens; and if we are, we demand the right to serve as all French citizens do."[34] There was loud applause; Diagne had made his point, and the question of the originaires' military status was now referred to committee for study. This was Diagne's maiden speech in the Chamber; but in the years to come he was to establish himself as one of the most fluent and effective orators in parliament.[35]

By July, Diagne's proposal had been carefully examined in committee, but still he feared delay. The Minister of Colonies remained sympathetic, but the Minister of War had prepared his own version of Diagne's proposal for presentation to the deputies. Frustrated, and sensing that he already had the support of many deputies, Diagne arose on July 1 during debate and demanded immediate action. During the discussion period, he said, various bureaucrats at the Ministry of War had voiced doubts about incorporating the originaires in the regular army because there were no cadres to train them. He pointed out that the tirailleurs had already fought for eleven months; what better cadres could one ask? Outraged, he attacked the Ministry's inconsistency.

When the Minister of War, as of August 10, 1914, gives to foreigners (under a protectorate, it is true—I'm not talking about their courage, and I am referring to the Tunisians) the right to enlist without restriction in any branch of the French army, it is scandalous to refuse the same right to us, who are able to come and sit on these [parliamentary] benches.[36]

Diagne charged the director of colonial troops with saying that Africans were not capable of fighting in French uniforms, and accused him of harboring "monstrous prejudices." Finally, amid loud applause, Diagne asked for the immediate passage of his proposal. Although the vote was postponed for one more week while details were worked out, it was apparent to most of those involved that Diagne had won, and that his proposal, in one form or another, was going to be adopted.

On July 8 the Chamber convened and Diagne was confronted by a most determined opponent: Henri Labroue, deputy from Marseille, who was closely associated with the Bordeaux and Marseille business interests. Labroue ridiculed the notion that originaires were any different from other Africans; they were judicially *sujets français*, he argued, even though they might possess certain historic rights by accident. He demanded that if Africans were considered for regular-army service at all only those who knew how to read and write French should be admitted, and then only to a special contingent of troops enlisted for the duration. If the Chamber gave the right to serve in the French army to these voters, it would be obliged to give the vote to all foreigners who were serving under the French flag.[37]

Diagne replied to this attack by reading a letter sent him by Governor-General Ponty just before Ponty's untimely death in June. Ponty expressed hope that Diagne's proposal would be considered, and added that although the ministries had so far not asked for information on the matter he felt sure of success. Diagne continued by pointing out that the French army already included a number of Senegalese, Soudanese, Guineans, and other Africans who had been in France at the outbreak of war. They had been enlisted in the regular army and were serving on the front lines with Frenchmen at that very moment.[38]

Labroue received no applause for his closely reasoned case, whereas Diagne was warmly applauded throughout his speech. The Marseille deputy obviously represented special interest groups, and his knowledge of Africa was deficient. He made a fool of himself at one point by calling a Guinean a Bambara; and Diagne even teased him for making an error in his French. Diagne, by contrast, appeared cool and knowledgeable. But above all, he played on the liberal sympathies of the Chamber. In this he was aided by an impressive array of co-sponsors to his proposal: Paul Bluysen, Gratien Candace, René Boisneuf, Albert Grodet, Ernest Outrey, and others. Labroue capitulated, and the proposal easily passed by a voice vote.

The battle had tested Diagne's political mettle and clearly revealed his talents for political maneuver and debate. In the space of a year, he had acquired enough allies to reverse the associationist line that most French colonialists had adopted. With no extensive base of support in France, an obscure African whose own status was tenuous had been able to convert the Governor-General and the Ministry of Colonies to his idea, circumvent the hostile Ministry of War, and move the question directly to the floor of the Chamber. (Diagne knew that ultimate power on all questions lay with the Chamber, despite the fact that colonies were ruled by decree law and few colonial questions came up for consideration.) And most important, Diagne won the day because he was offering to provide France with a much-needed commodity: men for the army.

Diagne was jubilant, but he realized that a new battle was ahead: persuading the originaires to volunteer for service. The initial burst of patriotism was now gone. Thousands of men had gone to the front without returning, and Africans were no longer anxious to volunter for the ominous trenches of France. After his victory in the Chamber, Diagne wrote his constituents that he had kept his word, that the law allowing them to serve in the regular French army was an accomplished fact; but now they must fulfill their part of the bargain by volunteering.[39] During the next few months no more than a dozen men came forward. Diagne wired Galandou Diouf to set an example by volunteering himself. Diouf did so, but with little effect.

Diagne returned to the colony in December, to explain the implications of the new law and exhort his friends to take advantage of it. He was greeted by Jules Sergent, Thiécouta Diop, and a newcomer to the Diagne organization, Creole Louis Guillabert. (Diouf had tried to organize a traditional welcoming ceremony with drummers and singers but was denied permission.) On December 15, he spoke to the people of Rufisque, whom *La Démocratie* described as "skeptical."[40] The next day he spoke to the young people of Saint-Louis, who were most receptive. A special *vin d'honneur* was given on Diagne's behalf at the General Council building. The new Governor-General, François Clozel, an old colonial with moderate ideas, spoke approvingly of Diagne's project. He added: "It's just too bad the people of France don't know the history of Senegal."[41] Diagne himself took the opportunity to announce his further intentions.

The war, despite its horrors . . . has become for the people of Senegal an instrument of social reform. . . . The question of people born outside the Four Communes but descended from those born inside the Communes remains unanswered. The local tribunals will be notified of this, and I will call it to parliament's attention. This will bring the stubborn bureaucracy, which has neither the right nor the power to deform the law, to its senses. The offspring of the natives of the Four Communes, regardless of where they were born, are citizens and nothing less.[42]

Diagne tried to calm the jealousies of Africans in the Protectorate by calling for the political union of all Senegal and the extension of communal privileges to the bush. But on this point his rhetoric did not impress the backland peasants, who knew very well that he had been hard pressed even to win the concession for the originaires; they also knew, for a certainty, that originaires enlisting under the dispensation won by Diagne were treated very differently from their own people serving in the colonial regiments (see Table 5). For the first time, numerous Africans from the Protectorate came forward to claim status as originaires. Such a claim was difficult to prove or disprove: many civil registers were either missing or had been poorly kept; and many Africans changed names, used pseudonyms, or had been registered under variously spelled names by different clerks. The Young Senegalese, who had so far resisted the recruiters, were now inducted into the army as their respective military classes were called up. The Wolof fishermen under the political protection of Justin Devès, however, were reluctant to be called and created many problems, which were only resolved by Devès's sudden death in June 1916. Thus passed from the scene one of Senegal's most colorful political figures—and the Creole community's last real hope of regaining political power.[43]

The Law of October 19, 1915 was the first of the "Blaise Diagne Laws." Its promulgation in the colony was a source of concern for Acting Governor Antonetti, who by now had become an outright foe of the originaires, and his reports deplored the new law's effect in the colony.

Much enthusiasm among the young people, especially the Young Senegalese party, who consider the law a perfect means of assimilating the blacks to the whites. Defiance and unrest among the older people, who see the new law only as a dangerous innovation for their youngsters, who will be torn from traditional ties. Between these groups is the mass of the people, who cannot really comprehend the full import of the law and its consequences for the community.[44]

The application of this law will undoubtedly prove to be the most serious occurrence in the history of the Communes. I have never seen the populace so excited and so disorderly.[45]

Antonetti noted three potentially dangerous results of the new law. First, a dangerous rift was developing between Communes and Protectorate because of the inequalities of military service; this was ex-

TABLE 5
*Comparative Service Conditions for Originaires
and Protectorate Africans, ca. 1915*

| Condition | Originaires in regular army | Colonial troops |
|---|---|---|
| Service liability | Initial three-year enlistment | Same |
| Pay | Same as French soldiers | One-half originaires' pay |
| Quarters | Barracks, with bed | No provision for beds; sleep on ground or floor; blankets issued |
| Food | European food; food allowance 3.76 francs per ration | Traditional African food prepared by Senegalese women accompanying the troops; allowance 1.68 francs per ration |
| Promotion | Same as Frenchmen; can become officers in regular army | No promotion beyond noncommissioned rank; authority over African troops only |
| Pension (25 years service) | 1,500 to 1,800 francs | 437 to 572 francs |

SOURCE: Military service dossier, ARS, 17-G-241-108.

acerbated by originaires who haughtily referred to Protectorate troops as paid mercenaries. Second, it now seemed clear that Diagne eventually wanted Senegal's urban Africans to assume complete control of the local government—and most originaires knew this. Third, thanks to the pressure exerted by Diagne, the law was being applied not only to local originaires but also to Africans who claimed originaire parents.*

* See Antonetti's political report for the third trimester, 1916 (ARS, 2-G-15-6). Governor-General Clozel was infuriated by the third point, and penciled in the margin of Antonetti's report: "Mais non! Jamais de la vie!" He passed the report on to the Ministry of Colonies with a complaint about Diagne's strongarm tactics in unofficially extending the scope of the law. Paris blandly replied that the enlistment of Africans living outside the Communes was highly irregular and should cease at once. One of the victims of this ruling was Lamine Guèye, a founding member of the Young Senegalese. Many of Guèye's ancestors had been respected originaires of Saint-Louis, and his grandfather, Bacre-Waly, had sat in the General Council; but because his parents had been living in the French Soudan when he was born he was accorded the same status as an African from the Protectorate. When Guèye wrote his doctoral dissertation for the Faculty of Law at the University of Paris, this experience prompted him to deal with the problem of the originaires. See Guèye, *De la situation politique des sénégalais originaires.*

Returning to Paris, Diagne realized that his 1915 law left two questions unsettled. First was the issue of extended originaire status. Second was the issue of French citizenship. It was clear in his own mind that originaires were French citizens; but French officials in Paris and Dakar did not take a similar view. Even the originaires themselves were uncertain, except for the Young Senegalese, who proclaimed their status to the world. Clearly, further parliamentary action would be necessary.

By September Diagne had induced the Chamber to consider a simple resolution: "The natives of the full communes of Senegal, and their descendants, are and remain French citizens subject to the military obligations imposed by the Law of October 19, 1915."[46] So enormous were the war's demands on manpower, and so persuasive was Diagne's appeal to the Chamber, that no one arose to attack the proposal. It was passed by a voice vote, without discussion. In slightly more than two years Diagne had kept his campaign promise to make Senegalese originaires eligible for military service; and by doing so he had finally resolved the citizenship question, which had perplexed courts, governors, and ministers since 1848. Henceforth there was no doubt that originaires—or their children, wherever born—were full-fledged French citizens. This was a belated victory for the old theory of assimilation.

### Consequences of the War in Africa

Senegal was slowly drained of its French administrators and businessmen during the long war years. Only those not fit for military service or considered indispensable to the administration of the colony stayed. African chiefs in some areas found they had regained part of their old authority in the absence of French administrators. French business interests complained that the Lebanese traders, who as foreigners were not subject to conscription, were taking over small businesses and agencies vacated by Frenchmen. War needs dictated that more peanuts should be grown; but because the market had become unstable, many peasants had switched to subsistence crops and refused to produce for the war effort.[47] And many chiefs reported that it was impossible to meet government schedules for the harvest because so many young men were at the front.

All elections had been cancelled until the end of the war, which meant that the impending showdown between French, Creoles, and Africans was postponed.[48] The death of Justin Devès in 1916 made a place for Louis Guillabert—a skilled Creole politician who had served his family's interests for many years. But Guillabert realized that Diagne's party was the wave of the future, and when he took over the presidency of the General Council it was with the understanding that he was a Diagne man. His family and friends objected, but Guillabert was one of the few Creoles who could see that political change was inevitable.[49]

Diagne's most important aides were fighting in the armies. Diouf had volunteered and was serving in the front lines in France; d'Oxoby was called up and turned over *La Démocratie* to Sergent, who employed a succession of substitute editors until 1919. Amadou Duguay-Clédor, Lamine Guèye, Papa Mar Diop and other Young Senegalese went off to France. (Diop, regarded by his young colleagues as a possible successor to Diagne, died at the front.) M'Baye sold his share of ownership in *La Démocratie* to Louis Pellegrin in 1916 and retired to Diourbel to pursue his activities as an écrivain public. Both M'Baye and Thiécouta Diop were slow to adjust to the idea that Diagne had become the commanding figure in local politics; they supported Diagne as deputy but were too individualistic to replace Diouf and d'Oxoby as Diagne's lieutenants. Guillabert and Sergent stepped into the vacuum, fully conscious that at war's end there was bound to be a conflict.

Meanwhile, France created a new ministry to coordinate her war effort. When Georges Clemenceau, the Premier, also became Minister of War in November 1917, one of his first concerns was the hideous total of French casualties during the past three years. To hold her own, France would have to find more men for the army.[50] Albert Duchêne, the director of political affairs for the Ministry of Colonies, also voiced concern about the strains of the war. He and General Mangin, who had suggested the expansion of African troops almost a decade before, now conferred on the possibility of recruiting additional troops from West Africa, even though administrators and chiefs there were already complaining about the number of conscriptions. Mangin studied the question for several weeks, then presented a report to Clemenceau and the Minister of Colonies, urging that a vigorous attempt be made to raise new troops by sending a special recruiting mission to West Africa.[51] The man chosen to lead the mission was Blaise Diagne.

So far, Diagne's formal speeches in parliament had been limited to efforts on behalf of the 1915 and 1916 laws. Since that time he had intervened in various debates to protect the interests of African soldiers on the front. He helped arrange furloughs that allowed many of them to spend part of the winter in southern France, where the climate was closer to that of Africa. He fought vigorously when Germany presented a demand that France take her black troops out of combat; to him, this was nothing but racial prejudice.[52] Diagne had functioned as deputy, critic, and lobbyist. Now he was being asked to join the cabinet (at a secondary level) and take charge of an administrative responsibility that would give him rank and prestige comparable to that of the Governor-General of West Africa. The appointment of an African to such a post was unheard of in the colonial world. But this was wartime France, and Clemenceau was growing desperate for men.

Diagne hesitated, however, at becoming a member of the administration. Until now he had fought the administration on behalf of his constituents, many of whom had not understood the need for passing the military laws, for requiring that young men march off to war so they could become citizens. How many Senegalese would understand, now that the laws were passed, why Diagne should come and demand more men, especially if he came not as their defender and representative but as a government commissioner? Diagne's appointment was a logical one, since he had supported African aid for the French military effort from the beginning. But now he was being asked to sanction continued recruiting in the face of thousands of African casualties—indeed, to recruit men himself.

There was a further consideration. Governor-General Joost Van Vollenhoven, who had replaced Clozel in early 1917, was firmly opposed to the idea of recruiting more Africans. Van Vollenhoven and his chief adviser, Maurice Delafosse, were convinced that many areas of French West Africa, already openly hostile, were on the verge of revolt owing to widespread dissatisfaction with the war and with colonialism.[53] The new recruiting scheme was directly contrary to Van Vollenhoven's policy of making West Africa a source of supplies for the war effort, which required that the federation's manpower stay where it was.[54] Reluctantly, the Governor-General gave in and worked out a plan to recruit more Africans. He then resigned in protest, asked to be reassigned to his regiment, and was killed in action a few months later.*

---

* Van Vollenhoven also rejected the idea that his powers as Governor-General could be shared with anyone. He was skeptical of Diagne's new post, which appeared as a direct threat to his authority. Whether he thought Diagne himself was a threat is not known; but the idea of sharing authority with a representative of the colonized people was novel for the day. (From private materials.)

Diagne prepared for his new assignment with confidence. He did not leave France, however, until Clemenceau and Minister of Colonies Henry Simon had put a series of concessions in writing and promulgated them in the *Journal Officiel*. The government agreed to give all Africans serving under the French flag a number of special privileges. They were to be exempted from taxation and the *indigénat*, and their families were to receive larger allotments. Provision was made for some colonial soldiers to apply for French citizenship, which would give them the same options as originaires. Veterans' hospitals and rest homes were authorized for each colony in West Africa, and the government promised to establish agricultural schools, a lycée, and a medical school for Africans in Dakar. Finally, certain jobs were to be held open for returning soldiers. These were not extensive reforms, but they would greatly ease the burden of increased conscription on African homes.[55]

Diagne returned to Paris in August 1918. From the French point of view, his mission had been an overwhelming success: sent to recruit 40,000 men, Diagne's team had enlisted more than 60,000, and another 20,000 were recruited later. As Buell remarks, "The political effect of this appointment on the development of black prestige was considerable."[56] Diagne was lauded by French officials in France and Africa; and Clemenceau offered him the Légion d'Honneur, which he politely refused, explaining that what he had done was strictly in the line of wartime duty.

This refusal was undoubtedly influenced by the African side of the matter. Although the multitude had been overawed by the sight of an African travelling as the equal of the Governor-General, there were many complaints.[57] Africans outside of the Communes were envious of the superior treatment given originaires in the service; they felt the war was a European conflict, and they had little identification with France. The many revolts, outbreaks of violence, and incipient rebellions in Soudan, Niger, Dahomey, and Ivory Coast during 1916–17 indicated the depth of African frustration with the war and a widespread desire to rise up against the French colonial regime.

Moreover, regional and local chiefs across West Africa thought Diagne had overextended his mandate by presuming to speak for all of French-speaking Black Africa. (The trip did indeed give Diagne the sense of having a larger mandate, for the next year he renamed *La Démocratie*, calling it *L'Ouest Africain Français*.) Diagne's recruiting mission made his name a household word throughout much of West Africa—a name that inspired respect in some quarters but for the first time gave Diagne the image of a collaborationist in other quarters. Diagne was clearly pleased with his title and rank, and with the deference shown him by French colonial officials; but his refusal of the Légion d'Honneur suggests his personal chagrin and ambivalence.

Once again, Diagne had turned a difficult problem into a means of gaining concessions for his constituent Africans—in this case, not only for the Senegalese, but for Africans throughout the federation. For another decade Frenchmen and Africans alike would debate Diagne's motives in serving as recruiting commissioner: whether he really believed the concessions were worth the price of 60,000 more soldiers, and whether he had served to repay political debts for the passage of the 1915 and 1916 laws. The new hospitals, schools, jobs, and other improvements guaranteed by Clemenceau did help to give French West Africa more than the token structure of social services and institutions that had characterized it before the war. But were these concessions worth the thousands of Africans killed and wounded during the war? Diagne apparently believed his actions would bring all Africans closer to the political assimilation that he had won for the originaires of the Communes; but most Africans were skeptical and continued to regard the originaires with envy and bitterness.[58]

As for the originaires who had joined the French army, they found a new saying: "We have paid the blood tax." For those who had won political assimilation, this was to be a password in the postwar world of Senegalese politics.

## CHAPTER 11

# The African Accession to Power in the Four Communes

DURING THE long war years the local government of Senegal had vegetated. With most French councilmen in the army, the municipal councils met infrequently. Caretaker staffs ran the municipal governments, since there had been no special elections to fill vacancies. The only body that met regularly was the General Council, but this had lost the importance it had enjoyed under its former president, Justin Devès. Louis Guillabert, the new president, worked to keep the Council securely in Creole hands; but he knew that once the war ended a day of reckoning with Diagne would come. By allying himself with Diagne, Guillabert hoped to influence the postwar political makeup of Senegal.*

The registered electorate had increased by almost 50 per cent since 1914, for several reasons. After the ratification of the 1915 law, hundreds of Africans rushed to urban courts to prove their claim to originaire status and French citizenship. The procedure used was the *jugement supplétif*, in which the petitioner brought two friends to court to swear that he had been either born in the Communes or born of originaire parents. Civil registers to substantiate these claims had been kept in Saint-Louis since the eighteenth century and in all the Communes since the nineteenth century; but many Senegalese Muslims had been hostile to the idea of registering births and deaths with officials whom they considered aliens. Some records had been lost; names had been changed, improperly recorded, and recorded twice. Fraudulent or doubtful cases were frequent, and by 1922 it was required that petitioners also swear on the Koran before the local Muslim judge (*cadi*).[1] Many rural African women who were expecting children now made a practice of moving to a Commune temporarily so that their children would be born as originaires. Fi-

---

* Governor Levecque of Senegal noted on March 15, 1920, that Guillabert "was the prisoner of a party to which he owed his election and the political success he could not obtain otherwise." Note in ARS, 4-E-13.

nally, hundreds of men had become citizens by serving in the French army. The total electorate of the Communes in 1914 was 7,882; by 1919 it had swelled to 13,035.[2]

### The Campaign and Elections of 1919

As political campaigning began in 1919, it might have appeared to a casual observer that the 1914 drama was about to resume after a short intermission. The candidate of the Lebous and the Young Senegalese was Blaise Diagne, and the candidate of the Bordeaux-Creole alliance was François Carpot. The issues, except for African citizenship, were also much the same. Even the campaign posters resembled those of 1914, and in some cases they were unchanged. Two local newspapers, *L'A.O.F.* and *La Tribune*, supported Carpot; *L'Ouest Africain Français*, the successor to *La Démocratie*, defended the incumbent deputy. Diouf, d'Oxoby, and other Diagne lieutenants returned from the army, joining Sergent, M'Baye, and others who had waited out the war in Senegal. Most conspicuously absent were the interests of Justin Devès, who had not left a political heir.

Carpot and his backers took the view that Diagne's victory in 1914 had been purely fortuitous. Now, they intended to reestablish French and Creole control of local politics. This faction included such important Bordeaux houses as Vézia and Maurel et Prom, as well as a number of French administrators. Some of these Frenchmen were outright racists who found it incredible that an African should have advanced so far in politics. Others simply feared that Diagne would remove them from office if he continued in power. This fear was not unfounded, since Diagne had become an intimate of the Minister of Colonies, Henry Simon; in fact, Paris newspapers now spoke of the Ministry's "official" support for Diagne's candidacy and labeled this new threat to colonialism *simono-diagnisme.**

The resulting effort to discredit Diagne extended to Paris. *Le Soir* charged that Diagne's influence had penetrated the entire colonial establishment, and alleged that he was personally responsible for having Simon transfer Governor-General Gabriel Angoulvant from his post in Dakar.[3] Another Parisian newspaper, *La Démocratie Nouvelle*, warned its readers that the Clemenceau ministry would probably support Diagne's candidacy, which it termed "prejudicial to the national interest."[4] Several papers published stories that seemed

* A phrase coined by Jean de Medina, columnist for *Le Soir*. See his article in *Le Soir*, September 26, 1919. The phrase was later shortened to *diagnisme* with the passing of Simon from the Ministry of Colonies and with Diagne's continuing electoral successes.

to confirm Diagne's rumored intention of controlling the Ministry of Colonies from behind the scenes.[5]

*Le Soir* claimed that Diagne intended to gradually remove all French officials from posts in West Africa, replacing them with "natives who would owe everything to Diagne and who would permit the rapid and certain development of Diagnist imperialism."[6] Simon was criticized for acting as though Diagne expressed the wishes of all France's black Africans. Moreover, he was called naïve for believing that Georges Barthélemy, the head of a newly formed association of government employees in West Africa, was independent; it was charged that Barthélemy was a mere creature of Diagne's, and that Diagne and Barthélemy were in no way representative of France's colonial interests.[7]

The conservatives were delighted when a new Governor-General, Martial Merlin, took office in the summer of 1919. Merlin was at the end of a long colonial career that had begun in Senegal in the early 1890's and had taken him all over Africa. He opposed the "progressive" ideas of men like Van Vollenhoven, and intended to reestablish strong French rule in West Africa and bring Diagne's party into line. Not long after Merlin took over he was informed that Diagne would arrive in October to start campaigning. He wired the Ministry asking how Diagne should be received: as a deputy, as a recruiter of African troops, or as a commissioner on a special mission? The Ministry replied that Diagne was going to Senegal in his capacity as deputy for the campaign. Merlin then ordered a simple, unimpressive welcoming ceremony that would hopefully attract little attention.[8]

Diagne's arrival was nonetheless a major event in the Communes, where thousands of returned veterans welcomed him as a kind of patron saint. *Le Courrier Colonial* reported an incident that had taken place in September among African troops waiting at Saint-Raphaël on the Riviera for shipment back to Senegal. As French General Guerin inspected the troops, he was bombarded with shouts of, "We want to go home!" (A decree in July had kept some 40,000 Africans in the army.) The General tried to calm the Africans, but had his cape torn off and was jostled about. He was finally rescued by aides as the troops chanted, "C'est Diagne qu'il nous faut, oh, oh, oh!"[9] Such veterans were a powerful source of support—provided they could return to Senegal before the elections.[10]

Carpot attempted to duplicate Diagne's successful tactics of 1914 by organizing large-scale political rallies. The first was an enormous open-air meeting in the Médina, a new Dakar suburb that had been built to house the thousands of Africans who had migrated to the capital during the war.* Only thirty-odd Africans attended, although Carpot had even invited his African supporters from Saint-Louis. This fiasco was explained away as proof that Saint-Louisian Wolofs and Dakar Lebous did not like to mix. There was actually much truth in the apology, for the proud originaires from Saint-Louis did tend to regard their counterparts in Dakar and Rufisque as upstarts.[11]

In marked contrast to the Carpot rally was a Diagne gathering a few days later. Over a thousand Africans surged around Diagne, cheering and acclaiming his candidacy, so that it was impossible for him to speak.[12] Immediately after the crowd had cleared, a Carpot meeting was begun. The Creole candidate tried to convince the few Africans who remained to listen that because French citizenship had been available to Senegalese since the promulgation of the Civil Code in 1833, Diagne had actually not brought them citizenship. The ex-deputy was jeered, hissed, and finally escorted to safety by the police, who broke up the meeting. Later the same evening, a second rally for Diagne drew 5,000 to 6,000 cheering Africans.

The Carpot forces were particularly annoyed by one of Diagne's newest lieutenants, Amadou Duguay-Clédor. Clédor had not been active during the 1914 campaign, since he had been teaching school in the Protectorate. But in 1919, after he had served in the army, his speaking and writing talents made him one of Diagne's most trusted aides. Writing in *L'Ouest Africain Français*, Clédor spelled out part of Diagne's program: "We want the unacceptable institution of local civil servants, also known as native civil servants, to disappear as rapidly as possible; we need a system in which all aspirants, whether Senegalese or from the metropole, would be admitted under the same conditions."[13] The French editors of *L'A.O.F.* pointed to this assertion as proof positive that Diagne intended to create a single corps of bureaucrats that would soon be entirely African; this would give Diagne control of the colony, just as the Paris newspapers had warned.[14]

Clédor also demanded that French merchants change their hiring policies: "We want the commercial world to stop judging an individual only by the color of his skin; it should consider how he works

---

* It also housed Africans who had been relocated from other districts of Dakar—not because of discrimination, but because the squalor in their old neighborhoods had sometimes led to epidemics. See Betts, "The Establishment of the Medina in Dakar."

and the results he obtains, and he should be paid accordingly." The Bordeaux press replied that it was one thing for Diagne and his lieutenants to meddle in the status of government employees but quite another to question the employment practices of private businessmen.[15] In actual fact, Africans were still employed mostly at the lower levels of French commercial operations—that is, as agents in the bush or clerks and accountants in the towns. Galandou Diouf's former position as chief accountant for a French firm had been a notable exception.

Carpot and his Bordeaux backers did not seem to comprehend that 1919 was not 1914, that the war and Diagne's rise to power had raised new political issues. "Pascal Dumont" (the pseudonym of a high colonial official who wrote attacks on Diagne's campaign) could only sputter and rage when Clédor suggested: "We Africans, under French guidance, of course, want to control the political destiny of our own country."[16] This seemed to confirm rumors in Paris that Diagne was at heart a separatist; and that although he might appear loyal in France, his policies were clearly opposed to French colonialism in Senegal. Diagne's French lieutenants, Sergent and d'Oxoby, were considered traitors for supporting such a program.

Diagne's 1915 and 1916 laws were also criticized. It was argued that only children by the first wife of a Muslim originaire could be considered legitimate under the French codes; this interpretation would surely lead to the disintegration of the traditional African family, with disastrous consequences for all Senegal.[17] The problem became a major issue of the campaign. The French press claimed that parliament had not really understood the legal implications of the originaires' retaining their right to Muslim institutions. "In fact," argued L'A.O.F., "the Chamber thought the Diagne law would abrogate the special privileges of the Senegalese Muslims, since these were not mentioned in the text of the law."[18] It was also alleged that important reports from Governor-General Clozel and Acting Governor-General Angoulvant had been ignored when the Chamber passed Diagne's 1916 law without discussion. Angoulvant had supposedly written: "If this concession is made to our subjects, it means the negation of our social organization, civilization, and genius."[19]

Diagne himself was so unobtrusive during the campaign that he was rumored to be suffering from a temporary illness. He seldom appeared in public, and let his lieutenants manage the rallies and debates. But behind the scenes, he was laying the foundations for the first permanent political party in French-speaking Africa: the Republican-Socialist Party of Senegal. In 1914, Thiécouta Diop had refused to give up leadership of the Young Senegalese, whom Diagne wanted to convert into a political party; and much the same situation existed at the beginning of the 1919 campaign. Seeing no chance for breaking Diop's hold on his youthful followers, Diagne announced that *L'Ouest Africain Français*, which as *La Démocratie* had carried the phrase "organ of the Young Senegalese party" on its masthead, would henceforth speak for the new Republican-Socialist Party. He sent Diouf and Clédor through the direct rule areas and the western Protectorate to solicit subscriptions for the journal and contributions for his campaign. At the same time, campaign committees were created in towns outside the Communes. Local notables who had helped Diagne in the last election or during the war were enlisted in these committees, which became the backbone of the new party.[20]

A formal party organization was dictated because Diagne intended to organize a list of African candidates for all four municipal councils, as well as the General Council. Previously, no more than a handful of Africans had ever served on any particular council, and they had invariably been elected on French and Creole lists. Diagne was determined to create a party that could put Africans on all the councils, besides winning the deputyship. His posters announced: *Vive la France! Vive le Sénégal! Vive la république sociale!* And for the municipal elections, Diagnist posters called the voters "to the defense of the African proletariat."[21]

Carpot and the Bordeaux interests, meanwhile, were still thinking in terms of the rigged elections of a decade earlier. The cashier's windows of many large Bordeaux firms were opened for the usual electoral payoffs two weeks before the ballots were to be cast. According to Governor Levecque, "important sums of money were paid out, but the Africans later voted as they pleased."[22] Levecque admitted that Carpot was an unpopular candidate, but pointed out that the French-Creole group could find no one else to oppose Diagne. A. N. Federici, a government employee and journalist who spoke for the petits colons, French clerks, and small agents, had aspired to the candidacy; but he was rejected by the Bordeaux agents who held the purse strings. Another possibility was the former police commissioner of Dakar, Monsieur Abbal, who had long been an articulate opponent of Diagne. (It was rumored that Diagne had engineered Abbal's transfer from the police service to the army during the war.) But Carpot, who had carefully planned his comeback during the war, won out after Abbal was booed publicly by Africans in Saint-Louis and Rufisque.[23] Jean Renaud, a mulatto customs collector, and Isaac Diop, an African employee of the colonial treasury, also ran, but their candidacies were not taken seriously.[24]

Levecque complained that the campaign against Diagne had become far too violent—especially since French administrators were illegally joining in the torrent of abuse. Many articles for *L'A.O.F.*, he said, were written by a high official in the Ministry of Education and sent to Senegal for the anti-Diagne campaign.[25] And a broadside called *L'Intransigeant* had become so offensive that Levecque called for the resignation of the administration employee who was editing it. To be fair, Levecque admitted in his report that he himself was pro-Diagne. In fact, it was he, as Governor of French Guiana, who had given Diagne permission to leave that colony and begin a political career in 1914.

On November 30, the voters overwhelmingly declared their allegiance to Diagne, who received 7,444 votes as compared to 1,252 for Carpot and 20 for Isaac Diop.[26] And in the municipal elections, which followed in December, Diagne's Republican-Socialist Party elected every man on its ticket, gaining complete control of local government in all Four Communes. The only Frenchmen elected were those who had supported Diagne.[27] The non-African elite had simply been unable to field the experienced candidates who had served before the war. Many experienced French politicians had been killed in the war or had stayed in France after 1914; and the Creole community had continued to decline, producing fewer and fewer young men of the caliber of Louis Guillabert. At the same time, the African majority had become increasingly politicized and had found a dynamic leader to carry them to power.

The possibility of an African majority in the city halls of the Four Communes, which had been feared by French merchants after the 1914 election, was now a reality.[28] This minor revolution in colonial politics finally alarmed Frenchmen in Paris, who now believed the old rumors that Diagnism was a political force to be reckoned with. The election of 1914 had occasioned mild interest, but had quickly been eclipsed by the war. Paris in 1919, however, was not totally preoccupied with the peace settlement; and journalists, politicians, and colonials all expressed concern about the radical changes taking place in Senegal. Even before the elections, I. P. Greslé called attention to the new state of mind in Black Africa:

All of this new population is now gaining consciousness of itself . . . . There is definitely such a thing as African public opinion, an outlook that spreads in a very short time even to [Africans] in the most remote forests. . . . Yet the existence of this native opinion is scarcely suspected. For one thing, it lacks the means to express itself publicly.[29]

In most cases, the African councilors were new to politics. Many of them were veterans just returned from the war; others were clerks or businessmen with some experience in administration; and others were farmers or landlords. A few were plainly political opportunists, recruited at the eleventh hour to fill Diagne's lists. The list on p. 204 is, in a way, a historic document: it was the first African slate elected in modern French Africa.* In a fair election, with no fraud charged at the polls, Africans had come to power within the colonial system. And they had been certified by parliamentary law as full-fledged French citizens.

Diagne's closest associates were three of the mayors: Clédor, Diouf, and Sergent. He also was in touch with Ambroise Mendy and Armand Angrand in Gorée, Michel Sangué and Louis Pellegrin in Dakar, and Birahim Camara in Saint-Louis. Thiécouta Diop was elected to the council in Saint-Louis, but his relationship with Diagne remained distant. Of Diagne's inner circle only d'Oxoby had not tried for office, and he was a candidate in the General Council elections, which took place a few days later on January 4, 1920.

Many of the same names appeared on the winning Council slate, for Diagne was again triumphant.[30] The one-time preserve of the Creoles now passed to African hands. To be sure, Louis Guillabert remained president, but he followed Diagne's orders. Elected were:

*First Arrondissement (Saint-Louis)*

Blaise Diagne | Thiécouta Diop
Amadou Duguay-Clédor | Charles Pellegrin
Birahim Camara | Louis Guillabert
Saër Dièye Bakary | Antoine Guillabert
Antony Alexis | Pierre Chimère

*Second Arrondissement (Cape Verde)*

Galandou Diouf | Jules Sergent
John Kâ | Ambroise Mendy
Jean Daramy d'Oxoby | Louis Pellegrin
Al Hajj Amadou Fall | Lamine Diagne
Michel Sangué | Durand

* Election Dossier of 1919, ARS, 20-G-69-23. Frenchmen are indicated by *F* and and Creoles by *C*. It is impossible to give absolutely faithful spellings, since French clerks would often not know how to spell African names, or Africans were not sure how their names should be put into French. Also, it is difficult to ascertain who were French and who Creoles; since names are hard to differentiate, I have relied heavily on my interviews for clarification.

## SAINT-LOUIS

Mayor: Amadou Duguay-Clédor
First Assistant: Ibrahima Sarr, notable
Second Assistant: Birahim Camara, notable

*Councilors*

Saër Dièye Bakary, merchant
Charles Legros Diallo, printer
Alassane Bercy Niang, notable
Léon Cavialle, watchmaker (*F*)
Babakar N'Diaye, agent
Pierre Chimère, landowner
Amadou Guèye Saliou, agent
Thiécouta Diop, notable

Antony Alexis, lawyer (*F*)
Alioune Dièye, landowner
Abdoulaye Samba, landowner
Moussé Guèye, mason
Birahim Balla Diop, merchant
Charles Pellegrin, merchant (*C*)
N'Gor N'Diaye, merchant

## DAKAR

Mayor: Jules Sergent (*F*)
First Assistant: Louis Pellegrin, wholesaler (*C*)
Second Assistant: Jean Mayras, wholesaler (*F*)

*Councilors*

Michel Sangué, landowner
Faly Bâ, mason
Edmond Lacave, agent (*F*)
Léo Ramadé, merchant (*F*)
Omar Guèye, adjuster
Daour Guèye, agent
Mabigué Madiaga, carpenter
Paye N'Diaye, agent

Cellé Diop, farmer
Diouga Diop, farmer
Bayemour Paye, agent
Baye Gagne Diagne, farmer
Alassane Codou Faye, tailor
Thierno Diagne, farmer
Mamour Diagne, farmer

## RUFISQUE

Mayor: Galandou Diouf
First Assistant: John Kâ, agent
Second Assistant: Mour N'Diaye M'Bengue, merchant

*Councilors*

Ousmane Kane, merchant
William Jean Pierre, shipper (*C*)
Momar Sène, merchant
Alexandre Angrand, agent (*C*)
Amadou Mangara, farmer
M'Baye Diamé, merchant
N'Doye Seck, farmer

Laty Guèye N'Doye, landowner
M'Baye Niasse, farmer
Al Hajj Amadou Fall, merchant
Momar Guèye, merchant
Moussé Hesse Seck, farmer
Atoumane Seck, farmer

## GOREE

Mayor: Pierre Cissé, landowner (*C*)
First Assistant: Pierre Sarre, clerk

*Councilors*

Antoine Diadhiou, carpenter
Adrien Allègre, merchant (*C*)
Sougui Seck, shipper
Banda Seck, jeweler

Ambroise Mendy, agent
Roboth Dolly, accountant (*C*)
Cossene Sène, landowner
Armand Angrand, restaurateur (*C*)

The Guillabert brothers and the two Pellegrins kept Creole representation alive, and Frenchmen such as Alexis and Durand kept company with Diagne stalwarts d'Oxoby and Sergent; but the Africans had a clear majority. The political ferment of the past two decades had finally given the Africans control of local government in Senegal.

## The Consolidation of African Gains

Diagne and his followers consolidated their positions. They were extremely careful to stay within the laws and hence were generally able to escape government persecution. Governor-General Merlin established a special network of police agents in the African community in order to keep track of the new African politics. But he constantly found news from his own confidential dispatches appearing in the Parisian press or in *L'Ouest Africain Français*, for Diagne, too, had an intelligence service.[31] Many African clerks and messengers in the administration habitually brought important information to the attention of Clédor or Diouf, who transmitted it to Diagne.

Perhaps the greatest benefit gained by the Africans in 1919 was widespread publicity. For several years after the campaign, the Parisian press discussed the rising "specter" of Diagnism, a political term never clearly defined. One of Diagne's lukewarm Creole supporters, Adrien Allègre, tried his hand at explaining the elements of Diagne's policy in 1922.[32] Diagnism, he said, was the state of mind of those who supported Diagne's policies on faith alone; in fact, many Africans did not know precisely what these policies were, and gave their support to Diagne as a person. There is no doubt that this statement was substantially true: some of Diagne's constituents even attributed supernatural powers to their deputy. And Diagne's whirlwind success in all his political maneuvers convinced Africans and French alike that the French colonial regime would have great difficulty containing him.

About this time merchants in Senegal began to peddle Diagne souvenirs. Diagne calendars and statuettes were everywhere, and even Diagne-endorsed perfumes appeared. The Mélia Company of Algeria, whose cigarettes were sold throughout West Africa, printed packs with Diagne's photo on them, flanked by the tricolor and captioned, "To all my racial brothers—Vive la France!" Diagne's continuing association with the Freemasons, instead of discrediting him, was regarded as further proof of his supernatural powers. Even the Muslim community overlooked both his Freemasonry and his Catholi-

cism, for his defense of the Muslims' special privileges had won him
the official endorsement of all the principal marabouts.³³

Diagnism as a political phenomenon, however, was more than the
cult of one man. In the French press it became a synonym for Africanization, and this is what most French observers meant by the word.
Frenchmen feared that if local politics could be Africanized in Senegal, Africans throughout the French possessions would soon demand
the same. The French in business would also suffer. In short, Diagnism came to be equated with separatist movements, radicalism, and
incipient nationalism.

A number of incidents following the great electoral victories of
1919–20 seemed to confirm these assumptions. In January 1920 the
*Joyeuse*, a French cruiser from Morocco, called at Dakar and took
Diagne to Monrovia, where he represented the French government
at the inauguration of Liberian President C. D. B. King. At a dinner
that he gave for King, Diagne spoke frankly. "I am one of your
brothers, of the same race and family as yourselves. Since I have
already met [your officials], I know I can count on them to show the
entire world that blacks are as capable as whites of governing themselves, running their own country, and carrying the Republic of
Liberia to the peak of economic and social development."* True,
Liberia was already independent. But to Frenchmen it seemed that
the rest of Africa was hanging on Diagne's every word.

After Diagne returned from Liberia, another incident took place.
While Governor Levecque was visiting the *commandant du cercle* in
Kaolack, an African delegation headed by Diagne called on him.
Diagne announced that he and his friends wanted the commandant,
Administrator Siadous, to resign, and that he expected Levecque to
help them. Levecque refused to dismiss Siadous, and there was a
sharp exchange of words. Diagne left, but returned within an hour
at the head of an angry mob, which chanted: "Down with Siadous!

* Notes on Diagne's mission to Liberia, ARS, 17-G-234-108. Diagne had met the
Liberian officials at the Pan-African Congress organized by W. E. B. Du Bois in
Paris in February 1919. Du Bois had encountered difficulty in convening the Con-
gress, but Diagne persuaded Clemenceau to give permission for the meeting.
Diagne presided over the sessions, which were not radical for the time (Du Bois
was mainly interested in the fate of Germany's African colonies). Although the
Congress was reported in the French press and in Senegal, it had little impact upon
politics in the Four Communes (see *L'A.O.F.*, July 24, 1919). However, it was important to the nucleus of Africans who grew into an expatriate community in
Paris during the 1920's and 1930's. Diagne also attended part of the 1921 Pan-
African conferences; but he then broke with the movement, fearing it would become dominated by Bolsheviks and Garveyists. In general, the Pan-African ideal
was too abstract for the many originaires preoccupied with the intrigue of Communes politics.

Down with the Governor!" Levecque tried to calm the crowd, but his words had no effect. Next day, the tension continued: schools in Kaolack were closed, and young Africans declared their support for Diagne. Siadous found it difficult to restore order. Other incidents of the same sort had been occurring of late, and he demanded leave to visit Paris and defend himself against "these Jacobins," as well as the charges of corruption brought against him by Africans in the General Council. Levecque, humiliated by the affair, broke with Diagne and wrote to Paris: "France, I fear, no longer commands in this country."[34]

By now, Diagne was quite accustomed to intervening in Protectorate politics, and he continued to act as though he were a spokesman for all French-speaking Africans.* For example, he proposed in 1921 that the African troops should have their own Unknown Soldier, to be "solemnly glorified on African soil."[35] Diagne's office in Paris became so filled with African petitioners that in 1920 he applied to the General Council for a yearly subsidy of 30,000 francs to defray the cost of helping his constituents. Sergent defended Diagne's request in the Council, and said that he personally had seen hundreds of people turning to Diagne for help in France. Diouf added:

We have in this country a kind of life you might call true socialism: all for one and one for all. When one of our compatriots is in France, the circumstances are different, and often he finds himself without resources. He usually asks for aid and protection from the deputy who is obliged to put him up. The deputy is sought out not only by his constituents but by people from all over Africa—Soudanese, Congolese, and so forth. He is considered the deputy of all the blacks.[36]

Governor-General Merlin ordered a secret study of Diagne and of the implications of present African politics in Senegal. The resulting report charged that Diagne had used his recruiting mission to spread ideas of political equality throughout West Africa, that he had tried to lower the status of Europeans in African eyes. In Guinea, Diagne had reportedly called a French administrator, Maurice de Coppet (later to become Governor-General of West Africa), simply by name, refusing to use his title; at the same time, he had demanded that de Coppet address him as Commissioner. The report also claimed that Frenchmen who had not turned out to greet Diagne at Khombole, a town in Senegal, were later ordered to active duty in the army be-

* In fact, many Africans thought of him in this light. My 1963 interview with Mme. Diop, mother-in-law of Alioune Diop (editor of *Présence Africaine*) and mother of the late Senegalese poet David Diop, revealed that in her native Cameroun after World War I Diagne was considered "our deputy."

cause of Diagne's machinations.[37] Finally, several incidents were listed to show how the Senegalese had "acquired an independent spirit" because of Diagnism.

In July 1920, Senegalese crew members led a mutiny on board a Fraissinet Company steamer.

In 1920, insubordination of Senegalese toward the French administration at Boghé in Mauritania.

In 1921, racial disputes in Tivouane, home of Malick Sy. French police obliged to quit the city when mobs became uncontrollable, shouting, "Kill the whites! Kill the whites!"

In 1921, at the Fête of Joan of Arc in Dakar, French shops looted and stoned by African rioters.[38]

In the Kaolack incident, Diagne had been directly responsible; but Merlin now became certain that any unrest in the colony resulted from the spirit of separatism and resistance fostered by Diagne.

Some groups in Paris began to share Merlin's concern. A conservative colonial organization, the Comité d'Action Républicaine aux Colonies, held a number of dinners in 1920–21 to discuss African politics. At one dinner, Monsieur Vidal, a French attorney recently returned from Dakar, claimed that the only way to solve the Senegalese problem was to work with the traditional chiefs and back them up. Diagne's followers, he said, were all of humble origin. "Among them you will find no descendants of Senegal's great traditional African families. Servants or sons of servants, coolies, lackies—these are the backers of M. Diagne . . . . Let's not make the same mistake we made in Indochina by recruiting from the lower classes."[39]

In 1921 Diagne helped found *L'Effort Colonial*, a Paris newspaper intended to strike back at his three principal adversaries: Merlin, former Governor-General Angoulvant, and the new Minister of Colonies, Albert Sarraut. But after three months the journal died for lack of funds.[40] Diagne then took to the lecture circuit to defend his ideas. Since his 1910 debate with Governor-General Augagneur after their feud in Madagascar, he had enjoyed visiting various French cities to explain his politics. He now found an enthusiastic reception in many cities where Frenchmen were still grateful for the fact that colonial subjects in far-off Africa had sent their sons to fight for France. Before a cheering crowd of 3,000 or more in Rouen, Diagne outlined his political program, interspering his remarks with selections by a military band. He advocated more education in the colonies, wanted bigger financial investments, and called on France to help liberate "an oppressed race." The speech was eulogized in the provincial press.[41]

Diagne later visited Antwerp to tell Belgian audiences about African politics in the French colonies. He declared that close cooperation between Africans and Europeans was necessary, and that a kind of "marriage" between European and native civilizations was both possible and desirable.[42] Remarks like this gave many the impression that Diagne deliberately spoke as an apologist for colonial rule when in Europe but continued to attack it when in Senegal. Even so, his notoriety in Senegal only brought him greater popularity in France, especially after he came to blows in the aisles of the Chamber with Marcel Cachin, editor of the Socialist *L'Humanité* and a critic of Diagne since 1916.[43]

Diagne continued to work for greater African political participation. In 1920, France reorganized the Conseil Supérieur des Colonies, an elected body that advised the Ministry of Colonies. Diagne thought the new Conseil might conceivably wield some influence and therefore insisted to Governor-General Merlin that Senegalese voters be allowed to help select its members (a small college of French electors ordinarily chose the Conseil). This point was granted; and in June 1920 Diagne touched off an investigation of his old foe Antonetti, now Governor of Ivory Coast, who had allegedly influenced the vote for the Conseil of Senegalese originaires residing in that colony.[44]

Diagne consistently favored increasing the number of communes-mixtes in Senegal and creating others elsewhere in West Africa. Eventually, these cities could be converted into full communes with municipal councils and mayors like those of Senegal's Four Communes. In fact, the French government had considered this plan in 1918, when it was studied by the civil affairs section of the Government-General. Administrator Fousset, in charge of the study, reported: "To create full communes in Senegal and make all their inhabitants voters without doing the same for the inhabitants of cities in our other colonies would be to commit a great injustice, which would create unrest among all interested parties."[45] Fousset said that many inhabitants of French West Africa had already demanded the same status as the originaires of Senegal. He thought that more municipal governments with voters should be set up, but did not believe that each colony should be given a deputy in Paris; rather, he suggested creating a West African Colonial Council with African delegates.[46]

Diagne's own views on the matter were succinctly presented in an interview printed by *La Presse Coloniale* in 1924. Giving Africans parliamentary representation, he claimed, was not only a badly needed reform, but also good political insurance. He feared that educated Africans would soon find ideas like Bolshevism attractive unless they were drawn into the existing political process.* Asked whether Africans should have representatives in Paris or in Dakar, Diagne replied that a voice in Paris was vital for all "evolved" Africans. "It's not a question of giving in one massive dose all the rights of French citizenship to people who may not understand their duties. I think such people should keep their separate codes and figure on separate electoral lists."[47] Diagne admitted that this was not an ideal solution, but thought it practical and "a hundred times better" than the existing situation, in which sujets français were little better than serfs. And those Africans who qualified as full French citizens should not be placed in a separate electorate, for they could make a greater contribution to the general welfare by being mixed in with French voters.

Diagne's plan was criticized because it would make voters out of sujets and leave the door open for them to become citizens. Diagne thought this was no problem, since French constitutional law did not require voters to be citizens: "It's not necessary to make the natives French citizens in order to give them basic rights. France has already agreed to respect their traditional customs and beliefs."[48] If one of these "half-citizens" were elected deputy, asked the interviewer, what would happen in colonial politics? Diagne said this possibility was not inconsistent, citing his own election in 1914. Moreover, he argued there were now Alsatian deputies in the Chamber who had sat in the Reichstag when Alsace was German. Since these men had no better claim to French citizenship than the Africans, there would surely be no problem for noncitizen Africans elected to Parliament.

Diagne went on record as advocating the following representation: One deputy for each colony or group of adjoining colonies in West Africa; one deputy for the federation of colonies in Equatorial Africa; and one deputy for Madagascar.[49] These ideas were rejected by the Chamber in the early 1920's; but they became part of France's plan for African participation in colonial affairs after World War II.

---

* Diagne himself had been accused of being a Bolshevist at one time; but after the early 1920's he used the threat of Bolshevism as a political device for showing what might occur in Africa unless France were more liberal.

## Reform of the General Council

Diagne could not muster enough support to create full communes outside Senegal or have further deputies created; but he was able to surmount the panicky opposition generated by Diagnism and bring reforms to Senegal itself. Ever since the General Council's responsibility had been limited to the direct rule areas and the Protectorate put under direct control of the Governor, the Councilors had discussed the desirability of creating a Colonial Council that could debate and act for the entire colony. By 1919 the idea had many advocates. Diagne and the Republican-Socialists favored it because it would bring Protectorate Africans into politics. Liberal French administrators favored it for the same reason. And even conservative administrators like Merlin favored it because it might restrict the powers of the Senegalese urban elite.

Governor-General Angoulvant (who succeeded Van Vollenhoven and preceded Merlin) wrote the Minister of Colonies in February 1919 that the time had come to create a Colonial Council. He was undoubtedly spurred on by the fact that the General Council had been uncooperative during his term of office and had refused to vote a number of optional expenses for Senegal's budget. Angoulvant argued that the only way to bring order into the present chaotic situation was to establish a single Council to represent the entire colony and to give it control of budgets for both the Protectorate and the direct rule areas.[50] In June Minister Simon replied that he had conferred with Diagne, Governor Levecque, and Inspector-General of Colonies Revel; all agreed that Revel should prepare a detailed report on the matter.

By October Revel's report was ready. He had found that the average attendance at Council sessions was only five or six of the twenty members. Many Frenchmen did not attend because they were traveling in the interior or in France on business; and Councilors from Dakar, Rufisque, and Gorée found it inconvenient to journey to Saint-Louis. Thus the Council continued to be dominated by Louis Guillabert and the Creoles of Saint-Louis. Revel recommended a Colonial Council made up of elected originaires and appointed Africans from the Protectorate—not precisely what Diagne had originally proposed. (Revel claimed that Diagne had finally agreed to the revised proposal because he thought it essential to have at least a few Council members from the Protectorate, however they were se-

lected.) The new council was to meet in Saint-Louis, which gave
Diagne an opportunity to undermine the Creole oligarchy in that
city.[51]

The new Colonial Council was instituted by the Decree of December 4, 1920. By this time it was apparent to the African elite that
the French favored the change, and Diagne's African members in
the General Council were put in the curious position of having to
defend the new, government-sanctioned Council. The switch to a
colony-wide Council, in fact, annoyed a number of Africans, especially Saint-Louisians, who could see that their dominant position
in the General Council would be undermined. Instead of having
approximately half the Council members, Saint-Louis would share
twenty elected members with the Cape Verde cities, and the administration would appoint twenty African chiefs from the Protectorate.

Elections for the new Council were held in June 1921, and Diagne's
Republican-Socialist party was again victorious. A group of Wolof
dissidents in Saint-Louis, led by several young schoolteachers, had
openly opposed Diagne, forming an opposition list that had little
success at the polls. They were joined by Thiécouta Diop, who finally
broke with Diagne when Saint-Louisian interests were threatened.[52]
After the voting, the Diagnists announced that the colony was no
longer divided, that one region would no longer dominate the Council, and that citizen and sujet could now work together in local
politics.

Governor-General Merlin was pleased with the new institution,
and expected to control it easily by influencing the African chiefs
who had been appointed as representatives of the Protectorate.[53] But
the local French and Creole communities, which had controlled
politics from the beginning, saw the creation of the new Council as
the final blow to their long hegemony. Several months after the election, *L'A.O.F.* surveyed the political scene in Senegal and came to
the conclusion that a new era had begun:

Look what has happened in Dakar, in Rufisque, and in Saint-Louis: The
Diagnists who now hold power, blacks or half-blacks, are clearly anti-French.
All of the whites who used to hold office have been replaced by blacks. Occasional whites may still be found in the local assemblies, but there is no use
having any illusions about their future; for sooner or later, despite their flexibility and adaptability, they, too, will be swept away. We must conclude that
today in the Four Communes the former subjects have become the masters—
and what masters![54]

## CHAPTER 12

# The Significance of African Local Rule

BLAISE DIAGNE had never talked about Senegalese independence as an immediate goal for the African movement he led. Rather, like such contemporaries as Herbert Macauley in Nigeria and Casely Hayford in Gold Coast, he was interested in working within the colonial system to gain further political advances for Africans. Clearly, the political activities of the Four Communes do not bear comparison with the nationalistic independence movements that have characterized the breakup of European empires since World War II. But in the world of the 1920's, colonial officials like Martial Merlin, Albert Sarraut, and others considered the appearance of Africans in local politics an ominous portent for the future of French rule in Africa. Merlin tried to manipulate the African chiefs in the new Colonial Council and undermine the influence of the citizen members. Sarraut blocked the appointment of certain French administrators to posts in West Africa because they were rumored to be Diagnists. The Union Coloniale in Paris actively lobbied against Diagne and his projects; and the Comité d'Action Républicaine proposed creating a double electoral college in Senegal, with only persons living under the French civil code admitted to the higher college.[1]

The electoral victories of Diagne and the Republican-Socialists in 1919–20 forced the French administration to consider whether African political activity should be allowed to grow and spread elsewhere, or whether it should be contained and, if possible, diminished. The second policy was the one adopted. Between 1924 and 1928 control of the police and public sanitation services was transferred from the Communes to the French colonial administration. The Circumscription of Dakar was created in 1925, placing territory around the federal capital under the control of a new, separate administration. For all practical purposes, Africans stayed in control of the municipality; but there was repeated conflict between the African officials of Dakar and the new French administrator.

Diagne found it increasingly difficult to fight both the colonial administration and the attacks of Bordeaux commerce. In 1923 he held several meetings with members of the Bordeaux syndicate of merchants who were active in Senegalese trading. It was agreed that Bordeaux would henceforth support Diagne in return for representation on his councils and in his party. This "Pacte de Bordeaux" was applauded by the Ministry of Colonies, loyal Diagnists, and the new Governor-General, Jules Carde, who had been appointed to ease the tension. The pact inaugurated a decade of cooperation between Bordeaux, the administration, and Diagne's party that ended with Diagne's death in 1934.[2]

A good many Africans were not at all pleased with Diagne's new alliance. In Paris there arose several groups of African radicals (veterans, workers, students, and political expatriates) who became angry critics of Diagne. Typically, these men had sought political asylum in the metropole because they were wanted in the colonies as potentially dangerous agitators. Among their leaders were Lamine Senghor, Kojo Tovalou Quénum, and Tiémoko Kouyaté. They accused Diagne of really being uninterested in winning African emancipation; they founded the Ligue de Défense de la Race Nègre, tried to organize labor unions for the thousands of Africans working in France's port cities, and sought to create an alternative to Diagnism. Some Senegalese students in France were attracted to Kouyaté and Senghor, and to other African and West Indian radicals. Although these intellectuals were relatively powerless against the efficient Diagne organization, they helped to stir up opposition in both France and Senegal.[3] (Tovalou visited Senegal in 1928 to campaign with Diouf against Diagne's reelection.)

In Senegal, a number of dissidents from the 1921 General Council election—notably Thiécouta Diop—joined forces with the young Lamine Guèye (recently returned from Paris with a doctorate in law) to oppose Diagne. They accused Diagne of selling out to Bordeaux and the government. Guèye, Diop, and other dissatisfied Wolofs anxious to sweep out Diagne and the Lebous entered the 1924 elections for deputy; but they made the mistake of putting up a French candidate (lawyer Paul Defferre), who was soundly beaten.[4] By this time, the African electorate insisted on having an African in Paris.

Even the Republican-Socialist party was unhappy with the Pacte de Bordeaux. Diagne's lieutenants remained loyal at first, but began to drift away within a few years. Jean D'Oxoby left in 1926. Galandou Diouf, piqued by Amadou Duguay-Clédor's accession as Diagne's chief lieutenant in Senegal, enlisted Lamine Guèye's support and challenged Diagne for the deputyship in 1928. Diagne won the election, but only with the connivance of the colonial administration, which preferred to keep him in office rather than admit Diouf, whom they considered a greater radical.[5] Diagne's Republican-Socialist party was likewise too strongly entrenched to be put out, and it held on in the municipal and Council elections in 1929 and 1930. Diouf opposed Diagne again in 1932 and was once more defeated. After Diagne's death, Diouf was elected in a 1934 by-election, and won again in 1936; on both occasions his opponent was Guèye. Diouf organized his own political party and controlled local politics until 1940, when Senegal's local political institutions were abolished by the Vichy government.

The African victory of 1919 inaugurated two decades during which the African politicians struggled to improve their position and to strengthen their grip on local politics. Diagne's Republican-Socialist Party became the model for the urban elitist parties that flourished in 1920–40 and 1945–48.[6] Among these were Diouf's Republican-Nationalist Party, Guèye's Senegalese Socialist Party, and the French SFIO (Socialist Party); the last was the first metropolitan party to take root in Senegal.[7] In addition, there were numerous political action groups. The Young Senegalese had disbanded in 1921, when Thiécouta Diop broke with Diagne,[8] but many similar organizations took their place: the Kamara youth group in Dakar, the Mulattoes' Mutual Alliance, the Senegalese Veterans, and a short-lived chapter of Marcus Garvey's Universal Negro Improvement Association were typical.[9] Political committees flourished in the Communes and the larger towns (such as Diourbel, Kaolack, and Zinguinchor), and personal representatives of Diagne, Diouf, and Guèye ran the smaller railway and market towns. Any party in power was able to exercise patronage, since certain jobs in the secretariats of the city councils and the General Council, as well as numerous municipal jobs, were reserved for Africans.

Diagne's possession of his own newspaper (*La Démocratie* and later *L'Ouest Africain Français*) was emulated by Diouf (*Le Sénégal*) and Guèye (who took over *L'A.O.F.*). In addition, more than two dozen minor political journals appeared and vanished during the interwar period. Some of these were produced by Africans attempting to modify local politics; others by French petits colons bent on gaining political power, and others by liberal Frenchmen who wanted to bring social reform to the colonies.[10] The politics of the urban areas became increasingly literate.

During the period of French-Creole domination the most important institution in the colony had been the General Council; but Diagne made the deputyship the key to local politics. Orders went from Paris to Diagne's lieutenant in Senegal—first Diouf and then Clédor. This practice was carried on by Diouf when he became deputy and named ambitious petit colon Alfred Goux as his lieutenant for local affairs. The Colonial Council, though more representative than the General Council, was overshadowed by the deputy, who was able to intervene directly in Paris with the Chamber, the governmental committees, and the Ministry of Colonies. The high point of the deputy's influence was reached during the early 1930's, when Diagne served as Deputy Minister of Colonies in two cabinets.

Politics during the era after 1919 helped to train Africans for future positions of leadership. In this regard, Diagne made a number of contributions before adopting a more conservative approach in his later years. First, he emphasized the participation of Africans as political candidates, government functionaries and members of political organizations (action groups or parties). Second, he conveyed an immense pride in his race and his people—he strongly believed they should have parity with Frenchmen because fundamentally they were no different as human beings. The only difference he admitted was one of education and training. Third, to liberal Europeans Diagne appeared as an example of what "enlightened" Africans might aspire to become, and his career created sympathy for African political ambitions in such important officials as Robert Delavignette.[11] Diagne (and to a lesser extent Diouf) created an impression on the French colonial establishment that lasted even as late as 1945, when it was recommended that all French African colonies should have deputies to the new National Assembly.

### Conclusions

The year 1920 was a turning point in the development of modern politics in Senegal. Embryonic local political institutions had evolved until 1848, when the first guarantee of participation for Africans (as distinct from Frenchmen or Creoles) was made in the parliamentary election instructions. From 1848 to 1900 there was only minimal participation of Africans in the municipal councils and the General Council because the French-Creole entente controlled local politics. By the turn of the century, however, a new attitude was in the making among Africans—a veritable *prise de conscience* in political matters. There was increasing unrest and increasing interest in politics, especially after Galandou Diouf's election in 1909. Finally, the victory of Blaise Diagne in the epochal election of 1914 gave the Africans great confidence and a capable and determined leader. Employing the powers of Senegal's deputy to a maximum, Diagne was able to win a clarification of status for the originaires, gain concessions, and complete the Africanization of local political institutions with the electoral victories of 1919–20.

In conclusion, we may profitably examine several aspects of African politicization that will emphasize the continuity of Senegalese political tradition and clarify the growth of African concern for political matters.

Initially, political activity in Senegal was made possible by the pragmatism of French colonial rule from the Revolution through the Third Republic. The first African mayors and advisers were essentially convenient links between the Governor and the urban Africans. But separation from the metropole at various periods allowed these embryonic institutions to develop; and even though they were only tacitly sanctioned by the Bourbon restoration, they continued to function. The Ordinance of 1840 brought a colonial council to Senegal and a representative to the metropole. And the events of 1848 established the principle that Senegal should be represented in France by a deputy. As a result, when the Third Republic was established Senegal was immediately given a deputy, soon received formal recognition of her municipal institutions, and was eventually endowed with a General Council.

Senegal's local institutions were clearly an outgrowth of France's assimilation theory, and it was presumed that local inhabitants participating in them would be assimilated to French culture and life, as the Creoles already were. The fact that most voters in the colony were unassimilated Africans did not pose a problem in the nineteenth century, since few Africans were candidates for office. But after 1900 the number of young, educated urban Africans increased at the same moment that hostility to assimilation grew in official circles. After French colonial policy had been reexamined and modified, the privileges of Senegal's originaires came under attack; but this action only spurred the Africans to take a greater interest in political matters. The fact that Frenchmen were still sentimentally attached to the ideal of assimilation (and needed additional manpower) allowed Diagne to gain passage of the citizenship laws of 1915 and 1916, the high point of assimilation in tropical Africa before 1945.

There was another dimension to assimilation, however. The African quest for citizenship was not a quest for total assimilation into

French culture (although some elitist Africans, such as Clédor, in essence became "black Frenchmen"). For the overwhelming majority of Senegalese originaires, and for those who aspired to originaire status, the goal was political parity with the French: political and civic rights, combined with enough Western education and skills to allow participation in an urban market economy. At heart, the Senegalese wanted to remain African.[12] Diagne realized this, and he made the retention of the originaire's special status the cornerstone of his policy. The few Senegalese who studied or worked abroad and became greatly assimilated suffered intense alienation—people such as Léopold Senghor and others who later took part in the *négritude* movement, for example.[13] On the other hand Galandou Diouf was perhaps the best example of an African who adopted only the minimum of French culture in order to compete in business and politics; otherwise, he was considered thoroughly African both by his constituents and by Frenchmen.

Urban politics provided a focus for African resistance to French occupation, which had begun in the rural areas after Faidherbe began the conquest of the traditional states. The defeat of Lat-Dior and other traditional chiefs ended overt resistance; but the rise of a dynamic Islamic movement in town and countryside began a covert resistance. Resistance to French domination was taken up by the urban political elite and broadened to mean resistance not only to French administrative domination but also to economic exploitation by Bordeaux commerce and the Creole oligarchy. This was resistance by a group with a common color consciousness and sense of religion, opposed to the alliance of mulattoes, whites, and Catholics. The identity of color and religion were essential elements in local politics.

The Africans of the Communes were not radical until the conquest of the interior stimulated resistance to the French. By the same token, the interior was introduced to modern politics when it sought redress for its grievances. By 1920 it was apparent that political action in Senegal, though technically limited to the Four Communes, was slowly spreading to encompass the entire geographic heartland of Senegal. The influence of originaires in the Protectorate did much to prepare rural Africans for politics when suffrage was finally extended to them in 1946.

The larger significance of the emergence of black African politics in Senegal lies in the example the Four Communes set for the rest of French-speaking Africa. Urban Senegal became a test area for local politics at a time when political activity was proscribed elsewhere in colonial Africa. Students from all of French Africa, studying at the William Ponty school near Dakar in the 1930's, learned their first lessons in politics by watching the Communes. These men were to become the political leaders of the 1940's and 1950's. The African awakening in 1900 and the consolidation of African rights during the next twenty years produced a system of politics that was extended to the other colonies of French tropical Africa after 1945.[14] Deputies were given to all colonies, municipal government on the Senegalese model was established in urban centers, and territorial councils were created that approximated Senegal's General Council.

The deputy's role as party leader and his involvement in metropolitan politics, as exemplified by Diagne, became the norm for African politicians in West and Equatorial Africa. The form and style that characterized politics in black French Africa after 1945 were those evolved in the Communes after 1900. The originaires' success in their quest for political power and recognition was an important step toward the political independence of all French-speaking Africa. It prepared the way for pressuring France to make all Africans citizens and voters, and was one of the first breaks made in the colonial armor. It was an early and accurate portent of the growing intention of Africans all over the continent to achieve independence and self-determination.

◇◇◇◇◇◇◇◇◇◇◇◇◇◇◇◇◇◇◇◇◇◇◇◇◇◇◇◇◇◇◇◇◇◇◇◇◇◇◇◇◇◇◇◇◇◇◇

# Notes

COMPLETE authors' names, titles, and publishing data for the works cited will be found in the Bibliography, pp. 244–55. Further information on interviews will be found in Part II of the Bibliography. The following abbreviations are used in the Notes:

ARS   Archives de la République du Sénégal, Dakar. Contains Archives de l'Afrique Occidentale Français and Archives du Sénégal. Materials from mid-nineteenth century through 1920.

FOM   Archives de la Ministère de la France d'Outre-Mer, Paris. (Formerly the Ministry of Colonies Archives.) Materials from the Bourbon Restoration through 1920.

IFAN   Institut Français d'Afrique Noire, Dakar. Special collections, especially notes and correspondence of French administrators.

The Notes referring to private sources or confidential materials involve documents that I was allowed to see only on the condition that they would not be cited by name.

CHAPTER 1

1. Mille, pp. 77–78. See also the reactions of Inspector Verrier, Ch. 4.

2. The outstanding geographical synthesis for Senegal is Jacques Richard-Molard's *Afrique occidentale française*.

3. Mauny divides most of Senegal into two belts, each part of a larger zone stretching across Africa. Roughly the northern half of Senegal is placed in the Southern Sahel belt, which has light vegetation and is excellent for grazing; the southern half is placed in the North Sudanic belt, which has enough rainfall to support mixed farming and more trees and vegetation. Mauny, pp. 219–22.

4. My interviews with Senegalese indicated that the hivernage provided almost the only chance for Africans to advance in business and civil-service jobs.

5. For a study of the most important ethnic group in the Casamance, see L. V. Thomas, *Les Diola*.

6. Richard-Molard, p. 34.

7. Fouquet, pp. 31–33.

8. It should be noted that modern scholars see few differences between the Toucouleurs and the Fulbe; indeed, the two speak the same language and can be considered essentially of the same ethnic group. For details on the Toucouleur peoples, see, *inter alia*: Boutillier *et al., La moyenne vallée*

222 *Notes to pp. 8–14*

*du Sénégal;* Bâ, "La polygamie en pays toucouleur." A primary source for Tekrour and Fouta Toro history is Delafosse and Gaden, *Chroniques du Fouta Sénégalais.* David Robinson (Columbia) and James Johnson (Wisconsin) are currently completing Ph.D. dissertations on the Toucouleurs in the nineteenth century which will be important contributions; John Willis of Berkeley is writing a full-length biography of Al Hajj Umar Tall.

9. See Brigaud, *Histoire traditionnelle du Sénégal,* pp. 37–41; David Robinson, "The Tradition of the Islamic State in the Fouta Toro in the 18th and 19th Centuries" (unpublished paper).

10. On the Wolofs, see *inter alia:* David P. Gamble, *The Wolof of Senegambia;* Thiam, "Hiérarchie de la société ouolove"; Chabas, "Le droit des successions chez les Ouolofs"; David Ames, "The Economic Base of Wolof Polygyny," *Southwestern Journal of Anthropology,* XI, No. 4 (1955), pp. 391–403; Witherell, "The Response of the Peoples of Cayor to French Penetration."

11. For an interesting account of Wolof origins that is accepted by a minority of qualified observers, see Cheikh Anta Diop, *L'Afrique noire précoloniale,* pp. 173–77. Diop's assumptions are also based on analogies between totemic family names of the Nuer and Wolof. See also Brigaud, *Histoire traditionnelle,* Ch. III; Coifman, "History of the Wolof State of Jolof until 1860, Including Comparative Data from the Wolof State of Walo."

12. Brigaud, *Histoire traditionnelle,* pp. 49–53.

13. Carrère and Holle, p. 113.

14. On the Sereres, see, *inter alia:* Aujas, "Les Sérères du Sénégal"; Bourgeau, "Notes sur la coutume des Sérères"; Klein, *Islam and Imperialism in Senegal.*

15. On the Lebous, see, *inter alia:* Balandier and Mercier, *Particularisme et évolution: Les pêcheurs lebous du Sénégal;* Angrand, *Les Lébous de la presqu'île du Cap Vert;* Faure, *Histoire de la presqu'île du Cap Vert et les origines de Dakar.*

16. Angrand, pp. 55–65. For the French viewpoint (Angrand was a Creole of Lebou ancestry), see the untitled manuscript by Alfred Goux in ARS, 1-G-26-104. For a recent assessment by an African, see Sylla, "Une république africaine au XIXᵉ siècle, 1795–1857." Also useful is a memoir by French administrator Claude Michel, "L'Organisation coutumière de la collectivité léboue de Dakar," *Bulletin du Comité d'Etudes Historiques et Scientifiques de l'A.O.F.,* XVII (1934), No. 3, pp. 510–24.

17. Angrand, pp. 55–65. See also Cheikh Anta Diop, pp. 55–57.

18. The following analysis is based on several items: conversations with André Hauser, Paul Mercier, and Abdoulaye Diop, who have been concerned with social stratification in Senegalese urban areas; Brigaud, *Histoire traditionnelle,* pp. 7–44 (Toucouleur), 45–60 (Wolof), 123–40 (Lebou), and 141–71 (Serere); Paul Mercier, "Aspects des problemes de stratification sociale dans l'ouest africain." See also: Klein, pp. 8–11; Sy, pp. 76–81; L. V. Thomas, pp. 1005–56.

19. See the discussion by Fallers, "Are African Cultivators To Be Called Peasants?"

20. It has been surmised that the term badolo comes from the Fulbe expression "baydolo," meaning "not to have power." See Brigaud, *Histoire traditionnelle,* p. 58.

21. The earliest French observer to offer a description of the Senegalese family was the naturalist Michel Adanson, who lived in Senegal from 1749 to 1754. See especially pp. 40–41 of his *Voyage to Senegal.*

22. Adanson, p. 39. Other European visitors, such as Golberry, Milligan, and Labat, also commented on female freedoms.

23. The standard work on Islam in Senegal is Paul Marty's study based upon many years of first-hand contact with Senegalese Islam as a French native affairs officer, *Etudes sur l'Islam au Sénégal.* See also the relevant chapters in Trimingham, *Islam in West Africa,* and the general discussion in Gouilly, *L'Islam dans l'Afrique occidentale française.* For the Mourides, see Sy, *La confrérie sénégalaise des mourides,* and Cruise O'Brien, *The Mourides of Senegal.*

24. Early Portuguese accounts tell of Wolof chieftains having Moors in their entourages as wise men but say that few Wolofs themselves practiced Islam. Gamble, p. 70; Behrman, "The Islamization of the Wolof," pp. 102–5.

25. Froelich, pp. 222–27.

26. For a general study of the Tijaniyya, see J. Abun-Nasr, *The Tijaniyya, a Sufi Order in the Modern World* (London, 1965).

27. *Ibid.,* pp. 232–38; see also Marty, I, 175–206.

28. Sy, *La confrérie;* Cruise O'Brien, *The Mourides.*

29. Marty, pp. 222–94; Froelich, pp. 227–31.

30. "Les confréries islamiques en A.O.F.," a report by the Governor-General of French West Africa dated September 8, 1915. ARS, 19-G-1. On marabouts, see Maurice Delafosse, "Les confréries musulmanes et le maraboutisme dans les pays du Sénégal et du Niger," *Afrique Française,* No. 4 (Apr. 1911), pp. 81–90.

31. Marty, I, 320–34; personal communication from Dr. Cheikh Tidiane Sy, Dakar; interview with Amadou Assane N'Doye, 1964.

32. For an account of this period, see Abdoulaye Ly, "Le site et les origines de Saint-Louis," *Notes Africaines,* No. 58 (Apr. 1953), pp. 52–57.

33. *Ibid.,* p. 55.      34. See Delcourt, p. 322.

35. Adanson, pp. 38–41.      36. Villard, p. 64.

37. Cultru, pp. 248–49.      38. Hargreaves, "Assimilation," p. 181.

39. *Ibid.,* p. 182. See Hargreaves' reference: Durand, I, 218–20.

40. The following two paragraphs are based on Hargreaves, "Assimilation," pp. 180–83.

41. Golberry, pp. 154–55.

42. Jore, pp. 216–17.

43. Hargreaves, "Assimilation," p. 180.

44. *Annuaire de Gouvernement Général de l'Afrique Occidentale Française* (Paris, 1922).

45. See Delafosse, *Histoire,* p. 110.

46. Carrère and Holle, p. 12.

47. Governor of Senegal to Minister of Colonies, Apr. 19, 1849. FOM, Sénégal VII-50.

48. Villard, pp. 131–32.

49. Brunschwig, *La colonisation française,* p. 88.

50. See Faidherbe, *Le Sénégal, la France dans l'Afrique occidentale.*

51. Quoted in Delavignette and Julien, p. 249.

52. Angrand, pp. 97–101.

53. Villard, pp. 164–65.

54. Alvarez de Almada, a Portuguese traveler who visited Senegal in 1560, noticed peanuts growing around peasant huts and reported that a goodly number were harvested each year for household use. Cited in Fouquet, p. 19.

55. Some of the Mourides were overly zealous in clearing land of its cover, and were responsible for much erosion. Sy, Chapter IV.

56. Economic report, Governor Cor to Governor-General Ponty, 1911. ARS, 2-G-11-7.

57. See *La Démocratie*, Jan. 29. 1914; and the 1917 report of Governor Levecque on the Lebanese problem, ARS, 2-G-17-5.

58. On the migration of Africans, see: 1908 report on Dakar, ARS, 2-G-8-9; 1913 report of Governor Cor, ARS, 2-G-13-8.

59. For a short history of Thiès, see Savonnet, pp. 13–33.

60. My remarks on Saint-Louisians are based on interviews in Saint-Louis, Dakar, and Paris, 1963–64.

CHAPTER 2

1. Certain materials in this chapter are also discussed in Johnson, "The Development of Local Political Institutions."

2. See, for example: Olivier, *Le Sénégal*; Deschamps, *Le Sénégal et la Gambie*; Exposition Universelle de 1900, Paris, *Le Sénégal* (Paris, 1900).

3. Jore, p. 257.

4. *Ibid.*, p. 258.

5. These requests were presented to the National Assembly on 14 March 1794. *Ibid.*, pp. 136–37.

6. See pp. 55–62.

7. Alquier, pp. 277–320, 411–63. There are 452 orders preserved, dating from 1789 to 1807.

8. This view was held by such an eminent legal scholar as P. Dislère, and was argued in his *Traité de législation coloniale*. Dislère, however, had undoubtedly never seen the dispatches in the Senegal archives.

9. Alquier, p. 295.

10. *Ibid.*

11. *Ibid.*, p. 297.

12. Commandant of Senegal to Minister of Marine, Nov. 12, 1823. FOM, Sénégal VII-8.

13. Commandant of Senegal to Minister of Marine, 1824. FOM, Sénégal VII-8.

14. Analysis of petitions for municipal organization of Senegal, Feb. 14, 1872. FOM, Sénégal VIII-51. Among the non-French signers were Guillabert of the Army engineers and Foy, "wealthy indigenous merchant and father-in-law of Gaspard Devès." The Ministry noted that the petitions of 1869 and 1870 had a greater number of local notables' signatures.

15. Petition and letter to de Fongaufier, Saint-Louis, Jan. 15, 1872. *Ibid.*

16. De Fongaufier to Minister of Marine, Feb. 12, 1872. *Ibid.*

17. *Ibid.*

18. Minister of Colonies to de Fongaufier, Mar. 12, 1872. *Ibid.*

19. Letter from petitioners to de Fongaufier, May 15, 1872. *Ibid.*

20. Decree of August 10, 1872: Article II, Paragraph 11.

21. *Ibid.*, Article VIII.
22. Ballay to Minister of Colonies, July 27, 1898. FOM, Sénégal VII-68.
23. Report of municipal election, Dakar, Oct. 2, 1898. ARS, 20-G-11.
24. See the discussion in Jore, pp. 129–30.
25. Jore observes that this document, *Addresse des habitants du Sénégal*, was probably the work of Lamiral alone, and that the Senegalese had not seen it. However, Lamiral signed it "au nom et par pouvoir des habitants du Sénégal." My impression is that Lamiral had actually become an unofficial Paris representative for the citizens of Saint-Louis and was not acting strictly in self-interest, as Jore insinuates. *Ibid.*, pp. 130–31.
26. See the biographical note on Lamiral, *ibid.*, p. 139. Lamiral's motives have been questioned by Jore and Mercier, among others; i.e., they imply that he was more concerned with keeping slave-trading alive in Senegal than with political or human rights. The fact that he was probably the real instigator of the *cahier* of Saint-Louis in 1789, however, before the slave trade was in peril, indicates his interest in political rights. His later writings on behalf of slavery damaged his reputation with later historians. See Jore, pp. 126–39; Roger Mercier, pp. 180–86.
27. Hardy, *La mise en valeur*, p. 231.
28. Commandant Gerbidon to Minister of Marine, June 8, 1827. FOM, Sénégal VII-7.
29. Governor of Senegal to Minister of Marine, Feb. 10, 1837. *Ibid.*
30. There is a gap in the archival material at this point in the early 1840's; we know little about Calvé except that he was elected.
31. Undated memo in FOM, Sénégal VII-7. See also Hardy, *La mise en valeur*, p. 231.
32. Minister of Marine to "Commissioner of the Republic of Senegal," May 10, 1848. FOM, Sénégal VII-44.
33. *Ibid.*
34. Official report on election of October 30, 1848. FOM, Sénégal VII-44.
35. Official report on election of August 12, 1849. *Ibid.*
36. *L'Ordre* (Paris), Oct. 12, 1851.
37. Undated memo in FOM, Sénégal VII-44.
38. *Moniteur du Sénégal*, Apr. 4, 1871.
39. Governor of Senegal to Minister of Marine, Mar. 14, 1871. FOM, Sénégal VII-45.
40. ARS, 20-G-17 (17).
41. *Le Réveil du Sénégal*, Sept. 13, 1885.
42. *Ibid.*
43. *Ibid.*, Oct. 11, 1885.
44. *L'Union Africaine*, Dec. 5, 1896.
45. Minister of Colonies to Governor-General of Senegal, Apr. 10, 1896. FOM, Sénégal VII-7b.
46. *Tableau des élections à la Chambre des députés*, Archives of the Chamber of Deputies, Paris.
47. Hardy, *La mise en valeur*, pp. 227–29.
48. Memo in FOM, Sénégal VII-7.
49. Minister of Marine to Governor of Senegal, Feb. 25, 1834. FOM, Sénégal VII-4.

50. The Ordinance of January 17, 1822, created the Conseil du Gouvernement; that of July 9, 1830, created the Conseil Privé.
51. Memo in FOM, Sénégal VII-4.
52. Analysis of the Ordinance of 1840. FOM, Sénégal VII-9.
53. *Ibid.*
54. Mager, pp. 96, 107; see also the election reports for September and October 1879, in FOM, Sénégal VII-33.
55. Buell, I, 696–74. See also Idowu, "Conseil Général," pp. 306–70, on the Council's powers.
56. Buell, I, 979. Buell was writing after some powers of the Council had been diminished by the reorganization of 1920–21. Kenneth Robinson agreed with Buell that the Council had greater powers than its counterparts elsewhere in Black Africa; see Robinson, "Political Development in French West Africa."
57. Sierra Leone's council is covered on p. 43 of Martin Wight's *The Development of the Legislative Council, 1606–1945* (London, 1946), a study of councils throughout the British Empire. Wight claims Sierra Leone developed British Africa's first legislative council in 1863. (See also pp. 66–69, 73–78.) For Nigeria, see James Coleman, *Nigeria: Background to Nationalism* (Berkeley, 1958). For Gold Coast, see David Kimble, *A Political History of Ghana* (Oxford, 1963).
58. This analysis is based on the minutes of the General Council, 1879–1920, issued annually by the government printers at Saint-Louis. See also: Governor of Senegal to Minister of Marine, Nov. 4 and 11, 1891, ARS, 20-G-8; an article by Lamine Guèye in *L'A.O.F.*, Jan. 4, 1936; and an article by Jean Daramy d'Oxoby in *L'Ouest Africain Français*, May 25, 1925.

CHAPTER 3

1. Bouna N'Diaye, the Bourba of Djolof, served in the French army during World War I, was appointed to a French chiefship, and served in the Colonial Council after its creation in 1920. Although he was aggressive, intelligent, and independent, his great prestige among the Senegalese derived almost entirely from his hereditary title. In 1923, when the Bour of Sine died, the French announced that no one would be appointed in his stead. Yet Africans saw no reason to stop honoring the next in line, since traditional legitimacy was not an issue to be decided by the French. From France's viewpoint, these deposed rulers and their heirs were simply pretenders.
2. From personal interviews with Senegalese active in politics during 1900–1920. Dakar, Rufisque, and Saint-Louis, 1964.
3. On the organization and administration of Senegal, see: Olivier, Pt. III; Deschamps, *Le Sénégal et la Gambie*, Pt. III; and Buell, I, Chaps. 61–63, 67, and 69.
4. See Villard, pp. 184–85.
5. As we have seen, however, a similar kind of council certainly existed during the last years of the *ancien régime*.
6. This statement is based on my examination of the quarterly and annual reports of the Governor of Senegal to the Governor-General, 1898–1934 (ARS, Series 2-G), and on the reports of the Governor-General to Paris (same series). I found it remarkable that so many important items were omitted from the summaries sent to Paris.

7. In 1926, when Buell visited Senegal, there were 110 chiefs of villages and cantons still in office. Most of the traditional chiefs in the Thiès district of Senegal (Wolof and Serere peoples) were under appointed chiefs who had been administrative clerks—and this in an area where there were many educated claimants to legitimate authority who could have been appointed. Buell, I, 990–91. See also discussion in Crowder, *West Africa*, pp. 187–94.

8. Election dossier, 1921 Council elections. ARS, 20-G-74(23).

9. Olivier, pp. 169–85; Solus, pp. 13–34, 508–22.

10. By 1905, the federal government had appropriated 78 percent of Senegal's revenues; in return it assumed only 39 percent of the expenses formerly covered by these funds. This argument was given before the Council of State in the 1908 hearings (see Buell, I, 933). The General Council argued that its right to customs receipts had been given it by parliamentary statute, and that a presidential decree could not take this away. The Council of State observed that the General Council did not have exclusive jurisdiction over taxation in Senegal and could levy only those taxes that the federation government chose to authorize (arrêté of May 29, 1908).

11. Van Vollenhoven, Decree of July 28, 1917.

12. Buell, I, 932.

13. *Le Soir*, Nov. 11, 1904. For a fuller discussion of Roume's role in centralizing authority, see Newbury, "Formation of the Government General."

14. He made a name for himself by trying to halt domestic slavery and setting up "freedom villages," as Faidherbe had done, and by giving released slaves advances in seed and grain. ARS, 21-G-127(108).

15. *La Démocratie*, June 20, 1915.

16. *L'A.O.F.*, June 14, 1915.

17. Many of these are printed in the memorial volume published by his colleagues: Van Vollenhoven, *Une ame de chef*.

18. Roberts, I, 134. Not impressed with France's centralizing tradition, Roberts continued: "Most of the ordinary affairs in colonial life are determined by the dictates of the permanent officers in Paris; add to this the lack of self-government in the colonies, and it will be obvious why France is a century behind England in this regard." Roberts, like most writers on French colonial theory or policy, never ventured into the colonies to see the system at work. His remarks about the central administration are quite accurate, but he is less authoritative on matters outside Paris.

19. Cowan, p. 51. See also Cohen, *Rulers of Empire*, for an important study on the formation of colonial administrators, with special reference to French West Africa.

20. British Naval Intelligence Division, *French West Africa* (Oxford, 1943), I, 249–50.

21. See, for example: Roberts, *History of French Colonial Policy*; Thompson and Adloff, *French West Africa*; Buell, *The Native Problem*; Betts, *Assimilation and Association*; Deschamps, *Méthodes et doctrines*.

22. Crowder, *Senegal, A Study of French Assimilation Policy*; Amon d'Aby, *La Cote d'Ivoire dans la cité africaine*. English-speaking Africa has fared much better, and there are individual studies of colonies by Coleman, Kimble, Apter, Gann, Rotberg, and others.

23. Betts, p. 15.

24. Crowder, *Senegal*, p. 2.

25. Deschamps, *Méthodes et doctrines,* p. 121.
26. Betts, p. 20.
27. For a discussion of this literature, see *ibid.,* especially Chaps. 4 and 6.
28. Michael Persell, "The French Colonial Congresses." Unpublished seminar paper, Stanford University, 1965.
29. Betts, p. 8.
30. See also Hubert Deschamps, "Et maintenant, Lord Lugard?" *Africa,* XXXIII, No. 4 (1963), pp. 293–306.
31. Cowan, p. 36.
32. *Ibid.,* p. 44.
33. Their most important arguments are reproduced in Forgeron, pp. 75–95.
34. Cowan, p. 45.

CHAPTER 4

1. Guèye, *Etapes et perspectives,* p. 24.
2. *Ibid.,* p. 30. See also Guèye's discussion of the period 1789–1833, pp. 21–26.
3. Report of Inspector-General Verrier on the Senegalese election lists, extracts of June 25, 1905. ARS, 20-G-17(17).
4. *Ibid.*
5. Verrier ignored the Declaration of 1795, the Order of 1830, and the Law of 1833. These were used later by such men as Lamine Guèye to show the historic antecedents of African political rights.
6. Verrier to Minister of Colonies, July 21, 1905. FOM, Sénégal VII-7b.
7. Roume to Minister of Colonies, July 8, 1950. *Ibid.*
8. Arrêté of July 24, 1907.
9. Runner, p. 22.
10. Decree of May 20, 1857. Runner (pp. 20–21) notes that the Court of Appeal had always avoided pronouncing on the status of Africans between the decrees of 1830 and 1857.
11. See Paul Mercier, "L'Evolution des élites sénégalaises."
12. Memo on migration to the city of Dakar, 1908, ARS, 2-G-8-9; report by Governor Jore, 1926, ARS, 2-G-26-10.
13. For an important discussion of caste in contemporary Senegal, see Silla, "Persistence des castes."
14. Even after World War II and the extension of politics to the interior, ethnic groupings were far less important in Senegal than in most African colonies. (Contrast with Nigeria or Kenya, for example.)
15. On the Lebanese as a political pressure group, see *La France-Coloniale,* May 31, 1928. The Comité Libano-Syrien of Dakar is described in ARS, 21-G-133-108.
16. Election dossier for 1909. ARS, 20-G-18.
17. Governor-General Gabriel Angoulvant called the members of the Communes "a true civil and political aristocracy based on the chance of birth." ARS, 17-G-241-108.
18. The many editorials and columns published by Amadou N'Diaye Duguay-Clédor are an illustration of this. For example, Clédor reprinted Faidherbe's laudatory speech delivered to the School for the Sons of Chiefs,

claimed that the Africans were working for the same goals that André Brüe had sought (*La France Coloniale*, May 8, 1930), and sought to describe the feelings of elite Africans toward France in a series of articles called "Pensées vers l'idée de patrie" (which began in *La Démocratie*, Aug. 22, 1915). Masylla Diop, an African poet, tried his hand at evoking the African past in "Epopée sénégalaise" (*La Démocratie*, Nov. 20, 1913).

19. This was the periodic theme of special and regular reports from the Governor of Senegal to the Governor-General (most included in Series, 2-G, ARS, Dakar). Communications usually broke down on this point, however: the Governor (regardless of the man actually occupying the position) was usually less sympathetic toward the originaires than his superior was.

CHAPTER 5

1. Villard, pp. 96–97.
2. The Devès family did not officially recognize its Senegalese offshoot, but the two were often associated in business enterprises during the nineteenth century.
3. I have discussed some of the following ideas with Professor Roger Pasquier of the Sorbonne, who is working on a study of Senegal's economic history in the nineteenth century. Pasquier's *thèse*, when finished, will shed much light on trade, shipping, and commerce in Senegal, and on Bordeaux's role in these enterprises.
4. For the beginnings of the sociétés de prévoyance, see a special report dated 1909, ARS, 2-G-9-7.
5. Report on Lebanese in commerce, 1914, ARS, 2-G-14-6.
6. A. Bibé, *Comptes rendus de 1922* (Saint-Louis du Sénégal, 1922).
7. R. L. Buell, during his visit to French Africa, was impressed with the influence and organization of the chambers of commerce, which were "of a type unknown to Anglo-Saxons." The chambers were supported by a license tax on all merchants, whether or not they were members. It was the administration's policy to consult the chambers on a number of economic questions. Buell, I, 927.
8. A survey from private materials (ms. held by Robert Delmas of Dakar) revealed the following about the composition of chambers of commerce in the Communes. In all cases, African merchants formed the majority of the total membership and possessed the right to vote; but candidates for executive positions were drawn only from the upper membership categories, which were made up of Frenchmen and Creoles. From 1870 to 1940, only 17 Africans served on the governing boards, as follows. *Saint-Louis*: Bacre-Waly, Abdoulaye Mar (1880's); Ogo Seck, Malick Fall, Moctar Dia (1920's); Malick Fall, Yare Fall (1930's). *Dakar*: Mody Camara, Matar Guèye (1920's); both of these, plus Samba Ba and Wagane Diouf (1930's). *Rufisque*: Omar Sy, Alioune Yamar Guèye, Ibra Seck (1920's); Badiane Salif, Madiama Diop, alternates Amadou Seck and Mawa Doukouré (1930's). No Africans served at Gorée.
9. See *L'A.O.F.*, Jan. 11, 1914.
10. Material taken from genealogical tables in Robert Delmas ms.
11. Suret-Canale, p. 222.          12. Note in FOM, Sénégal VII-4.
13. Suret-Canale, pp. 221–22.       14. *Ibid.*, p. 224.

15. This attitude appears in the reports of the Governors of Senegal after the 1902, 1906, 1910, and 1914 elections for deputy (all are in the ARS 20-G series). See also ARS, 2-G-10-13, which indicates the attitude of Governor Justin Devès toward Africans as voters and supporters. But it would be incorrect to say that Senegal's electorate was politically ignorant solely because of the Bordeaux merchants and certain Creole families. Until the twentieth century Senegal had no educational facilities that could teach Africans about politics as practiced in France during the Third Republic. The situation changed when the development of more schools produced a literate African elite.

16. By 1920, however, many petits colons found it advantageous to cooperate with the Africans in politics. Interview with M. Charles Graziani, August 1964.

17. The Director of the Guinea railway noted: "Mr. Daramy is intelligent, works hard, and has some good qualities; but he has the capital fault of being unable to live within his means. Therefore, he'll just never make it as a railway agent." See ARS, 17-G-233-108.

18. *La Démocratie*, Nov. 5, 1913. French journalism during this period was often polemical because articles and editorials were paid for by interested parties.

19. *La Démocratie*, Jan. 24, 1914.

CHAPTER 6

1. See two articles on French women in West Africa: *L'A.O.F.*, Mar. 3, 1928; *L'Ouest Africain Français*, Sept. 7, 1929.

2. Based on interviews with two modern Creole political leaders: André Guillabert, Vice-President of the National Assembly (1964); and the late Louis Legros, Mayor of Saint-Louis and former Ambassador from Senegal to the Vatican (1964).

3. Villard, p. 157; interviews with André Guillabert and Aby Kane Diallo.

4. Villard, pp. 96–98.

5. I disagree with Villard (p. 97), who asserts that few Creoles were educated. In the colonial archives in Paris, there are indications that Creoles did go on to France for higher education (see FOM, Sénégal X series). François Carpot and Justin Devès were two noted Creoles who studied in Paris and Bordeaux.

6. Villard, p. 98.

7. Governor-General to Minister of Colonies, May 3, 1902. FOM, Sénégal VII-7b.

8. *Ibid.*

9. See the version of Roume's report in ARS, 20-G-12.

10. Election dossier of 1902. *Ibid.*

11. Rally of Apr. 16, 1902. ARS, 20-G-12.

12. Rally of Apr. 25, 1902. *Ibid.*

13. Police report, Apr. 28, 1902. *Ibid.*

14. Report of Délegué de Dakar, Apr. 28, 1902. *Ibid.*

15. Rally of Apr. 25, 1902. *Ibid.*

16. Excerpts from election posters. ARS, 20-G-12.

17. Election dossier of 1902. ARS, 20-G-12.

18. The letter was confiscated by French agents and given to the Governor-General, who was greatly annoyed. Carpot to Abdoulaye Faye, Jan. 19, 1906. *Ibid.*
19. Governor of Senegal to Governor-General, May 10, 1906. ARS, 20-G-15.
20. Profession de foi, Teisseire. *Ibid.*
21. Profession de foi, Carpot. *Ibid.*
22. Carpot, 2,857 votes; Marsat, 1,878; Teisseire, 857. Report of May 22, 1906. *Ibid.*
23. He had replaced the Creole Léopold Angrand as the leader of Gorean politics. Interview with Armand Angrand, 1964.
24. Gaspard Devès is one of the nineteenth century's most fascinating figures, but there is no biography of him. There are numerous references in Hargreaves' *Prelude to the Partition of West Africa.*
25. Mlle. Elisabeth Devès, daughter of Justin Devès, in a private interview asserted: "Même la politique de la famille Devès était à la base de la pénétration française du fleuve." Dakar, 1964.
26. See ARS, 20-G-7.
27. Governor-General to Minister of Colonies, May 29, 1908. ARS, 20-G-17.
28. Election reports, ARS, 20-G-14.
29. Governor to Governor-General, political report, 1904. ARS, 2-G-4-7.
30. Guy to Governor-General, May 27, 1904. ARS, 20-G-14.
31. Governor of Senegal to Governor-General, July 10, 1909, ARS.
32. Personnel dossier of Galandou Diouf, ARS, unclassified; interview with Moustapha Diouf, 1964.
33. *La Presse Coloniale*, Oct. 4, 1910.
34. Presidential decree of Jan. 5, 1910.
35. For a discussion of Carpot's campaign ideas, see the copies and clippings of *Le Radical Sénégalais* in ARS, 20-G-19.
36. Justin Devès's brother Hyacinthe polled 130 votes, but was not considered a serious candidate. Report on elections of Apr. 24, 1910, ARS, 20-G-19.
37. *Ibid.*
38. The depositions are in FOM, Folio 13, Sénégal VII-51b. See also records of the investigation conducted in the Protectorate and on the railway line between Saint-Louis and Dakar, ARS, 2-G-10-13.
39. Guy to Governor-General, political report of third trimester, 1910. ARS, 2-G-10-13.
40. Guy to Governor-General, May 7, 1912. ARS, 20-G-17.
41. Five Africans were elected in Dakar. Election reports, *ibid.*

CHAPTER 7

1. There were many such outbreaks. Administrator Chautemps of Baol and Police Chief Bourdennec of Rufisque were both assassinated (ARS, 13-G-77). The African postal workers struck, refusing to wear uniforms in place of their traditional robes; and African employees in general demanded at least one full day of rest each week (*Le Petit Sénégalais*, June 6, 1914). Some Africans in Rufisque even demonstrated for the right to play their traditional drums at certain hours (ARS, 13-G-72).
2. A good example of this *mentalité* can be found in Hardy, *Une conquête morale*, especially pp. 1–4.

3. Decree of May 25, 1912, *Journal Officiel de l'Afrique Occidentale Française*, 1912, p. 395.

4. Delafosse, "Les confréries musulmanes," p. 89.

5. See Marty, *Etudes sur l'Islam*, I, 186. "Ce n'est pas une idée ou une doctrine commune qui constitue le lien intime qui réunit les indigenes: c'est un homme." This was in reference to Al Hajj Malick Sy, one of Senegal's most respected marabouts, but it succinctly summarizes the general situation.

6. Sy, p. 105; Cruise O'Brien, p. 39. Behrman (p. 28) maintains that Thioro Diop was Lat-Dior's sister.

7. Marty, *Etudes sur l'Islam*, I, 222–23.

8. Médioune Thiam, *Cheikh Ahmadou Bamba* (Conakry, 1964), pp. 6–8.

9. Private communication from Dr. Cheikh Tidiane Sy, Dakar.

10. There are indications that Bamba might have contemplated armed resistance in 1903. According to rumor, he had privately voiced Allah's desire that the French be driven from the country; and pilgrims descended on his headquarters with gifts of horses, arms, and money (no regulations on carrying firearms were enforced in Senegal until World War I). Bamba refused to go to Saint-Louis, so 150 infantrymen and 50 spahis were sent to take him to Mauritania (political report, 1903, ARS, 2-G-3-7). The Governor of Senegal noted in his 1910 political report to the Governor-General that Bamba was "behaving well" since the French had issued an ultimatum giving precise indications of what he could and could not do (political report for third trimester, ARS, 2-G-10-13).

11. When Marty wrote, the Mourides were just entering the towns, usually as day workers who returned to the country after several months of labor. After 1919, however, a slow migration of Mourides to the urban areas began.

12. Political report for second trimester, 1911. ARS, 2-G-11-7.

13. On Cheikh Anta M'Backé, Bamba's brother, see Marty, *Etudes sur l'Islam*, I, 237–38.

14. Cheikh Anta M'Backé is a good example: technically without political rights in the Communes, he wielded considerable influence in local politics from 1914 through 1928, when he was finally deported to the French Soudan.

15. Marty, *Etudes sur l'Islam*, I, 208.

16. *Ibid.*, p. 180.

17. *Ibid.*, p. 203.

18. The comments in this paragraph are excerpted from a pronouncement made by Malick Sy on September 8, 1912. *Ibid.*, p. 208.

19. Report in ARS, 2-G-22-9. When Malick Sy died in 1922 he was mourned by Tijani, Mourides, and French alike. Even Amadou Bamba sent his brother Cheikh Anta M'Backé to attend the funeral.

20. The breakdown by Communes was as follows. *Saint-Louis:* 77 marabout teachers, 72 of them Wolofs; about half were Tijaniyya, and most of these were followers of Malick Sy; of the 2,011 students, 300 also attended French schools. *Dakar:* 30 teachers, 13 of them Lebous; 28 were Tijaniyya, most affiliated with Sy; 672 students, with 49 attending French schools. *Rufisque:* 14 teachers, 12 of them Tijaniyya; Sy's influence strong; 240 students, 12 attending French schools. These survey figures are in Marty, *Etudes sur l'Islam*, II, 48–49, 63, 85–87.

21. See Van Vollenhoven, pp. 189–210.

22. Report on the lower Senegal by the Secretary-General of French West Africa, 1903. ARS, 2-G-3-7.

23. Unclassified personnel dossiers in ARS.

24. Dossier on Mody M'Baye, ARS, 13-G-77.

25. Notation of Ponty on a letter from Cor to Ponty, Oct. 8, 1907. ARS-G-77.

26. Mody M'Baye to Governor-General, May 12, 1904. *Ibid.*

27. Depositions taken by Aubry Lecomte, Inspector of Administrative Affairs, Sept. 3, 1907. *Ibid.*

28. Cor to Ponty, Feb. 1909. *Ibid.*

29. *L'Eveil Colonial*, May 25, 1922. For a discussion of early newspapers in Senegal, see Pasquier, "Les débuts de la presse"; Boulègue, "La presse au Sénégal avant 1939."

30. The article by Senator Isaac is in *L'Afrique Occidentale*, Sept. 15, 1896.

31. Dossier on Mody M'Baye, ARS, 13-G-77. Also see Klein, *Islam and Imperialism*, Chapters X–XII, for background on Brocard.

32. M'Baye dossier, ARS, 13-G-77.

33. François de Pressensé to Minister of Colonies, undated. ARS, 13-G-77.

34. Ponty to Cor, June 1913. *Ibid.*

#### CHAPTER 8

1. Delafosse, in Hanotaux and Martineau, p. 100.

2. Abbé P. D. Boilat, *Esquisses sénégalaises* (Paris: E. Bertrand, 1853).

3. Villard, *Histoire du Sénégal*, p. 96.

4. Guy to Governor-General, political reports for 1904. ARS, 2-G-4-7.

5. Colonie du Sénégal, rapport d'ensemble, 1903. ARS, 2-G-4-7.

6. *Ibid.*

7. Tables 3 and 4 are compiled from the education reports for 1910. ARS, 2-G-10-2.

8. Péter, p. 265.

9. See the critique of Senegalese education printed in *La Démocratie* (Aug. 22, 1915) and signed Lélo Valdor (probably a *nom de plume*).

10. In fact, in later years some Africans praised the advantages of receiving a Catholic education from the Frères de Ploërmel. Galandou Diouf, whose opinions were probably typical of the urban Muslim community, was reported as saying that the priests had done a better job of teaching than the state teachers. Excerpts from deliberations of the General Council, session of December 1920. Quoted in ARS, 4-E-13.

11. One of the first issues taken up by *La Démocratie* after its founding was the Lebou land question. *La Démocratie*, Nov. 20, 1913.

12. This material was recorded in interviews; for a written evaluation, see the article signed by Alioune M'Baye, *Paris-Dakar*, July 31, 1937.

13. See Chapter VI. To be sure, other Africans had served before Galandou Diouf (notably Bacre-Waly, the grandfather of Lamine Guèye). But none of them had Diouf's independence, originality, and crusading spirit. It was ironic that the Lebous elected Diouf, since generally speaking they detested Saint-Louisians. The feeling was reciprocal, and the aristocratic citizens to the north held the Lebous in low esteem.

The material on the following pages is drawn from personnel files on

Diouf at ARS (non-classified), and from interviews with his son Moustapha Diouf, his former colleague Maurice Guèye of Rufisque, and his former supporter Aby Kane Diallo, who served as mayor of Saint-Louis when Diouf was deputy.

14. To my knowledge, Diouf always thought of himself as purely African, and not part of the Creole community. It is probable that his father's name came from an ancestor who was a Catholicized African rather than a Creole.

15. Election dossier for General Council elections of 1909.

16. Report for the third quarter, 1910. ARS, 2-G-10-13.

17. Report for the fourth quarter, 1910. *Ibid.*

18. Procès-verbal of the General Council, Nov. 6, 1912.

19. Galandou Diouf, signed article in *La Démocratie*, July 18, 1915.

20. Much of the following is based on my interviews with former members of the Young Senegalese: Lamine Guèye, president of the National Assembly; Aby Kane Diallo, former mayor of Saint-Louis; and Amadou Assane N'Doye, former Dakar municipal councilor.

21. Guèye, *Itinéraire africain.*

22. *Ibid.*, pp. 18–19.

23. *La Démocratie*, Nov. 13 and Dec. 25, 1913. The first excerpt was signed by "Merlo," who may have been Mody M'Baye.

24. Procès-verbal of the General Council, Nov. 6, 1912.

25. *La Démocratie*, Nov. 5, 1913 (first issue).

26. *La Démocratie*, May 19, 1915.

27. *Ibid.*, Jan. 15, 1914. D'Oxoby commented: "The politics of combat followed by *La Démocratie* [has] embarrassed this candidate. . . . *La Démocratie* will wait and enter the political arena in due time with a candidate of its own choice."

CHAPTER 9

1. *L'A.O.F.*, May 11, 1912.

2. Interview with Raoul Diagne, son of Blaise Diagne, Dakar.

3. Quoted in Cros, p. 14.

4. *Journal Officiel du Sénégal*, Aug. 7, 1890.

5. This quotation and other materials in this section are taken from classified archival sources that cannot be cited (see note in Bibliography).

6. Possibly Michel Sangué, who was one of Diagne's political lieutenants during the 1920's.

7. From confidential materials.

8. Augagneur and Diagne met in a series of public debates in Lyon, Lille, and Paris. *L'A.O.F.*, Apr. 19, 1913.

9. *Ibid.*

10. Gratien Candace, speech at Bordeaux, June 4, 1934. Printed in *Le Franco-Sénégalais*, June 28, 1934.

11. Excerpts from the remaining sections of this chapter have appeared in G. Wesley Johnson, "The Ascendancy of Blaise Diagne."

12. Emile Masson, for example, was an agent for the Bordeaux house of Maurel Frères.

13. Report of Governor Cor, n.d., FOM, Sénégal, VII-81.

14. Interview with Amadou Assane N'Doye, son of Assane N'Doye.

15. See FOM, Sénégal VII-81.
16. Meeting of Young Senegalese, Saint-Louis, Mar. 20, 1914. *Ibid.*
17. *Ibid.*
18. *Ibid.*
19. Diagne rally of May 8, 1914; FOM, Sénégal VII-81. Although this particular extract is from a later date, it closely resembles M'Baye's rhetoric in the earlier speeches.
20. Speech of Apr. 27, 1914. *Ibid.*
21. *Ibid.*
22. Candidates listed in a telegram of Apr. 12, 1914, from Governor-General Cor to the Minister of Colonies. FOM, Sénégal VII-81.
23. Governor-General to Minister of Colonies, Dec. 1909. FOM, Sénégal VII-7b.
24. Memorandum of Minister of Justice to Minister of Colonies, Jan. 10, 1914. *Ibid.*
25. *L'A.O.F.*, Apr. 30, 1914.
26. *La Démocratie*, Nov. 20, 1913.
27. *Ibid.*, Dec. 25, 1913.
28. Based on political reports in FOM, Sénégal VII series, and ARS, 2-G and 21-G series. Also, debates of the General Council and personal interviews with participants in Senegal.
29. *L'A.O.F.*, Apr. 27, 1914.
30. Rally at Saint-Louis, May 8, 1914. FOM, Sénégal VII-81.
31. Posters filed in *ibid.*
32. This anticipated the idea of the Grand Conseil de l'A.O.F., which was created after World War II.
33. Profession de foi, ARS, 30-G-21.     34. *Ibid.*
35. *L'A.O.F.*, Apr. 11, 1914.            36. Election reports, ARS, 20-G-21.
37. *L'A.O.F.*, Apr. 30, 1914. Governor-General to Minister of Colonies, May 1, 1914. FOM, Sénégal VII-81.
38. *La Démocratie*, May 2, 1914.
39. See Diagne and Sergent's telegram of complaint to the Minister of Colonies, May 4, 1914. FOM, Sénégal VII-81.
40. *L'A.O.F.*, May 5, 1914.              41. *L'A.O.F.*, May 2, 1914.
42. *La Démocratie*, May 2, 1914.         43. *Ibid.*
44. Diagne and Sergent's telegram of May 4, 1914. FOM, Sénégal VII-81. See also: Governor-General to Ministry of Colonies, May 27, 1914, *ibid.*; *La Démocratie*, May 16, 1914.
45. *Le Petit Sénégalais*, May 2, 1914.
46. *L'A.O.F.*, May 2, 1914.
47. Procès-verbal, election of May 10, 1914. FOM, Sénégal VII-81. See also ARS, 20-G-21. Out of 8,677 registered voters, 5,321 went to the polls—the second highest turnout in the Four Communes' history to that time.
48. Acting Governor of Senegal to Governor-General, political report for second trimester, 1914. ARS, 2-G-14-6.
49. Political report, ARS, 2-G-11. By contributing to the 1914 campaign, the Mourides continued a practice apparently begun in 1902 when they supported François Carpot, who arranged Bamba's release from exile. For 1902, see Cruise O'Brien, p. 44; for 1914, see ARS, 2-G-11. The practice became

standard among certain Islamic sects down to 1940. After the Second World War, with the suffrage extended to the countryside, the situation was reversed; politicians arranged subsidies for rural marabouts in return for delivering the vote.

50. Acting Governor of Senegal to Governor-General, second trimester, 1914, ARS, 2-G-14-6.

51. Governor-General to Minister of Colonies, June 24, 1914. ARS, 20-G-21. *La Démocratie* had agitated since January 1914 for the adoption of the secret ballot, which it claimed was more necessary in Senegal than elsewhere because so many voters were easily intimidated.

52. Article by Robert Chot, who knew Diagne in Paris in 1914. *Le Petit Parisien*, May 20, 1934; reprinted in *Le Franco-Sénégalais*, May 31, 1934.

53. Antonetti to Ponty, June 10, 1914; Ponty to Minister of Colonies, June 24, 1914. Both in ARS, 20-G-21.

54. Antonetti to Ponty, June 10, 1914. *Ibid.*

55. *Ibid.*

56. Anonymous source, quoted in *ibid.*

57. *Ibid.*

58. Ponty to Minister of Colonies, June 24, 1914. ARS, 20-G-21.

59. Ponty to Minister of Colonies, June 15, 1914. ARS, 18-G-234-108.

60. Lamine Guèye, *L'itinéraire africain*, p. 30.

61. *Ibid.*, p. 31. The report is filed in ARS, 20-G-21, and was printed in full in the *Journal Officiel de la République Française*, Chamber Debates, session of July 7, 1914, pp. 2735–37.

62. Here the committee stretched a point by saying that Diagne "because of special circumstance" was not affected by the Law of July 20, 1895, which required all members of parliament to have satisfied their military obligations. *Ibid.*

63. *La Démocratie*, May 16, 1916.

64. *Ibid.*, Apr. 28, 1914.

CHAPTER 10

1. Mendy was a Christian *gourmet* from Gorée who had known Diagne for years; he was also associated with the Young Senegalese. See obituary in *France-Coloniale*, June 7, 1928.

2. *La Démocratie*, Sept. 5, 1915.      3. *Ibid.*, Dec. 25, 1913.

4. Duboc, *Les Sénégalais*, pp. 23–24.   5. *Ibid.*, pp. 24–25.

6. *Ibid.* See also Buell, II, 5.        7. Duboc, pp. 24–25.

8. See Davis, pp. 15–55.

9. See the article by Moustaph Malic Gaye on Senegalese heroes in the French army, *France-Coloniale*, Mar. 22, 1928.

10. *L'Union Africaine*, Nov. 28, 1896.

11. Colony of Senegal, General Report, 1903, ARS, 2-G-3-18.

12. *Annales de la Chambre des Députés, débats parlementaires* (1910), pp. 1217–19.

13. Mangin, *La force noire*.

14. Buell, II, 7; *Chambre des Députés, débats* (1912), pp. 1156–62.

15. Buell, II, 7.

16. *Ibid.*, I, 950.

17. Governor Cor to Governor-General Ponty, political Report for Third Trimester, 1913. ARS, 2-G-13-8.
18. Antonetti to Governor-General Ponty, political report for second and fourth trimesters, 1914. ARS, 2-G-14-6.
19. *Ibid.*
20. Buell, II, 7.
21. Georges Bonnefous, *Histoire politique de la Troisième République, Vol. II: La grande guerre, 1914–1919* (Paris, 1957), pp. 1–5.
22. *La Démocratie,* Aug 11, 1914.
23. *Ibid.*
24. *Ibid.,* Aug. 26, 1914.
25. *Ibid.,* Sept. 9, 1914. The troops from the Antilles, Guiana, and Réunion were already part of the regular army.
26. *Ibid.*
27. *Ibid.,* Sept. 23, 1914.
28. *Ibid.*
29. Diouf persuaded the General Council to support Diagne's plan. See ARS, 13-G-72.
30. *Le Petit Sénégalais,* Sept. 7, 1914.
31. Acting Governor Antonetti to Governor-General Ponty, political report for the first trimester, 1915. ARS, 2-G-15-6.
32. *Ibid.*
33. *Ibid.*
34. *Chambre des Députés, débats* (1915), pp. 1072–76.
35. Cros, p. 78.
36. *Chambre des Députés, débats* (1915), pp. 948–49.
37. *Ibid.,* pp. 986–87. 38. *Ibid.,* p. 991.
39. *La Démocratie,* July 28, 1915. 40. *Ibid.*
41. *La Démocratie,* Dec. 15, 1915. 42. *Ibid.,* Dec. 29, 1915.
43. Governor of Senegal, remarks on Justin Devès. ARS, 2-G-16-5.
44. Antonetti to Governor-General Clozel, Jan. 2, 1916. *Ibid.*
45. Antonetti to Clozel, Feb. 10, 1916. *Ibid.*
46. *Chambre des Députés, débats* (1916), Sept.
47. In fact, the Governor of Senegal, hoping to assure his charges' welfare, had persuaded many African farmers to plant millet instead of peanuts. The Union Coloniale in Paris, subsidized by peanut wholesalers, complained bitterly. See the political reports of the Governor to the Governor-General, ARS, 2-G-14-6, and 2-G-15-6.
48. They were postponed by a 1916 decree. See note in ARS, 20-G-22.
49. Interview with André Guillabert, 1964.
50. One of Clemenceau's intimates, General Mordacq, admitted that the Premier had talked of little else for days after becoming Minister of War. See Cros, p. 99.
51. Duchêne, *La politique coloniale,* p. 278.
52. Cros, p. 94.
53. See the special report prepared by Delafosse for Van Vollenhoven, "Situation politique de l'A.O.F. à la fin de l'année 1917," Dec. 12, 1917. ARS, 2-G-17-4.
54. Van Vollenhoven had reason to worry: by 1918 Senegal exported only

129,000 metric tons of peanuts, compared to 280,000 tons in 1914. Villard, pp. 190–91.

55. *Journal Officiel de la République Française*, Jan. 14, 1918, p. 51.

56. Buell, II, 9.

57. *Ibid.*, I, 955.

58. A special report (ARS, 17-G-241-108) states that 158,865 native tirailleurs had served in the colonial forces, and that 7,611 originaires had served in the regular army. This did not include Africans who had been in France at the war's outbreak and had been incorporated into the army there. Buell (II, 10) states that 181,000 Africans served during the war and cites Jean Fabry, "Rapport relatif à la constitution des cadres et effectifs," *Chambre des Députés, documents parlementaires*, No. 6087 (1923), p. 79.

## CHAPTER 11

1. Buell, I, 952–53. See also Runner, *Les droits politiques des indigènes des colonies*, pp. 20–25.

2. Comparative table of registered voters, ARS, 20-G-70-23.

3. *Le Soir*, Sept. 26, 1919. Diagne had opposed Angoulvant, who was Acting Governor-General, and may possibly have had some part in having him transferred. Merlin's appointment, however, was not influenced by Diagne but was a victory for the career officials over Minister Simon, who was a politician and not a professional colonial. From private materials.

4. *La Démocratie Nouvelle*, Oct. 18, 1919.

5. Such articles appeared in *Les Annales Coloniales, Le Temps, Le Soir, La Grande Revue, Le Cri de Paris, La Démocratie Nouvelle*, and *Parlement et Colonies*.

6. *Le Soir*, Sept. 26, 1919. See also clippings in ARS, 17-G-237-108.

7. *Le Soir*, Oct. 17, 1919.

8. Note in ARS, 17-G-233-108.

9. *Le Courrier Colonial*, Sept. 26, 1919.

10. See *La Dépêche Coloniale*, Oct. 22, 1919. It was also provided that 12,000 men per year would be recruited in West Africa for enlistments of three years. In 1919 eight regiments were authorized: two to serve at Saint-Raphaël, two in North Africa, two in West and Equatorial Africa, and two to be available for service on the Rhine or in Syria.

11. Reports of campaign meetings, election of 1919; rally of Nov. 21, 1919. ARS, 20-G-70-23.

12. Rally of Nov. 24, 1919. *Ibid.*

13. See *L'A.O.F.*, Nov. 4 and 6, 1919. To my knowledge, there are no surviving copies of *L'Ouest Africain Français* for the 1919 election; hence I have relied on *L'A.O.F.*, which printed much of what Clédor said in order to refute or ridicule him.

14. *Ibid.*, Nov. 4, 1919.

15. Clédor's statement and the French response are in *ibid.*

16. Quoted in article by Pascal Dumont, *ibid.*, Nov. 6, 1919.

17. *Ibid.*, Nov. 4, 1919.

18. *Ibid.*, Nov. 20, 1919.

19. *Ibid.*

20. *La France-Coloniale*, May 1, 1930; G. Wesley Johnson, "Political Ac-

tion Groups, Factions, and Parties in Early Senegalese Urban Politics," in *The Senegalese Political Tradition*, ed. by G. Wesley Johnson and William J. Foltz (forthcoming).

21. ARS, *Collection affiches electorales.*

22. Levecque to Governor-General Merlin, Dec. 25, 1919. ARS, 20-G-70-23.

23. *Ibid.* Also see ARS, 17-G-15, which indicates that Diagne and Abbal had become bitter enemies because of several personal incidents. In July 1916, for example, Diagne had apparently written to the Minister of Colonies asking why Abbal had been transferred from Dakar to Cameroun rather than being sent to the front.

24. Levecque to Merlin, Dec. 25, 1919. ARS, 20-G-70-23.

25. *Ibid.*

26. France, *Tableau des elections à la Chambre des députés* (Paris: Imprimerie de la Chambre des députés, n.d.).

27. Dossier for election of 1919. ARS, 20-G-69-23.

28. Acting Governor Antonetti to Governor-General Ponty, June 10, 1914. ARS, 20-G-21.

29. I. P. Greslé, *Essai de politique indigène* (Paris: Ernest Sagot, 1919), p. 38.

30. Election dossier, 1921, ARS, 17-G-234-108.

31. Note in ARS, 17-G-237-108. A police report (ARS, 17-G-234-108) observed: "the majority of native typists are in the habit of giving copies of documents originating in the Government General to Diagne's party headquarters."

32. Adrien Allègre, *Aperçu sur la situation politique au Sénégal, 1923.*

33. Information from interviews and private materials in Dakar, Saint-Louis and Rufisque.

34. Levecque to Governor-General Merlin, Jan. 29, 1920, and Merlin to Minister of Colonies, Feb. 2, 1920. ARS, 17-G-234-108.

35. *Le Courrier Colonial*, Oct. 28, 1921.

36. Session of General Council, Dec. 23, 1920. ARS, 17-G-234-108.

37. Memoir on the politics of the Senegalese deputy, 1921. ARS, 17-G-237-108.

38. *Ibid.*

39. *Le Courrier Colonial*, Nov. 25, 1921.

40. *L'A.O.F.*, March 8, 1922.

41. *Le Journal de Rouen*, Sept. 20, 1921.

42. *L'Eveil Colonial*, June 23, 1922.

43. *Les Annales Coloniales*, Oct. 10, 1921.

44. Elections to Conseil Supérieur des Colonies, 1920. ARS, 20-G-73-23.

45. Report by Administrator Fousset, 1918. ARS, 20-G-22.

46. *Ibid.*

47. Interview by Georges Joutel, *La Presse Coloniale*, Dec. 31, 1924.

48. *Ibid.*

49. *Ibid.*

50. Governor-General Angoulvant to Minister of Colonies, Feb. 12, 1919. ARS, 4-E-12.

51. Report of Inspector-General Revel, Oct. 28, 1919. *Ibid.*

52. The dissidents were led by Moustaph Malic Gaye, Papa Konaré, and

Hamet Sow Télémaque. With Thiécouta Diop, these men formed the first African opposition in urban Senegal, beginning a tradition that continued until independence and the institution of a one-party state. See election dossier for 1921, ARS, 20-G-74(23).

53. Governor-General to Governor of Senegal, Apr. 12, 1921. *Ibid.* At times Merlin and other officials did influence voting; but some chiefs allied with the citizens, and others followed an independent political line.

54. *L'A.O.F.*, March 8, 1922.

CHAPTER 12

1. *L'A.O.F.*, Apr. 26, 1923.

2. *L'Ouest Africain Français*, Apr. 27, 1925; note on *pacte de Bordeaux*, ARS, 17-G-237-108.

3. See Langley, pp. 71–92. James Spiegler of Roosevelt University is revising an important Oxford dissertation on interwar French-speaking expatriates in France that should shed much light on this period.

4. Defferre was the father of the later Socialist leader Gaston Defferre.

5. It was alleged that certain irregularities in voting procedures gave the victory to Diagne, whereas it should have gone to Diouf. See electoral analyses in ARS, 20-G-82-23.

6. Léopold Senghor organized the first rural-oriented party, the Bloc Démocratique Sénégalais, in 1948.

7. Archival records indicate that the SFIO had a Senegal chapter composed mostly of Frenchmen as early as 1926. By 1935 many Africans were allowed to join. Note on SFIO in ARS, 21-G-127-108.

8. When Diop left Diagne's camp, he dictated a fascinating memoir of his political views for Governor-General Merlin. See ARS, 17-G-234-108.

9. On Garvey's agents, see confidential reports, ARS, 21-G-133-108.

10. For a complete listing of the newspapers that appeared, see Thomassery, *Catalogue des périodiques.*

11. See Delavignette's eulogy on Diagne, ARS, 20-G-90-23.

12. The question of political versus cultural assimilation is treated in my "Reactions of the Senegalese Urban Elite," a paper presented at the SSRC-ACLS Conference on African Intellectual Reactions to Western Culture, Baltimore, 1969.

13. See Markowitz, *Léopold Sédar Senghor and the Politics of Négritude.*

14. This was true of Mauritania, Soudan (now Mali), Upper Volta, Niger, Ivory Coast, Dahomey, Chad, Oubangi-Chari (now the Central African Republic), French Congo, and Madagascar. Senegalese-style institutions were also introduced to some extent in the French mandates of Togo and Cameroun.

◇◇◇◇◇◇◇◇◇◇◇◇◇◇◇◇◇◇◇◇◇◇◇◇◇◇◇◇◇◇◇◇◇◇◇◇◇◇◇◇◇◇◇◇◇◇◇◇◇◇

# Note on Names and Terms

OF THE many languages that have influenced the history of Senegal, the three most important are Wolof, Arabic, and French. Wolof is the language of the largest ethnic group in the country and the second tongue for thousands of others, especially Africans engaged in commerce. Wolof is almost entirely a spoken language, and its small body of literature is written in either Roman or Arabic script. Arabic has influenced Senegalese Muslims, but only the more educated marabouts were literate in Arabic. Most talibés memorized verses from the Koran without becoming literate. Wolof and Arabic have furnished many of the special terms used in this book; however, since the great bulk of scholarly literature on Senegal is in French, and since French is the official language of the country and the primary language of instruction in the schools, I have decided to follow French practice in orthography.

Anyone who has read the French literature on Senegal for the eighteenth to twentieth centuries, or who has worked through archival materials in Paris and Dakar, is aware of the difficulty of categorizing individuals because of the many terms employed and the nuances of time, place, and current usage. It is often difficult to decide from references whether a hypothetical personage, let us say "Dubois," is (1) a Frenchman, (2) a mulatto, (3) a métis, (4) a gourmet, or (5) an African slave given his master's name. Only an African Muslim, who would probably retain his African clan name and employ an Islamic-derived given name, could be exempted in this case. Moreover, as a general rule, the more anyone in these categories was assimilated, the less likely were references to his color in dispatches, minutes, memoranda, etc.

In this study, I have preferred to group together mulattoes and métis (persons with one European parent or of mixed origin) as Creoles, a term commonly used in Senegal. In some cases, highly assimilated gourmets are linked so closely to the Creole community that they are also referred to as Creoles. All others are qualified as Africans, with a distinction between African Muslims, African Christians (the bulk of the gourmets), and African animists. I have also used the term "native" to refer to indigenous persons in Senegal, despite its unpleasant connotations of imperialism and European exploitation. "African" is often not specific enough, and indigène seems overly affected.

As stated, I have used French practice in rendering almost all Senegalese names and terms. At times, these spellings depart from the forms most commonly used in English. Moreover, purely French words sometimes have altered meanings in a Senegalese context. The following terms occur frequently throughout the text. For other terms useful in understanding Senegalese history see: Klein, pp. 261–63; Lucy C. Behrman, *Muslim Brotherhoods and Politics in Senegal* (Cambridge, Mass.: Harvard University Press, 1970); Cruise O'Brien, p. xxi.

*Bour.* The word for king in Wolof; used by both Wolof and Serere states to indicate the paramount ruler.

*Bourba.* The king of Djolof, the major Wolof kingdom.

*Creole.* In Senegal, a person of mixed European and African ancestry.

*Damel.* The king or paramount ruler of the Wolof kingdom of Cayor.

*Ecrivain public.* A public letter writer. In Senegal, an écrivain public often assumed the role of advocate; he was usually an educated African who could write down the complaints and petitions of African sujets and forward them to the proper French officials.

*Enfant du pays.* Used to denote a person, usually a Creole (but possibly French), born in Senegal.

*Gourmet, gourmette.* A person, usually a full-blooded African, who was assimilated to French culture and converted to Roman Catholicism.

*Habitant.* Usually a free African or a Creole; in some cases, a resident Frenchman.

*Hivernage.* Season of rain and high humidity from June to September. Traditionally, Frenchmen would leave Senegal for vacations in France during hivernage.

*Indigénat.* French code governing sujets français.

*Jugement supplétif.* Special court decisions after 1916 confirming Africans as originaires of the Four Communes.

*Marabout.* French corruption of the Arabic word for cleric (*murabit*). Marabouts were largely responsible for the spread of Islam in Senegal.

*Métis.* A person of mixed African and European ancestry.

*Mouridiyya.* The Mouride brotherhood founded by Amadou Bamba in Senegal.

*Notable.* In Senegal, a person of high standing in the community.

*Originaire.* Originally, a person from the Four Communes; later applied to any Senegalese with French citizenship.

*Palabre.* A long meeting given over to discussion, often political in character.

*Profession de foi.* Campaign platform statements of candidates for elective office.

*Qadiriyya.* The oldest and most common Muslim sufi tariqa in West Africa.

*Serigne.* Wolof word for marabout; probably a corruption of the Fula *sérén* (Muslim clerics).

*Sujet français.* During the colonial period, all Africans who were not originaires were in point of law sujets.

*Talibé.* Follower or student of a marabout.

*Tariqa.* Islamic brotherhood or fraternity.

*Tiédo.* Warrior class, originally of slave origin, which in many areas gained quasi-noble status by the nineteenth century.

*Tijaniyya.* A sufi fraternity founded in North Africa; the largest Muslim brotherhood in Senegal.

*Torodbé.* Among the Toucouleurs, the ruling class of clerics.

*Toubab.* A white person.

*Traitant.* Originally, a trader in gum arabic on the Senegal River, but later applied to merchants in the peanut trade.

*Traite.* In Senegal, the period when peanuts were shipped and sold.

◇◇◇◇◇◇◇◇◇◇◇◇◇◇◇◇◇◇◇◇◇◇◇◇◇◇◇◇◇◇◇◇◇◇◇◇◇◇◇◇◇◇◇◇◇◇◇◇◇◇◇◇

# Bibliography

PRIMARY MATERIALS on Senegalese politics are often difficult to obtain. My primary archival sources for this study were the documents deposited in the Archives of the Republic of Senegal in Dakar (ARS) and those formerly in the Ministry of Colonies in Paris (Archives de la Ministère de la France d'Outre-Mer, FOM). Although in theory both Paris and Dakar observe the fifty-year closure rule on archival deposits, I was able to see materials through 1920 in both collections. Some papers and unclassified materials are impossible to cite; and in some cases, I was given permission to see them on the proviso that they would not be cited. A more complete description of the materials available for Senegal can be found in two publications of my own: "The Archival System of Former French West Africa (*African Studies Bulletin*, VIII, No. 1 (1965), pp. 48–58); "Bibliographical Essay: Senegal" (*Africana Newsletter*, II, No. 1 (1964), pp. 10–12). Two additional sources of value are: Carlo Laroche, "Les Archives d'Outre-mer et l'histoire coloniale française" (*Revue Historique*, CCVI (1951), 213–53); Jacques Charpy, "Les archives du Gouvernement-Général de l'Afrique Occidentale Française" (*A.B.C.D.*, No. 12 (1953), pp. 317–22).

News of the French colonies was reported in several French newspapers during the years 1900–1920; but there was little reporting in depth except at election time or during an economic crisis. Nevertheless, although papers published in Senegal give a far more complete picture of Senegalese political life, metropolitan papers are essential to an understanding of the politics of Senegal's deputy in France. The following newspapers can be found either at the Bibliothèque Nationale or at the former Colonial Archives in Paris.

| | |
|---|---|
| *Les Annales Coloniales* | *Le Temps* |
| *La Dépêche Coloniale* | *Le Soir* |
| *La Presse Coloniale* | *La Petite Gironde* |
| *L'Action* | *L'Eveil Colonial* |

In Senegal, all the earliest newspapers were edited by French and Creoles. But after 1900 a few Africans began to write for papers in Saint-Louis and Dakar. Not until the 1920's did a press actually managed by Africans appear. It should be noted that Senegalese papers in the early years of this century were seldom properly filed, and did not survive intact in any case because of Senegal's tropical climate; quite often, an entire edition is represented by a single copy filed in Dakar or Saint-Louis. The following newspapers were used in this study (the date is that of the paper's first appearance).

*Moniteur du Sénégal* (1854)
*Reveil du Sénégal* (1885)
*Le Petit Sénégalais* (1886, 1912)
*L'Afrique Occidentale* (1896)
*L'A.O.F.* (1907)
*L'Ouest Africain* (1907)

*Le Radical Sénégalais* (1910)
*La Démocratie du Sénégal* (1913)
*La Tribune* (1917)
*L'Ouest Africain Français* (1919)
*L'Action Sénégalaise* (1922)
*Paris-Dakar* (1932)

This Bibliography is divided into two parts: Works Cited, and Interviews. Many of the persons listed in the Interviews (pp. 253–55) also allowed me to see letters, family documents, and other material relevant to my study.

## WORKS CITED

Adanson, Michel. *Voyage to Senegal*. London, 1759.

Allègre, Adrien Edgar. *Aperçu sur la situation politique au Sénégal, 1923*. Nice, 1923.

Allegret, M. E. *La situation religieuse des peuples de l'Afrique Occidentale et Equatoriale Française*. Paris, 1923.

Alquier, P. "Saint-Louis du Sénégal pendant la Révolution et l'Empire," *Bulletin du Comité d'Etudes Historiques et Scientifiques de l'A.O.F.*, (1922), No. 2, pp. 277–320.

Amon d'Aby, F. J. *La Côte d'Ivoire dans la cité africaine*. Paris, 1951.

Angrand, Armand-Pierre. *Les lébous de la presqu'île du Cap-Vert*. Dakar, 1950.

Arnaud, Robert. *L'Islam et la politique musulmane française en Afrique Occidentale Française*. Paris, 1912.

Aujas, L. "Les Sérères du Sénégal," *Bulletin du Comité d'Etudes Historiques et Scientifiques de l'A.O.F.*, XIV (1931), pp. 293–333.

Azan, Paul. *L'Armée indigène nord-africaine*. Paris, 1925.

Bâ, Oumar. "La polygamie en pays toucouleur," *Afrique-Documents*, No. 64 (1962), pp. 164–79.

Balandier, Georges, and Paul Mercier, *Particularisme et évolution: Les pêcheurs lebous du Sénégal*. Saint-Louis du Sénégal, 1952.

Batude, Fernand. *L'Arachide au Sénégal*. Paris, 1941.

Behrman, Lucy. "The Islamization of the Wolof by the End of the Nineteenth Century," in Daniel McCall, ed., *Western African History* (New York, 1968), pp. 102–31.

———— *Muslim Brotherhoods and Politics in Senegal*. Cambridge, Mass., 1970.

———— "The Political Significance of the Wolof Adherence to Muslim Brotherhoods," *African Historical Studies*, I, i (1968), pp. 60–77.

Bérenger-Feraud, L. J. B. *Les peuplades de la Sénégambie*. Paris, 1879.

Berlioux, E. P. *André Brüe ou l'origine de la colonie française du Sénégal*. Paris, 1874.

Betts, Raymond F. *Assimilation and Association in French Colonial Theory, 1890–1914*. New York, 1961.

——— "The Establishment of the Medina in Dakar, Senegal, 1914," *Africa*, XLI (1971), No. 2, pp. 143–52.

Boilat, Abbé P.-D. *Esquisses sénégalaises*. Paris, 1853.

Bouche, Denise. "Autrefois, notre pays s'appelait la Gaule . . . . Remarques sur l'adaptation de l'enseignement au Sénégal de 1817 à 1960," *Cahiers d'Etudes Africaines*, VIII (1968), No. 29, pp. 110–22.

Boulègue, Marguerite. "La presse au Sénégal avant 1939," *Bulletin de l'IFAN*, XXVII (1965), Series B, Nos. 3–4, pp. 715–54.

Bourgeau, J. "Notes sur la coutume des sérères du Sine et du Saloum," *Bulletin du Comité d'Etudes Historiques et Scientifiques de l'A. O. F.*, XVI (1933), pp. 1–62.

Boutillier, Jean-Louis. "Les captifs en A.O.F. (1903–1905)," *Bulletin de l'IFAN*, XXX (1968), Series B, No. 2, pp. 513–35.

——— et al. *La moyenne vallée du Sénégal*. Paris, 1962.

Brigaud, Félix. *Histoire du Sénégal, I: Des origines aux traités de protectorat*. Dakar, 1964.

——— *Histoire traditionnelle du Sénégal (Etudes sénégalaises No. 9)*. Saint-Louis du Sénégal, 1962.

Brunschwig, Henri. *L'Avènement de l'Afrique noire*. Paris, 1963.

——— *La colonisation française*. Paris, 1949.

——— *Mythes et réalités de l'impérialisme colonial français, 1871–1914*. Paris, 1960.

Buell, Raymond Leslie. *The Native Problem in Africa*. 2 vols. New York, 1928.

Camara, Camille. *Saint-Louis-du-Sénégal: Evolution d'une ville en milieu africain*. Dakar, 1968.

Capperon, L. "Bouet-Willaumez en Afrique Occidentale et au Gabon (1836–1850)," *Revue Maritime*, 1953, pp. 1085–1103.

——— "Protet, gouverneur du Sénégal," *Revue Maritime*, 1956, pp. 1415–36.

Carrère, Frédéric, and Paul Holle. *De la Sénégambie française*. Paris, 1855.

Carter, Gwendolen M., ed. *African One-Party States*. Ithaca, 1962.

Chabas, J. "Le droit des successions chez les ouolofs," *Annales Africaines*, No. 1 (1956), pp. 75–119.

——— "Le mariage et le divorce dans les coutumes des ouolofs habitant les grands centres du Sénégal," *Revue Juridique et Politique de l'Union Française*, VI, Oct.–Dec. 1952, pp. 474–532.

Chailley, Marcel. *Histoire de l'Afrique Occidentale Française, 1639–1959*. Paris, 1968.

——— et al. *Notes et études sur l'Islam en Afrique noire*. Recherches et documents, série Afrique noire, de CHEAM. Paris, 1962.

Charbonneau, Jean, and René Charbonneau. *Marchés et marchands d'Afrique noire*. Paris, 1961.

Cohen, William B. *Rulers of Empire: The French Colonial Service in Africa*. Stanford: Hoover Institution, 1971.

Coifman, Victoria B. "History of the Wolof State of Jolof until 1860, Including Comparative Data from the Wolof State of Walo." Unpublished Ph.D. dissertation, University of Wisconsin, 1969.

Collomb, Henri, and Henri Ayats. "Les migrations au Sénégal: Etude psycho-pathologique," *Cahiers d'Etudes Africaines*, II (1962), No. 8, pp. 570–97.

Comité d'Etudes Historiques et Scientifiques de l'Afrique Occidentale Française. *Coutumiers juridiques de l'Afrique Occidentale Française.* 3 vols. Paris, 1939.

Cornevin, Robert. *Histoire de l'Afrique, I: Des origines au XVIᵉ siècle.* Paris, 1962.

——— *Histoire des peuples de l'Afrique noire.* Paris, 1960.

Cosnier, Henri. *L'Ouest africain français.* Paris, 1921.

Courter, M. *Etude sur le Sénégal.* Paris, 1903.

Cousturier, Lucie. *Les inconnus chez eux.* Paris, 1925.

Cowan, L. Gray. *Local Government in West Africa.* New York, 1958.

Cros, Charles. *La parole est à M. Blaise Diagne.* Aubenas, France, 1961.

Crowder, Michael. *Senegal: A Study of French Assimilation Policy.* London, 1967.

——— "West Africa and the 1914–18 war," *Bulletin de l'IFAN*, XXX (1968), Series B, No. 1, pp. 227–47.

——— *West Africa Under Colonial Rule.* Evanston, 1968.

Cruise O'Brien, Donal B. *The Mourides of Senegal.* Oxford, 1971.

Cultru, Pierre. *Les origines de l'Afrique occidentale: Histoire du Sénégal, du XVᵉ siècle à 1870.* Paris, 1910.

Davis, Shelby C. *Reservoirs of Men: A History of the Black Troops of French West Africa.* Chambéry, 1934.

Decraene, Philippe. *Le panafricanisme.* Paris, 1959.

Deherme, G. *L'Afrique Occidentale Française: Action politique, action économique, action sociale.* Paris, 1931.

Delafosse, Maurice. *Afrique Occidentale Française, IV: Histoire des colonies françaises.* Paris, 1931.

——— "Le congrès panafricain," *Afrique Française*, Nos. 3–4 (1919), pp. 53–59.

——— "Sur l'orientation nouvelle de la politique indigène dans l'Afrique noire," *Afrique Française*, No. 7 (1921), pp. 145–52.

——— and Henri Gaden, eds. *Chroniques du Fouta sénégalais.* Paris, 1913.

Delavignette, Robert. *Afrique Occidentale Française.* Paris, 1931.

——— *Service africain.* Paris, 1946.

——— and Charles-André Julien. *Les constructeurs de la France d'Outre-Mer.* Paris, 1946.

Delcourt, André. *La France et les établissements français au Sénégal entre 1713 et 1763 (Mémoires de l'Institut Français d'Afrique Noire, No. 17).* Dakar, 1952.

Deroure, Françoise. "La vie quotidienne à Saint-Louis par ses archives, 1779–1809," *Bulletin de l'IFAN*, XXVI (1964), Series B, No. 26, pp. 397–439.

Deschamps, Hubert. *Méthodes et doctrines coloniales de la France.* Paris, 1953.

——— *Le Sénégal et la Gambie.* Paris, 1964.

——— "Pour une histoire de l'Afrique," *Diogène*, 1962, No. 37, pp. 113–20.

Despagnet, Frantz. *Essai sur les protectorats: Etude de droit international.* Paris, 1896.

Devèze, Michel. *La France d'Outre-Mer*. Paris, 1948.

Diagne, Abdel-Kader. *La résistance française au Sénégal et en A.O.F. pendant le guerre 1939–1945*. Thiès, Sénégal, ca. 1950.

Diop, Abdoulaye. "Enquête sur la migration toucouleur à Dakar," *Bulletin de l'IFAN*, XXII (1960), Series B, Nos. 3–4, pp. 393–418.

Diop, Cheikh Anta. *L'Afrique noire pré-coloniale*. Paris, 1960.

Doriot, Jacques. *Les colonies et le communisme*. Paris, 1929.

d'Oxoby, Jean Daramy. *Le Sénégal en 1925*. Paris, 1925.

—— *Les sociétés indigènes de prévoyance, de secours de prêts mutuels agricoles en Afrique Occidentale Française*. Paris, ca. 1936.

DuBert, M. *Nos sénégalais pendant le grande guerre*. Metz, 1922.

Duboc, General A. *L'Epopée coloniale en Afrique Occidentale Française*. Paris, 1938.

—— *Les sénégalais au service de la France*. Paris, 1939.

Duchêne, Albert. *Histoire des finances coloniale de la France*. Paris, 1938.

—— *La politique coloniale de la France*. Paris, 1928.

Durand, Jean B. L. *Voyage au Sénégal*. Paris, 1802.

Faidherbe, L. L. *Le Sénégal: La France dans l'Afrique occidentale*. Paris, 1889.

Faure, Claude. *Histoire de la presqu'île du Cap Vert et des origines de Dakar*. Paris, 1914.

Fédération Française de l'Enseignement Ménager. *La vie aux colonies: Préparation de la femme à la vie coloniale*. Paris, 1938.

Foltz, William J. *From French West Africa to the Mali Federation*. New Haven, 1965.

Forgeron, Jean-Baptiste. *Le protectorat en Afrique Occidentale Française et les chefs indigènes*. Bordeaux, 1920.

Fouquet, Joseph. *La traité des arachides dans le pays de Kaolack, et ses conséquences économiques, sociales, et juridiques*. Saint-Louis du Sénégal, 1958.

Froelich, J.-C. *Les musulmans d'Afrique noire*. Paris, 1962.

Gaffarel, Paul. *Comptoirs de l'Afrique Occidentale Française de 1830 à 1870*. Dijon, 1910.

—— *Le Sénégal et le Soudan Français*. Paris, 1890.

Gaffiot, Robert. *Gorée, capitale déchue*. Paris, 1933.

Gaillard, Jean. *L'Expansion française dans le monde*. Paris, 1951.

Gamble, David. *The Wolof of Senegambia*. London, 1957.

Gautherot, Gustave. *Le bolchévisme aux colonies et l'impérialisme rouge*. Paris, 1930.

Gayet, Georges. "Les libanais et les syriens dans l'ouest africain," pp. 161–72 in *Ethnic and Cultural Pluralism in Intertropical Communities* (Report of the thirtieth meeting of the International Institute of Differing Civilizations: Lisbon, April 15–18, 1957). Brussels, 1957.

Geismar, L. *Recueil des coutumes civiles des races du Sénégal*. Saint-Louis du Sénégal, 1933.

Girault, Arthur. *Principes de colonisation et de législation colonial*. Paris, 1943.

Golberry, S. M. X. *Fragments d'un voyage.* Paris, 1802.

Gorer, Geoffrey. *Africa Dances.* New York, 1962.

Goudal, Jean. *Le destin de l'Afrique.* Paris, 1933.

Gouilly, Alphonse. *L'Islam dans l'Afrique Occidentale Française.* Paris, 1952.

Greslé, I. P. *Essai de politique indigène.* Paris, 1919.

Guèye, Lamine. *De la situation politique des sénégalais originaires des communes de plein exercice.* Paris, 1922.

—— *Etapes et perspectives de l'Union française.* Paris, 1955.

—— *L'Itinéraire africain.* Paris, 1966.

Guiraud, Xavier. *L'Arachide sénégalaise.* Paris, 1937.

Guy, Camille. *L'Afrique Occidentale Française.* Paris, 1929.

Hardy, Georges. *Histoire de la colonisation française.* 3d ed. Paris, 1938.

—— *Histoire sociale de la colonisation française.* Paris, 1953.

—— *La mise en valeur du Sénégal de 1817 à 1854.* Paris, 1921.

—— *Nos grands problèmes coloniaux.* Paris, 1942.

—— *Une conquête morale: L'Enseignement en A.O.F.* Paris, 1917.

Hargreaves, John D. "Assimilation in Eighteenth-Century Senegal," *Journal of African History,* VI, 2 (1965).

—— *France and West Africa.* New York, 1969.

—— *Prelude to the Partition of West Africa.* London, 1963.

—— *West Africa: The Former French States.* Englewood Cliffs, N.J., 1967.

Hodgkin, Thomas. "African Reactions to French Rule," *West Africa,* Jan. 16, 1954, pp. 31–32.

Idowu, H. Oludare. "Assimilation in 19th-Century Senegal," *Bulletin de l'IFAN,* XXX (1968), Series B, No. 4, pp. 1422–47. Also in *Cahiers d'Etudes Africaines,* IX (1969), No. 34, pp. 194–218.

—— "The Conseil Général in Senegal, 1879–1920." Unpublished Ph.D. dissertation, Ibadan, 1966.

Johnson, G. Wesley. "The Ascendancy of Blaise Diagne and the Beginning of African Politics in Senegal," *Africa,* XXXVI (1966), pp. 235–52.

—— "The Development of Local Political Institutions in Urban Senegal," in Arnold Rivkin, ed., *Nations by Design: Institution-Building in Africa* (New York, 1968), pp. 208–27.

—— "Political Action Groups, Factions, and Parties in Early Senegalese Urban Politics," in G. Wesley Johnson and William J. Foltz, eds., *The Senegalese Political Tradition* (forthcoming).

Jore, Léonce. "Les établissements français sur la côte occidentale d'Afrique de 1758 à 1809," *Revue Française d'Histoire d'Outre-mer,* LI (1964), Nos. 182–85, pp. 9–252, 255–476.

Kesteloot, Lilyan. *Les écrivains noirs de la langue française.* Brussels, 1963.

Klein, Martin A. *Islam and Imperialism in Senegal: Sine-Saloum, 1847–1914.* Stanford, 1968.

Langley, J. Ayo. "Pan-Africanism in Paris, 1924–36," *Journal of Modern African Studies,* VII, No. 2 (1969), pp. 69–94.

Lebel, A. Roland. *L'Afrique Occidentale dans la littérature française (depuis 1870).* Paris, 1925.

Leca, N. *Les pêcheurs de Guet N'Dar.* Paris, 1935.

Legum, Colin. *Pan-Africanism: A Short Political Guide.* New York, 1965.

Lengyel, Emil. *Dakar: Outpost of Two Hemispheres*. New York, 1941.
LeVine, Victor T. *The Cameroons from Mandate to Independence*. Berkeley, 1964.
——— "Political Elite Recruitment and Political Structure in French-Speaking Africa," *Cahiers d'Etudes Africaines*, VIII (1968), pp. 369–89.
Ligou, Daniel. *Histoire du socialisme en France (1871–1961)*. Paris, 1962.
Little, Kenneth. *West African Urbanization*. Cambridge, Eng., 1965.
Ly, Abdoulaye. *La Compagnie du Sénégal*. Paris, 1958.
MacKenzie, W. J. M., and Kenneth E. Robinson, eds. *Five Elections in Africa*. Oxford, 1960.
Mademba, Abd-El-Kader. *Au Sénégal et au Soudan Français*. Paris, 1931.
Mager, Henri, ed. *Cahiers coloniaux de 1889*. Paris, 1889.
Mangin, Charles. *La force noire*. Paris, 1910.
——— *La mission des troupes noires*. Paris, 1911.
——— *Regards sur la France d'Afrique*. Paris, 1924.
Markowitz, Irving L. *Léopold Sédar Senghor and the Politics of Négritude*. New York, 1969.
Martini, Marien. *Les corses dans l'expansion française*. Ajaccio, 1953.
Marty, Paul, *Etudes sénégalaises (1785–1826)*. Paris, 1920.
——— *Etudes sur l'Islam au Sénégal*. 2 vols. Paris, 1917.
Mauny, Raymond. *Tableau géographique de l'ouest africain au moyen âge*. Dakar, 1961.
Mercier, Paul. "Aspects des problèmes de stratification sociale dans l'ouest africain," *Cahiers Internationaux de Sociologie*, XVII (1954), pp. 47–65.
——— "Etude du mariage et enquête urbaine," *Cahiers d'Etudes Africaines*, I (1960), No. 1, pp. 28–43.
——— "L'Evolution des élites sénégalaises," *Bulletin International des Sciences Sociales*, VII (1956), No. 3, pp. 448–60.
——— "Le groupement européen de Dakar: Orientation d'une enquête," *Cahiers Internationaux de Sociologie*, XIX (1955), No. 2, pp. 130–46.
Mercier, Roger. *L'Afrique noire dans la littérature française: Les premières images (XVIIe–XVIIIe siècles)*. Dakar, 1962.
Meunier, P. *Organisation et fonctionnement de la justice indigène en Afrique Occidentale Française*. Paris, 1914.
Milcent, Ernest. *Au carrefour des options africaines: Le Sénégal*. Paris, 1965.
——— and Monique Sordet. *Léopold Sédar Senghor et la naissance de l'Afrique moderne*. Paris, 1969.
Mille, Pierre. "The 'Black-vote' in Senegal," *African Affairs*, I (1901), pp. 64–79.
Monteil, Vincent. *L'Islam noir*. Paris, 1964.
——— "Lat-Dior, Damel du Kayor (1842–1886), et l'islamisation des Wolofs," *Archives de Sociologie des Religions*, VIII (1963), No. 16, pp. 77–104.
——— "Une confrérie musulmane: Les mourides de Sénégal," *Archives de Sociologie des Religions*, 1962, No. 14, pp. 77–101.
Moreau, Paul. *Les indigènes d'A.O.F., leur condition politique et économique*. Paris, 1938.
Morgenthau, Ruth Schachter. *Political Parties in French-Speaking West Africa*. Oxford, 1964.

Mortimer, Edward. *France and the Africans, 1944–1960*. New York, 1969.

Moulaert, G. *Un grand colonial: Le gouverneur-general J. Van Vollenhoven*. Brussels, 1919.

Mumford, W. Bryant and G. S. J. Orde-Brown. *Africans Learn To Be French*. London, ca. 1935.

Nadel, S. F. "La notion d'élite sociale," *Bulletin International des Sciences Sociales*, VIII (1956), No. 3, pp. 419–31.

Newbury, C. W. "The Formation of the Government-General of French West Africa," *Journal of African History*, I (1960), No. 1, pp. 111–28.

———— "The Government-General and Political Change in French West Africa," *St. Antony's Papers*, No. 10 (African Affairs, No. 1), London, 1961, pp. 41–59.

Ninine, J. *La main-d'oeuvre indigène dans les colonies africaines*. Paris, 1932.

Nyambarza, Daniel, "Le marabout El Hadj Mamadou Lamine d'après les archives françaises," *Cahiers d'Etudes Africaines*, IX (1969), No. 33, pp. 124–45.

Olivier, Marcel. *Le Sénégal*. Paris, 1907.

Padmore, George. *Pan-Africanism or Communism?* London, n.d.

Pasquier, G. *L'Organisation des troupes indigènes en Afrique Occidentale Française*. Paris, 1912.

Pasquier, Roger, "A propos de l'émancipation des esclaves au Sénégal en 1848," *Revue Française d'Histoire d'Outre-mer*, LIV (1967), pp. 188–208.

———— "En marge de la guerre de secession: Les essais de culture au Sénégal." *Annales Africaines*, 1955.

———— "Les débuts de la presse au Sénégal," *Cahiers d'Etudes Africaines*, VII (1962), No. 7, pp. 477–91.

———— "Villes du Sénégal au XIXᵉ siècle," *Revue Française d'Histoire d'Outre-mer*, XLVII (1960), pp. 387–426. Also in *Annales Africaines*, 1955, pp. 387–426.

Pelleray, Emmanuel. *L'Afrique Occidentale Française*. Paris, n.d.

Persell, S. Michael. "The French Colonial Lobby, 1899–1914." Unpublished Ph.D. dissertation, Stanford University, 1969.

Péter, Georges. *L'Effort français au Sénégal*. Paris, 1933.

Petit, Edouard. *Organisation des colonies françaises de protectorate*. Paris, 1895.

Peyrat, Joseph, "Un congrès pan-noir," *La Revue Indigène*, Nos. 151–53 (July–Sept. 1921), pp. 133–45.

Poquin, Jean-Jacques. *Les relations économiques extérieures des pays d'Afrique noire de l'Union française, 1925–1955*. Paris, 1957.

Prévaudeau, Albert. *Joost Van Vollenhoven, 1877–1918*. Paris, 1953.

Pulvenis, Claude. "Une épidémie de fièvre jaune à Saint-Louis-du-Sénégal (1881)," *Bulletin de l'IFAN*, XXX (1968), Series B, No. 4, pp. 1353–73.

Rau, E. "La question des terrains de tound," *Annales Africaines*, 1956, pp. 141–63.

Renouard, G. *L'Ouest africain et les missions catholiques*. Paris, 1904.

Richard-Molard, Jacques. *Afrique Occidentale Française*. Paris, 1949.

Ricord, Maurice. *France noire*. Marseille, 1939.

Roberts, S. H. *History of French Colonial Policy (1870–1925)*. London, 1929.

Robinson, Kenneth. "Political Development in French West Africa," pp. 140–81 in Calvin Stillman, ed., *Africa in the Modern World*. Chicago, 1955.

Roux, A. Charles. *L'Appeln de l'Afrique noire à la France*. Lyon, 1939.

Roux, Emile. *Manuel à l'usage des administrateurs et du personnel des affaires indigènes de la colonie du Sénégal*. Paris, 1911.

Runner, Jean. *Les droits politiques des indigènes des colonies*. Paris, 1927.

Sabatié, A. *Le Sénégal: Sa conquête, son organisation (1364–1925)*. Saint-Louis du Sénégal, 1925.

Saint-Geuest, Jean. *Un voyage de M. Albert Sarraut en Afrique*. Paris, 1922.

Saint-Martin, Yves. "Une source de l'histoire coloniale du Sénégal: Les rapports de situation politique (1874–1891)," *Revue Française d'Histoire d'Outre-mer*. LII (1965), No. 187, pp. 153–244.

Sarraut, Albert. *Grandeur et servitude coloniales*. Paris, 1931.

——— *La mise en valeur des colonies françaises*. Paris, 1923.

Satineau, Maurice. *Schoelcher*. Paris, 1948.

Savonnet, G. *La ville de Thiès*. Saint-Louis du Sénégal, 1955.

Schefer, Christian. *Instructions générales données de 1763 à 1870 aux gouverneurs et ordonnateurs des établissements français en Afrique Occidentale*. 2 vols. Paris, 1921.

Schnapper, Bernard. "La fin du régime de l'exclusif: Le commerce étranger dans les possessions françaises d'Afrique tropicale (1817–1870)," *Annales Africaines*, 1959, pp. 149–99.

——— "Les tribunaux musulmans et la politique coloniale au Sénégal (1830–1914)," *Revue Historique de Droit Français et Etranger*, 1961, No. 1, pp. 90–128.

Schoelcher, Victor. *Histoire de l'esclavage*. Paris, 1847.

Seck, Assane. "La formation d'une classe moyenne en Afrique Occidentale Française," pp. 159–63 in *Development of a Middle Class in Tropical and Sub-tropical Countries* (Record of the 29th Session of the International Institute of Differing Civilizations). Brussels, 1956.

Senghor, Léopold S. "De la négritude: Psychologie du négro-africain," *Diogène*, 1962. No. 37, pp. 3–16.

Silla, Ousmane. "Langage et techniques thérapeutiques des cultes de possession des Lébous du Sénégal," *Bulletin de l'IFAN*, XXXI (1969), Series B, No. 1, pp. 215–38.

——— "Persistence des castes dans la société wolof contemporaine," *Bulletin de l'IFAN*, XXVIII (1966), Series B, Nos. 3–4, pp. 731–70.

——— "Religion traditionnelle et techniques thérapeutiques des Lébous du Sénégal," *Bulletin de l'IFAN*, XXX (1968), Series B, No. 4, pp. 1566–80.

Solus, Henry. *Traité de la condition des indigènes en droit privé*. Paris, 1927.

Songy, Louis. *Au Sénégal*. Paris, 1905.

Suret-Canale, Jean. *Afrique noire occidentale et centrale, II: L'Ere coloniale (1900–1945)*. Paris, 1964.

Sy, Cheikh Tidiane. *La confrérie sénégalaise des mourides*. Paris, 1969.

Sylla, Assane. "Une république africaine au XIXe siècle, 1795–1857," *Présence Africaine*, nouvelle série, Apr.–July 1955, pp. 47–65.

Tharaud, Jérome, and Jean Tharaud. *La randonnée de Samba Diouf*. Paris, 1922.

Thiam, Bodiel, "Hiérarchie de la société ouolove," *Notes Africaines*, No. 41 (January 1949), p. 12.

Thomas, Louis Vincent. "Analyse dynamique de la parenté sénégalaise," *Bulletin de l'IFAN*, XXX (1968), Series B, No. 3, pp. 1005–56.

―――― *Les Diola: Essai d'analyse fonctionnelle sur une population de Basse Casamance.* 2 vols. Mémoires de l'IFAN, No. 55. Dakar, 1959.

Thomas, R. "La politique socialiste et le problème colonial de 1905 à 1920," *Revue Française d'Histoire d'Outre-mer*, 1960, pp. 213–45.

Thomassery, Marguerite. *Catalogue des périodiques d'Afrique Noire francophone (1958–1962) conservés a l'IFAN.* Dakar, 1965.

Thompson, Virginia, and Richard Adloff. *French West Africa.* Stanford, 1958.

Traoré, Bakari, Mamadou Lô, and Jean-Louis Alibert. *Forces politiques en Afrique noire.* Paris, 1966.

Trimingham, John Spencer. *A History of Islam in West Africa.* London, 1962.

―――― *Islam in West Africa.* Oxford, 1961.

Van Vollenhoven, Joost. *Une âme de chef.* Paris, 1920.

Vanlande, René. *Dakar!* Paris, n.d.

Villard, André. *Histoire du Sénégal.* Dakar, 1943.

Violette, Maurice, *et al. Afrique Occidentale Française.* Paris, 1913.

Webster, J. B., and A. A. Boahen. *West Africa Since 1800.* London, 1967.

Winder, R. Bayly. "The Lebanese in West Africa," *Comparative Studies in Society and History*, IV (1962), No. 3, pp. 296–333.

Wioland, François, and Maurice Calvet. "L'Expansion du wolof au Sénégal," *Bulletin de l'IFAN*, XXIX (1967), Series B, Nos. 3–4, pp. 604–18.

Witherell, Julian. "The Response of the Peoples of Cayor to French Penetration." Unpublished Ph.D. dissertation, University of Wisconsin, 1964.

Zuccarelli, François. "Le recrutement de travailleurs sénégalais par l'Etat indépendant du Congo (1888–1896)," *Revue Française d'Histoire d'Outre-mer*, XLVII (1960), Nos. 168–69, pp. 475–81.

―――― "Le régime des engagés à temps au Sénégal (1817–1848)," *Cahiers d'Etudes Africaines*, II (1962), No. 7, pp. 420–61.

INTERVIEWS

[In each instance the date given is that of the first interview; there were sometimes as many as five subsequent interviews. Only the more important interviews have been listed.]

Armand Angrand. Former Mayor of Dakar; one of Diagne's closest lieutenants in the later 1920's. Dakar, Feb. 28, 1964.

Alpha Bâ. Political intimate of Lamine Guèye since 1904; long-time Saint-Louis resident. Dakar, June 4, 1964.

Félix Brigaud. Formerly professor in the Lycée Faidherbe, Saint-Louis; French history teacher who taught two generations of future African leaders. Saint-Louis, Jan. 22, 1964.

Mme. Félix Brigaud. Daughter of Louis Guillabert (former President of General Council and Colonial Council). Saint-Louis, Aug. 2, 1964.

Monsieur Chamussy. Retired French director of Maurel et Prom for Dakar; in Senegal since 1920's. Dakar, Apr. 7, 1964.

Albert Charton. Former inspector of Instruction for French West Africa; resident of Dakar. Paris, Aug. 20, 1963.

Jacques Charpy. Former archivist of French West Africa. Quimper (Brittany), Aug. 18, 1963.

Dr. Adama Cissé. Physician interested in politics; well informed about the effect of Four Communes politics in the bush. Dakar, Jan. 1964.

Charles Cros. Former administrator in Senegal; member of General Council and deputy in French National Assembly; biographer of Diagne. Nice, Sept. 19, 1963.

Robert Delavignette. Former director of the Ecole Coloniale; directeur de cabinet of Ministry of Colonies; liberal writer on colonial policy. Paris, Nov. 14, 1964.

Robert Delmas. President of USIMA, Manutention Africaine, and other large commercial interests of the Delmas family in Senegal; member of Senegal's National Assembly. Dakar, Feb. 10, 1964.

Hubert Deschamps. Former Governor of Senegal; later Professor of African History at the Sorbonne. Paris, Mar. 16, 1963.

Mlle. Elisabeth Devès. Daughter of Justin Devès. Dakar, June 30, 1964.

Aby Kane Diallo. Member of Young Senegalese; former mayor of Saint-Louis, intimate of Diagne since 1914; former member of Colonial Council. Saint-Louis, Jan. 22, 1964.

Abdel-Kader Diagne. Formerly Dakar municipal council member; knew Blaise Diagne and Jean Daramy d'Oxoby; led resistance to Vichy regime in French West Africa; secretary of veterans' organization. Dakar, Nov. 1963.

Raoul Diagne. Son of Blaise Diagne. Dakar, Aug. 19, 1964.

Daniel Dias. From old Gorée family; active in politics and veterans' organizations. Dakar, Feb. 25, 1964.

Mme. Marie Diop. Intimate of Blaise and Mme. Diagne in Paris; a Camerounese who married Senegalese engineer; mother-in-law of Alioune Diop, of *Présence Africaine*. Dakar, Feb. 5, 1964.

Moustapha Diouf. Son of Galandou Diouf. Zinguinchor, Apr. 19, 1964.

Guy Etcheverry. French journalist in Senegal since 1945; personal adviser to President Senghor; interested in political history. Dakar, Feb. 21, 1964.

Prof. Sega Seck Fall. Teacher of physics in Lycée Van Vollenhoven, Dakar; knowledgeable about politics in the bush before the franchise was extended to all Senegalese. Dakar, Feb. 29, 1964.

Narda Filfilli. Lebanese businessman in Senegal since 1922; owner of largest plantation in modern Senegal. Rufisque, Apr. 12, 1964.

Françis Gomis. Senegalese formerly in French administration. Apr. 19, 1964.

Charles Graziani. Local merchant and politician; at first a foe and later a supporter of Diagne. Dakar, Aug. 18, 1964.

Lamine Guèye. Founding member of Aurora and Young Senegalese; supporter of Diagne; first African lawyer in French West Africa; one of first to oppose Diagne after 1923; later deputy for Senegal and president of National Assembly. Dakar, June 1964; Stanford University, Sept. 26, 1965.

Maurice Guèye. Long-time mayor of Rufisque; intimate of Diagne and Diouf. Rufisque, Aug. 26, 1964.

André Guillabert. Vice-president of the National Assembly; Creole lawyer;

son of Louis Guillabert and grandson of Louis Descemet. Dakar, Apr. 9, 1964.

Maurice Lapolice. Gorean Creole related to Daniel Dias; has written local histories of Gorée and the Creole community. Dakar, Mar. 11, 1964.

Jean-Aimé Le Franc. Frenchman employed at Saint-Louis city hall for several decades; supporter of Diagne. Saint-Louis, Aug. 3, 1964.

Louis Le Gros. Creole intellectual; former mayor of Saint-Louis; member of Colonial Council; Senegal's ambassador to the Vatican after independence. Saint-Louis, Jan. 22, 1964.

Abdoulaye M'Bodge. Official in Ministry of National Education; now preparing history of education in Senegal. Apr. 8, 1964.

A. M. M'Bow. Former professor in Lycée Faidherbe, Saint-Louis; later Minister of National Education. Saint-Louis, Aug. 2, 1964.

Ibrahima Seydou N'Daw. Honorary president of National Assembly; former opponent of Diagne; Saint-Louisian active in politics in the bush since 1920's. Dakar, June 26, 1964.

Amadou Assane N'Doye. Son of Assane N'Doye, one of Diagne's first supporters; former municipal council member in Dakar; Lebou merchant and businessman; former intimate and later opponent of Diagne; first Lebou in politics. Dakar, June 23, 1964.

André Ouatara. Former government printer in Saint-Louis; Diagnist; served in French army with originaires during World War I. Saint-Louis, Jan. 22, 1964.

Roger Pasquier. Former lycée professor in Senegal; historian of nineteenth-century Senegal. Paris, Mar. 25, 1963.

Mme. Françoise Salzmann. Wife of Creole politician who opposed Diagne in later 1920's and 1930's. Saint-Louis, Aug. 2, 1964.

Dr. Assane Seck. Professor of Geography, University of Dakar. Dakar, June 17, 1964.

Abdoulaye Sène. On staff of history section, IFAN. Dakar, Dec. 1963.

Léopold Senghor. President of the Republic of Senegal; knew Diagne as a student in Paris. San Francisco, Sept. 28, 1966.

Amadou Thiam. Notary public and former Diagnist; World War I veteran. Dakar, Apr. 8, 1964.

Christian Valantin. Creole government official; grandnephew of Louis Guillabert and descended from Durand Valantin, Senegal's first deputy (1848). Jan. 18, 1964.

Paul Vidal. French lawyer from Saint-Louis; former mayor of Saint-Louis. Saint-Louis, June 20, 1964.

# Index